DIALOGUE BETWEEN AN ORTHODOX AND A BARLAAMITE

A Global Academic Publishing Book

SAINT GREGORY PALAMAS

DIALOGUE BETWEEN AN ORTHODOX AND A BARLAAMITE

Translation by Rein Ferwerda
Introduction by Sara J. Denning-Bolle

For information, contact

State University of New York Press, Albany, NY

www.sunypress.edu

Imprint: *EPISTEME*

Cover image: "The Holy Trinity," in Janina Kłosińska, *Icons from Poland.*

Library of Congress Cataloging-in-Publication Data

Saint Gregory Palamas. *Dialogue between an Orthodox and a Barlaamite.* Translation by Rein Ferwerda. Introduction by Sara J. Denning-Bolle.

1. Saint Gregory Palamas 2. Theology 3. Philosophy.

ISBN 1-883058-21-X

Medieval Studies Worldwide

Center for Medieval and Renaissance Studies

Binghamton University

EPISTEME

Classical Greek and Latin Texts
with English Translation

In Memory of Father Meyendorff

TABLE OF CONTENTS

INTRODUCTION

In the fourteenth century a controversy arose in the Eastern empire between the Eastern Orthodox theologian Gregory Palamas and a philosopher and monk from Calabria in southern Italy by the name of Barlaam. Barlaam was working on the problem of union between the Roman and Byzantine churches in the 1330's and actually acted as the representative of the Orthodox church. In his discussions, in which he repudiated the use of *filioque* (the addition to the Creed of the Holy Spirit proceeding from the Father "and the Son"), he argued for the unknowable and unapproachable nature of God. Gregory did not take kindly to what he perceived to be agnostic tendencies in Barlaam's thought and he wrote a treatise about the procession of the Holy Spirit. However, it was particularly Barlaam's later attack on the hesychasts, a certain group of Orthodox monks, that led to a bitter debate between Gregory and Barlaam. Several basic issues were involved, centering on man's knowledge of God. The ideas that were defined in the debate by Palamas became crucial for the future of Eastern Orthodox thought.

Introductory Remarks to Palamas[1]

Gregory was born in 1296 to a large family of aristocratic origin in Asia Minor which later moved to Constantinople. After the death of his father Constantine when Gregory was six, he was brought up in the palace and educated by the Emperor Andronicus III. His education included the study of Aristotle which preceded Platonic metaphysics in the curriculum of the Byzantine universities.[2] However, it is John Meyendorff's contention that Palamas' education did not extend beyond the elementary and general course of study (viz., the *trivium* and *quadrivium*) of the basic educated man. Hence, it is likely that he did not seriously study Plato.[3]

When he was about twenty years old, Gregory entered a monastery. As first-born child, however, he had inherited not only his father's estate but also responsibility for the members of his family. Upon entering the monastic life, Gregory solved the problem of how to carry out his respon-

sibilities towards family members by convincing them to enter religious life with him. In all, his mother, two sisters, several servants, and his two brothers entered monasteries in Constantinople and Mt. Athos.

It is important to remember that Gregory did not spend his life cloistered from the world. It is true that he spent a good deal of time before his confrontations with Barlaam in hermitages and seclusion. The secluded life gave him intimate acquaintance with Eastern spirituality and prayer. But he was also ordained a priest in Thessalonica in the 1320's; the 1330's witnessed his involvement in the political and theological issues of the Empire, especially his dealings with Barlaam; in the 1340's he was elected archbishop of Thessalonica. In the 1350's he was captured by the Turks in Asia Minor which provided contact with Christian groups in the area along with Muslim theologians. After his release, he continued public debates with his theological opponents before returning to pastoral work in Thessalonica. There he died in 1359. His writings included treatises on the Holy Spirit, Christian morality, a set of sixty-three sermons, theological essays on God's revelation, and a defense of his fellow monks on Mt. Athos against Barlaam. We are dealing with a man who could argue theologically and write learned treatises but who was also engaged in issues of spirituality and everyday parish life. As priest and later archbishop he was particularly interested in pastoral problems and the involvement of the individual in the life and community of the Church. It is important to keep this dual role of his in mind when we turn to the specific problems he discussed with Barlaam. For Palamas, theology was never divorced or artificially separated from one's life in and commitment to the Church.

But what about Barlaam? Who was this philosopher-monk who journeyed to Constantinople in Orthodox garb and unwittingly involved the Eastern Church in one of the most bitter debates in its history?

Barlaam

Although Barlaam came from southern Italy his ancestors and language were Greek and he claimed Orthodoxy as his religious tradition. As Meyendorff points out he was "imbued with the spirit of the Italian Renaissance."[4] Around 1330 he arrived in Constantinople, working on some commentaries on Pseudo-Dionysius, and was considered knowledgeable in such disciplines as theology, philosophy, diplomacy and astronomy. Unfortunately, he does not seem to have warmed the hearts of his col-

leagues in Constantinople as he had a reputation for haughtiness and pride.

Nonetheless, Barlaam's original dispute concerning the Holy Spirit should have placed him squarely within the Orthodox camp. Superficially, such was the case. He wrote several treatises against the Latins, disagreeing with the insertion into the Creed that the Holy Spirit proceeds from the Father and the Son. This, of course, is a good solid Orthodox stance. What drew initial animosity from Palamas, who resided at the time in a hermitage at St Sabbas on Mt. Athos, was Barlaam's underlying argument. Barlaam said that since God is not knowable, it is not possible for anyone to show how the Holy Spirit proceeds. At best, the issue of the Procession should be limited to "private theological opinions."[5] At any rate, said Barlaam, it was not an issue that should jeopardize Church unity.

Barlaam's ideas sounded dangerously agnostic to Palamas. While he agreed that the Holy Spirit proceeded only from the Father (and not the Son) he felt that this could be demonstrated. In fact, Barlaam's insistence on God's unknowability stemmed from apophatic or negative theology evident in many Eastern writers, notably Pseudo-Dionysius. Apophatic theology attempts to describe God in negative terms: since God is so far above our human understanding, the best manner we have to "describe" him is by expressing what he is not. Pseudo-Dionysius, the enigmatic writer of the 5th or 6th century, was a master of such theology. Speaking of God, Dionysius says:

> He is known through knowledge and through unknowing. Of him there is conception, reason, understanding, touch, perception, opinion, imagination, name, and many other things. On the other hand, he cannot be understood, words cannot contain him, and no name can lay hold of him. He is not one of the things that are and he cannot be known in any of them. He is all things in all things and he is no thing among things. He is known to all from all things and he is known to no one from anything. This is the sort of language we must use about God...[6]

We will see later in our discussion that Pseudo-Dionysius was a cornerstone for both Palamas and Barlaam in their respective arguments over man's knowledge of God.

The Dispute over the Hesychasts

In spite of the disagreements between the two men regarding the theological issue of the Holy Spirit, the situation did not deteriorate until Barlaam came into contact with a certain group of monks in Thessalonica. The monks practiced a form of spirituality and prayer in which they claimed that the human body could experience the uncreated light of God and have a specific role in prayer. The monks practiced the spirituality known as hesychasm; those who practiced it were called hesychasts. *Hesychia* signified inner stillness and quiet and, as a term of Christian mysticism, was known from the fourth century.[7] The hesychasts took seriously the admonition of Paul "to pray continually" (1 Thess. 5:17) and they developed what came to be known as the Jesus Prayer which runs "Lord Jesus Christ, Son of God, have mercy on me."[8] The idea was that one should recite this prayer over and over until it became an unconscious, uninterrupted prayer. In fact, the monks used a psychosomatic method to achieve this. By fixing one's gaze on one's navel and resting one's chin on one's breast, one could make one's breathing coincide with the repetition of the prayer. The aim was to unite the heart with the intellect.[9] It was felt that the heart was the leader of the body and that the intelligence must descend into the heart. By making one's breathing coincide with the prayer until it became an unconscious repetition, one advanced spiritually to the vision of God. What is assumed here is solid biblical anthropology: God created body and soul at the same time with the result that the human being is good. A mystical vision of God includes the entire human, body and soul, and the hesychast strives to circumscribe the intellect within the body, not disengage it.

Barlaam's Platonic sensibilities were sorely offended by the hesychasts' claim to have a vision of God while fully embodied. A good Platonist should strive to free the soul from the material world, not include the body in the soul's upward journey. In his anger he referred to the monks as *omphalopsychoi*, "men-with-their-souls-in-their-navels" and he accused them of the heresy of Messalianism. The Messalians, known as Bogomils or, in the West, Cathars, rejected the sacraments as necessary for one's salvation, relied only on the leadership of charismatics, and claimed to have a vision of God with their earthly eyes.

It was Gregory who came to the defense of the hesychasts. This is

quite understandable. For one thing, the monks Barlaam attacked were from Mt. Athos, a conglomerate of monasteries where Gregory had also lived. Further, he himself was fully acquainted with the method of hesychast spirituality and he felt indignant at the accusations levelled by the vituperative Calabrian philosopher. Gregory's defense, known as the *Triads in Defense of the Holy Hesychasts*, was written in three stages.[10] The first *Triad*, written in the second half of the 1330's, is based on his personal discussions with Barlaam, though the philosopher is not named in the polemic. While Barlaam was in Avignon in 1339, trying to effect a union of the Church with Pope Benedict XII, Palamas wrote the second *Triad*. This second treatise quotes Barlaam directly from some of the philosopher's writings on the nature of knowledge, prayer and wisdom. Barlaam then wrote "Against the Messalians" in which he called the hesychasts Messalians, thus linking them to a group already declared heretical. Palamas' final *Triad* answers these charges.

Barlaam, however, took on far too significant an opponent. Not only did the monasteries of Mt. Athos back Palamas but the Council of Constantinople of 1341 supported him, officially repudiating Barlaam's positions. To make matters even more unpleasant for Barlaam, the Patriarch required that all copies of Barlaam's writings in Constantinople be handed over to him and that copies in any other towns be destroyed in public by church authorities. It is regrettable, therefore, that we have no complete set of Barlaam's work "Against the Messalians" which comprises his most significant theological treatise. We must rely instead on passages cited in other works by those who adamantly opposed him. In 1341, after the Council, Barlaam emigrated to Italy.

Before discussing the dialogue translated in this volume, it would be helpful to examine the basic issues in the debate between the two men as evidenced in the *Triads*. Acquaintance with the *Triads* will aid our understanding of the lesser-known and probably more specialized "Dialogue between an Orthodox and a Barlaamite." These discussions will also shed light on the relationship between Orthodoxy and Greek philosophy (specifically Platonism), a relationship greatly affected by the development of Palamite theology.

Triads in Defense of the Holy Hesychasts

The *Triads* are set up as a sort of dialogue between a disciple of Palamas and Palamas himself. The disciple opens the discussion by expressing his dismay over several accusations brought against the monks "by certain people." He turns to Palamas, his spiritual father: "I beg you, Father, to instruct me in what should be said in defense of the truth" (I.i.1). There is no ensuing discussion in the manner of an open dialogue; rather, Palamas speaks in a kind of instructional monologue. At certain points in this monologue, the disciple enters the discussion and describes particular arguments brought by the anti-hesychasts. By using the fictional and literary figure of the disciple, Palamas introduces different topics without losing the flow of his arguments. The disciple asks Palamas "to clarify our opinion on their views" (I.iii.1).

Right at the start of the *Triads* a major opposition between Palamas and Barlaam is evident: Barlaam apparently feels (remember that he is not called by name in the first *Triad*) that the hesychasts are unsophisticated, uneducated monks. The argument is described by the confused disciple:

> I have heard it stated by certain people that monks should also pursue secular wisdom, and that if they do not possess this wisdom, it is impossible for them to avoid ignorance and false opinions, even if they have achieved the highest level of impassibility; and that one cannot acquire perfection and sanctity without seeking knowledge from all quarters, above all from Greek culture (paideia), which is also a gift of God...(I.i.1).

The point of Barlaam's insistence on philosophy and secular education as prerequisites for enquiry into theological matters is that one is led to a knowledge of God by meditating on God's creatures. One proceeds, then, from effects to cause. Barlaam stresses the total transcendence of God; man can only have knowledge of Him indirectly through His created works. Seen in this light it makes sense that Barlaam should emphasize the necessity of secular knowledge as the foundation for theological study.

Palamas categorically rejects this idea. "By examining the nature of sensible things, these people have arrived at a certain concept of God, but not at a conception truly worthy of Him and appropriate to His blessed

nature," he says (I.i.18). He does agree that "the intellect of the pagan philosophers is likewise a divine gift insofar as it naturally possesses a wisdom endowed with reason." Alas, such wisdom, he maintains, has been "perverted by the wiles of the devil, who has transformed it into a foolish wisdom, wicked and senseless" (I.i.19). Later Palamas likens secular wisdom to a serpent, declaring that you must first kill it, meaning that you must overcome the pride that philosophy can produce (I.i.21). If one then dissects the serpent, one can extract the poison from what is beneficial; philosophy can then become "an instrument for good."

In spite of Palamas' angry assault on profane philosophy, let us not suppose that he attacks out of sheer ignorance. I mentioned earlier that Barlaam was well-known in Constantinople for his knowledge of such matters as astronomy and diplomacy. But Palamas must have been conversant in the sciences on some level, if only on a popular one. This is evident from his *150 Chapters*, translated by Robert Sinkewicz.[11] Sinkewicz dates this treatise to the late 1340's (1349-1350), about eight years after the Council of Constantinople officially backed Palamite ideas. Gregory's title for this treatise is telling: "150 Chapters on Topics of Natural and Theological Science, the Moral and the Ascetic Life, Intended as a Purge for the Barlaamite Corruption." The first chapters are devoted to refutations of what the "Hellene sages" have to say concerning such matters as the eternity of matter, the World Soul, celestial bodies, and the inhabited zones of the earth. Palamas relies to a great extent on biblical evidence to support his statements, e.g., we know about the beginnings of history because Moses instructs us, the earth is at the center of the universe because that is what Scripture and common sense tell us. Nonetheless, he had to be familiar in some manner (if not quite at the same level as Barlaam), with natural scientific ideas of the Greeks in order to refute them to his satisfaction.

The real problem in the debate seems to be the way in which the two men view man's knowledge of God. Barlaam, like Palamas, adhered to apophatic or negative theology (e.g., I.i.1). And both men continually refer back to Pseudo-Dionysius to bolster their arguments. Yet each uses Dionysius' negative theology in a different way. Meyendorff points out that, for Barlaam, negative theology was a species of philosophy and remained negative.[12] Palamas uses negative theology as a beginning for mystical knowledge. Hence, each man uses the same authority (Dionysius) but interprets him differently. "For God is not only beyond knowledge, but also beyond unknowing," says Palamas (I.iii.4). This "unknowing"[13]

harks back to Pseudo-Dionysius' *Mystical Theology* when he describes Moses as plunging "into the truly mysterious darkness of unknowing." Dionysius further describes this unknowing:

> Here, being neither oneself nor someone else, one is supremely united by a completely unknowing inactivity of all knowledge, and knows beyond the mind by knowing nothing.

Palamas uses the theme of unknowing in a paragraph in which he discusses how a human mind can attain to a vision of God. It is not the divine essence the mind can see; rather, it is "seeing God by a revelation appropriate and analogous to Him. One sees, not in a negative way—for one does see something—but in a manner superior to negation" (I.iii.4).

For Barlaam, then, negative theology reenforces the idea that man is unable to know God truly or to see him in a vision. Set in this context, it is no wonder that he became indignant with "uneducated" monks who claimed to have a vision of God with their own eyes! But if we consider that Palamas viewed negative theology not as an end but as a beginning, specifically a beginning for mystical knowledge, we can also understand his fury with the philosopher from Italy.

If both men argue for different positions vis-à-vis man's knowledge of God, what can be said regarding the mystic vision? What exactly *were* those monks up to on Mt. Athos, those hesychasts who practiced a psychosomatic form of prayer?

The Hesychasts' Vision and Man's Knowledge of God

Palamas discusses quite explicitly the hesychasts' manner of prayer. He stresses that beginners especially need help in learning self-discipline and he suggests that control of breathing is a good start. In this he is not proclaiming something new; several earlier masters of hesychasm had also seen breath control as a good way to begin. In fact, throughout the discussion of the hesychasts' method of prayer, Palamas refers either to earlier Christian writers or biblical figures (e.g., Moses, David, Paul); this has the effect of lending solid traditional evidence to the practice of the monks. Palamas does not consider impassibility to "consist in mortifying the passionate part of the soul, but in removing it from evil to good, and directing its energies towards divine things (II.ii.19). This is a good Orthodox posi-

tion in line with the biblical anthropology to which the Orthodox Church adheres. "It is the *misuse* of the powers of the soul which engenders the terrible passions" (II.ii.19), says Palamas. While Barlaam, in good Platonic fashion, sought to disengage the bodily passions from pure spiritual enquiry, Palamas insists that the body, being created by God, must be good as well. Power is power, he maintains. If it is used well, it will be directed toward God; if misused, it will lead to "terrible passions."

There is still the nagging question of what the monks saw in their vision of God and the manner in which they achieved the vision. The crux of the disagreement between Palamas and Barlaam centered on the Gospel story of the Transfiguration. Mt. Thabor was usually identified with the mount of the Transfiguration, where Peter, James and John saw Christ with Moses and Elijah. What exactly was the light that saturated the mount? Barlaam claimed that the light was meteorological in nature; it was a created light that disappeared once the phenomenon was over. Palamas adamantly disagreed. Using Basil the Great and Dionysius as support, he insisted that the light was not visible through the surrounding air. In fact, he exclaims, this light shone more brightly than the sun and yet people around the mount never saw anything (III.i.22). How could it possibly have been a meteorological phenomenon? He refers to theophanies in the Old and New Testaments in which God's glory appeared as overpowering light. The light on Mt. Thabor was divine light and was part of Christ's divine nature. The eyes of the disciples were changed for a moment so that they could see, in a way, what was always there in the divine sphere. That light, he says, "has no beginning and no end; it remained uncircumscribed (in time and space) and imperceptible to the senses, although it was contemplated...but the disciples of the Lord passed here from the flesh into the spirit by a transmutation of their senses."[14]

What, then, did the disciples see and what do those hesychasts experience? Barlaam, as a good Platonist, insisted upon the simplicity of the Godhead. God's essence and his actions are one because God is simple essence. God's operations, then, are either the same as the essence or are distinct from it. If distinct, then they must be created. And, for Barlaam, this meant that the light on Thabor had also to be created, if it was distinct from the essence of God. If the monks claimed to have a vision of God, he argued, then what they would have seen would have been the essence of God. This is absurd, he claimed! God as utterly transcendent and uncreated

cannot be seen in his essence by created beings. And if Palamas does not adhere to the simplicity of God's essence then he is breaking up God into pieces and worshipping, not one God, but two or perhaps more.

It is here that Palamite theology, as it is called, was crystallized. Palamas distinguished between God's essence and his operations or energies. We must note, however, that once again he is not originating doctrine but drawing upon tradition. Palamas completely agreed with Barlaam that God's essence cannot be participated in by created beings. Dionysius emphasizes this throughout his writings and Palamas quotes him continually. Concerning the distinction between essence (*ousia*) and operations, Palamas harks back to the Cappadocian fathers, who speak about God's knowable attributes, and Dionysius, who distinguishes between divine essence and its participable manifestations. He is also greatly influenced by Maximus Confessor (6-7th century) who writes explicitly:

> Indeed, the Holy Fathers say plainly that it is impossible for any nature at all to be or to be known apart from its essential activity. And if there is no such thing as a nature to be or to be known without its essential characteristic activity, how is it possible for Christ to be or be known as truly God and man by nature without the divine and human activities? For, according to the Fathers, the lion who loses its roaring ability is no lion at all, and a dog without the power to bark is not a dog.[16]

God's energies are uncreated because they are a part of God. But they are accessible to human beings; they are the link, so to speak, between divine and human. Only Christ as the God-man, as the hypostatic union of divine and human natures, has participated in the divine essence. When man has a vision of God, he sees not God's essence (which is impossible) but his energies. And the light of Thabor is uncreated grace in which man can share. Turning to Barlaam, Palamas exclaims: "Yet this quibbler...accuses us falsely of regarding God as sensible reality" (III.iii.10). Barlaam had insisted that if God could be seen with the sensible eyes, then what the monks saw had also to be sensible and tangible. Nonsense! retorts Palamas. You, Barlaam, he maintained, "imagine wrongly that the things around God—the natural attributes appertaining to Him—are identical with the inner being" (III.iii.10).

The fact that man can participate in God's energies leads to the oft-

misunderstood Eastern Orthodox idea of deification, *theosis*. Man, made in the image and likeness of God, is tarnished because of sin. But he can attain to his original likeness to God and become a "son of God" by grace. In his *150 Chapters*, Palamas gives us a clear expression of the concept of deification by quoting the Cappadocian father Basil:

> As souls that bear the Spirit are illumined by the Spirit they become spiritual themselves and send forth grace to others. Thence comes foreknowledge of the future, understanding of mysteries, apprehension of things hidden, distribution of spiritual gifts, citizenship in heaven, the dance with the angels, joy without end, divine distribution, likeness to God, and the summit of our longings, namely, to become God.[17]

When man "becomes" God, however, it is not implied that he has the ability to be God by nature, for man cannot share in God's essence. We should also note that, in good Orthodox fashion (and something that might have horrified Calvin and Luther) man must meet God halfway. This is the Eastern meaning of synergy: man attains salvation, not by waiting passively for God to dig him out of the mire, but by actively working toward God. In Chapter 78 of the *150 Chapters*, Palamas specifies that the participation in God's energies are "for those who approach by free choice to be near or to be far from God...(rational) beings alone are capable of wretchedness or blessedness. But let us hasten to attain blessedness."

Lest we accuse Palamas of becoming theoretical it is well to remind ourselves of his life as priest and archbishop. His life and, in turn, the lives of Orthodox Christians, are deeply rooted in the Church. Several times in speaking about the Transfiguration, he quotes Church liturgy from 6 August, the feast of the Transfiguration, and he specifically says that these "annual hymns" affirm the events on Thabor. He also stresses that it is God as a trinity who deifies us.[18] We can become sons of God because Christ assumed human and divine natures and the Spirit of grace flows from the Godhead. Mystical knowledge for Palamas is not Platonic intellection. What is Platonic about him regarding mystical union is the conviction that man *can* transcend himself and attain to the vision.[19] But then he parts ways with Barlaam. This mystical knowledge and union are achieved through a life of prayer, a life of action in Church liturgy and sacraments. The notion of deification is not new with Palamas; as an Orthodox Chris-

tian he accepts his tradition as authority and interprets it within the context of his historical and theological experience. But he insists, contra Barlaam, that man's mystical union is no disembodied affair. It involves body and soul. Naturally, he accepts with Barlaam that man's passions can wreck havoc with man's higher goals and good intentions. But as an Orthodox he was firmly convinced that passion need not be evil unless so used; if turned in the right direction, toward the good, it will only strengthen us in our attainment of virtue.

This, then, is what those monks, whom Barlaam viewed with such suspicion and, at times, downright disdain, busied themselves with. Psychosomatic prayer, navel-gazing as it were, and controlled breathing were not ends in themelves. They were meant to be starting points in the self-discipline of monks: an aid on the road to virtue. Through a life of prayer and activity in Church tradition and Church life, man could attain to a vision of God and reach the highest goal, to become a son of God. In his arguments with Barlaam, Palamas accused him and his cohorts of Messalianism (III.i.26; the same charge Barlaam brought against the hesychasts) and Eunomianism (III.ii.4; III.ii.18). Eunomius, an Arian, had said not only that the Spirit and the Son were creatures, but that man could have a knowledge of God that God had of himself. At the end of his *150 Chapters*, Palamas declares that the Barlaamites, agreeing with Eunomius, "say that the substance of God is visible through creatures" (Ch. 150). He closes these chapters with a final dramatic note of damnation:

> So the harvest of their impiety is abundant. We should therefore flee them and their company as one would a soul-destroying, many-headed serpent, or the manifold corruption of Orthodoxy.

Dialogue between an Orthodox and a Barlaamite

The text in this volume was written by Palamas in the form of a general dialogue that he envisioned could take place between an Orthodox and a Barlaamite, in general. However, let us not be fooled by the absence of names. Nor let us erroneously assume that because this is a dialogue in the old and familiar Platonic setting we are about to witness an objectively-portrayed discussion between two points of view. Palamas' full title

betrays his own prejudices from the outset: "Dialogue between an Orthodox and a Barlaamite which invalidates in detail the Barlaamite error." The text is certainly detailed: it consists of 57 chapters of varying lengths; the Orthodox begins the discussion and ends it with a fervent "Amen!" Whereas in the *Triads* Palamas ultimately wished to defend the knowledge of God claimed by the hesychast-monks, here the topic concerns the unity of God and how our knowledge about God reflects (or does not reflect) that unity.

The Dialogue is most easily understandable if read in conjunction with the *Triads*. Many of the essential ideas of the *Triads* resurface here but are directed toward slightly different paths. Two passages betray when the treatise was written (or, at least, when Palamas imagined the conversation would have taken place). The dialogue opens with the Orthodox enquiring into what charges the Barlaamites are bringing against them which occasions the present dispute. He launches into an immediate attack on Barlaam himself: "the heretic Barlaam (whose doctrine has been officially refuted by the synod" (I).[20] Palamas is referring here to the synod of 1341 which approved his ideas and condemned Barlaam. Later in chapter XII, Palamas inserts the parenthetical remark: "and the synod has found you out this year!" again referring to the synod of 1341. Hence, the dialogue must be read as having been written consequent to the official recognition of Palamas' ideas of the essence and energies of God which formed the essential topics of his *Triads*.

When Palamas makes the initial reference to the synod in his opening remarks, he is treading on sturdy ground: he has written this text knowing that he will be backed without question by the Orthodox Church. The Barlaamite replies by asking his colleague how he can defend "such obvious and admitted stupidities..." In spite of this rather rough start the Orthodox appears devoted to a peaceful dialogue. Thus, he begins the second chapter: "The Orthodox truth is really something difficult to ensnare and if you don't search for it like gold and silver (as the wise Solomon says) you will never get hold of it." Shortly thereafter, however, his tone again turns belligerent: "...you brag endlessly about your piety and, consequently, try to drag the masses along. In fact, you lead them astray from the orthodox truth in an unheard of manner!" In these first chapters, Palamas repeats the word "truth" by making it clear from the words of both interlocutors that they desire nothing *but* the truth. One cannot help but notice, however, that the tone of the Orthodox is decisively defensive and it is the Barlaamite who assumes an irenic pose: "Who doesn't desire peace and truth?" he

enquires halfway through the dialogue (XXIX).

The main topic is the unity of God. In its past, the Eastern Church had occasionally been accused of sundering the unity of God and, in fact, worshipping more than one deity. This is particularly the Barlaamite's worry. As a Platonist, the notion that God might not be one and simple was especially disturbing. His position was that God's essence was uncreated: "For we say that there is one uncreated being, the essence of God with three hypostases, and that all other beings other than that essence are created" (I). Naturally, such a statement about the unity and uncreatedness of God's essence would be acceptable to any right-thinking Christian. The snag concerned Palamas' distinction between God's essence and his activities, a distinction already formulated in the *Triads*. The Orthodox quotes the revered Maximus the Confessor: "Just as it is impossible to be without being, so it is not possible to be active without activity" (XXXI). Hence, if God is described as pure act then he must necessarily be active. How else can we get an idea of what God is unless we witness his activities in creation?

The Barlaamite disagreed that God's activities, particularly his deifying grace, are different from his essence. His argument was that whatever was not of God's essence must be created. Hence, the Orthodox's distinction between God's essence and his energies or activities was, for the Barlaamite, a distinction between what was uncreated and what was created. The Orthodox, so he claims, does not only destroy God's unity but he worships creatures as well as the Creator. Furthermore, if the Orthodox insists that essence and activity are separate then he will fall into the error of making God a composite creature.

Both men argue, then, for God's simplicity. Both argue that man cannot have a vision of God's nature: man cannot know God in his essence. And when man regains his original image and likeness of God, spoken of in Genesis, and further, becomes a "son of God" (based on 2 Peter 1:4), it will not be God's nature that he acquires. The Orthodox insists that we know God through his activities; on the surface, this argument sounds like the traditional philosophical line of proceeding from the effects to the cause. The Orthodox, however, rejects this and carefully quotes Basil. The creations of God do not proclaim his essence but only his activities. Both men are adamant that God cannot be circumscribed in human language: the

influence of negative theology upon Palamas has already been noted in connection with the *Triads*. There, Pseudo-Dionysius was quoted as an authority (see above, p.8). Here Dionysius' *On Divine Names* is used as the model for both discussants and both quote it at length to bolster their respective arguments. Discussing divinity, for instance, the Orthodox cites Dionysius when he calls divinity an "inimitable imitation" (XXI). In another place he quotes Gregory of Nyssa, described as "the most brilliant star dealing with those who oppose themselves to the divinity, the Spirit" (XVII): "(But) we know that the divine nature has no name which signifies it...the divine nature itself remains unspoken and unuttered; it exceeds all possibility of being revealed by name" (XVII).

If both men agree on so many of the basic points, how is it that the controversy, as it is reflected in this dialogue, takes on such a virulent tone?

It is clear that the Orthodox is on the defensive; he assumes a most passionate stance. His language, vocabulary, and reactions attest to his inability to make any compromise with his opponent. For example, when he charges the Barlaamite of worshipping two Gods, one created and the other uncreated, his tone witnesses to his severe agitation:

> You, then, who clearly suffer from the most despicable disease of believing in two Gods—and the synod has found you out this year!—spread that lie about us and all the saints who, through thick and thin, confess that God is one. For that sometimes the same God is seen and thought and participated in and other times He is invisible and unintelligible and imparticipable and that we call Him in all simplicity both wholly intelligible and unintelligible, the great Dionysius the Areopagite has taught us, too. But until today we had not yet heard that the same God is created and uncreated because He has admittedly a created and uncreated divinity (XII).

In the face of such accusations we would expect the Barlaamite, schooled as we would assume he was in the art of argumentation, to offer substantial retorts to these words. In the pen of Palamas, however, his response is limited to a single, humble sentence:

> We conclude from all these facts that there is one divinity (XIII).

This major hurdle overcome, the Orthodox resumes speaking, con-

tinuing with the same topic of whether God is composed of two parts. He asks his adversary:

> ...do you conclude in that way that there is one, or do you assert that that one divinity is composed of a created and an uncreated divinity? (XIII)

The Barlaamite replies:

> Come on, don't think we're *that* stupid! No, we raise the thinking part of our soul from the visible divinity up to the completely invisible and solitary uncreated divinity, and so, we revere the one uncreated divinity, the essence of God itself. (XIII)

Such an answer, one would imagine, would have greatly pleased the Orthodox. On the contrary. He uses this response as the occasion for grouping the Barlaamites with the "misleading doctrine of Eunomius," a fervent adherent of the Arian heresy.[21]

This is just one short illustration of how the dialogue proceeds. But it shows clearly how biting the Orthodox can be toward the arguments of his opponent. Indeed, though this is a dialogue, the Barlaamite is given very little space to air his own views. The greater part of the dialogue is devoted to the speeches of the Orthodox interspersed with questions addressed to the Barlaamite. In general, the Barlaamite's reactions tend to be submissive; for example: "It seems to me that in this point as well you reach the truth precisely" (XXXIV), and again: "Solve yet one more problem for me in a clearer fashion and I will believe you in every respect" (L).

The most basic position upon which neither theologian can compromise, and which accounts, I believe, for the vehemence with which the Orthodox argues, is the Palamite distinction between essence and activities. We saw earlier in discussing the *Triads* that Palamas does not offer new theological ideas here. As a member of Orthodoxy, tradition and the words of the fathers are of paramount significance. This is especially clear from the almost endless parade of citations, direct quotes and allusions to Orthodox writers made by both men. The list includes Basil, Gregory of Nyssa, Gregory the Theologian (Gregory Nazianzen in Western tradition), Pseudo-Dionysius, John Damascene, Maximus the Confessor, Athanasius, Cyril of Alexandria, and John Chrysostum. And Palamas bases his own

insights regarding essence and activities on the Cappadocian fathers, who speak about God's knowable attributes, and Dionysius, who distinguishes between the divine essence and its participable manifestations.[22] Many of the ideas, then, of the *Triads* resurface in the dialogue: only Christ as the God-man, the union of divine and human natures, has participated in the divine essence. The real problem with Barlaam, as Palamas formulated it in the *Triads,* was that he "imagined wrongly that the things around God—the natural attributes appertaining to Him—are identical with the inner being" (III.iii.10). In trying to describe the vision given to man, the Orthodox in our dialogue again turns to an earlier father, this time Basil: God leads us "from our humble state here on earth in order that the Incomprehensible (literally, the "uncontainable") is contained by a created nature in at least a moderate and most safe way" (XLIV). And what exactly does that mean? The Orthodox first cites Paul and then Basil before he gives us his own answer: "According to them we participate in God in a moderate way and, according to them, we see and think of Him dimly, one person more, the other less, one by his intelligence, the other by godlike power; each of us participates in them in agreement with his own purity..." (XLV). Only by accepting that we can participate in God's activities, insists the Orthodox, are we able to make any sense of the visions of the saints, the great event of the Transfiguration of Christ, or the experiences of his brothers, the hesychast monks of Mt. Athos.

How does the Barlaamite react to all this? If he was anything like his mentor Barlaam (and I think it is quite fair to assume he was) he would have been trained in philosophical argumentation. It would mean that no previous arguments or conclusions are acceptable without an initial critical enquiry into their validity. The Orthodox, however, did not use the philosophical method but a strictly theological one, based not so much on pure reason but first and foremost, on faith and the traditional sayings and earlier Church writings. Already from the outset, then, there is an enormous difference between this dialogue and a classical Platonic/Socratic discussion. In the latter, the philosophical method was assumed by the speakers; further, Socrates' basic contention was that we must admit our own ignorance in the matter under discussion and start with a clean slate. But this is hardly the stance taken by the Orthodox. There was no need for him to search for truth as one who had not yet found it; indeed, the truth was known already to any straight-minded Orthodox Christian, enshrined in the writings and teachings of old. If the Barlaamite had wanted to argue

along philosophical lines, he was given no chance to do so; the Orthodox had assumed that the only acceptable method here was a theological one.

This is certainly different from the problems which earlier Christian writers faced who also chose the dialogue form for apologetic purposes. Justin Martyr, an apologist of the second century, composed a dialogue between himself and a Jew, Trypho, in which it is clear that he wishes to show his friend the errors Judaism has made with regard to Christ. At the beginning of the dialogue Trypho enquires: "Do not the philosophers turn every discourse on God? And do not questions arise to them about His unity and providence? Is not this truly the duty of philosophy, to investigate the Deity?"[23]

Justin wholeheartedly agrees. And in describing his own conversion to Christianity, after making the rounds of all the major philosophical schools of his time, he says: "(But) straightway a flame was kindled in my soul; and a love of the prophets, and of those men who are friends of Christ, possessed me;...I found this philosophy alone to be safe and profitable. Thus, and for this reason, I am a philosopher."[24] For Justin, Christianity was the "true philosophy."

But the world in which Palamas found himself was far different from Justin's. As a priest and archbishop, he was a leader of Orthodox doctrine and had to safeguard Orthodoxy from devious thinking. His theological and dialogical weapons consisted of formulating traditional views and associating his opponent with heresy and condemned doctrines, including Arianism, Messalianism, and the heresy of Eutyches. Early in the dialogue we hear the Orthodox exclaim: "You do not (even) notice that you are rolling headlong down the slope of polytheism!" (III). For Palamas, the great problem is not so much the Platonic search for the Good; rather, the theological life must distinguish between right thinking and wrong, and the manner in which dialogue was used shifted accordingly. This accords well with Henry Duméry's observations in his *Phenomenology and Religion,* that once the Christian world separated itself from the Hellenistic, "culture embraces the relationship between philosophy and religion...as the relationship between reason and faith, between philosophy and theology."[25] This is clearly evident in Palamas' writings: there is no question

about the primacy of faith and the superiority of theology.

And what happens when the Barlaamite uses the very same authoritative figures in his own arguments? Though the Orthodox approves of their citation, he often dismisses their use, unceremoniously declaring to the Barlaamite that he has misread the fathers or simply misinterpreted them. For example, after the Barlaamite cites Dionysius and offers his interpretation of the passage, the Orthodox exclaims: "Not in the least! For you missed his trustworthy and divine insight to the utmost degree!" (XXII). The Barlaamite, however, is presented as one who easily accepts the interpretation of his opponent: "It seems to me that in this point as well you reach the truth precisely" (XXXIV). Other weapons used by the Orthodox are to accuse the Barlaamite of taking words of the fathers out of context, wrenching terms out of context, or not grasping the full import of what the Orthodox is trying to tell him, e.g., "One must carefully listen to the words that are spoken if one wants to arrive at their truth. Now you don't seem to understand the power of what I just said" (XX). As a theologian, a pastoral leader, a monk, and an archbishop, Palamas did not condone what appeared to him as misinterpretation or wrong-headed thinking. His job was to safeguard Orthodoxy not to engage in philosophical subtleties or argumentation in search for "the truth." For, after all, he already had the truth. In this respect, he stands in a long line of Christian writers of dialogue. Justin Martyr stood at the beginning of that tradition. Other examples include "Dialogue of Timothy and Aquila" (3rd century), "Dialogue of Athanasius and Zacchaeus" (4th century), "Dialogue between an Enquiring Jew and a Christian" of Peter Damian (11th century), and Peter Abelard's "Dialogue of a Philosopher with a Jew, and a Christian."[26] Most of the dialogues that deal with religious opponents are not imbued with the open Platonic spirit of enquiry. Often the tone is dogmatic and, in later dialogues, the opponent is converted in the end. The abiding characteristic of these Christian dialogues, including that of Palamas, is that the orthodox Christian (meaning, the "right-thinking" Christian) holds the keys to the truth and is given the forum in which to air his views and offer the keys to less enlightened folk.

Before addressing the question of whether such an approach merits our approval or censure, I would like to point out briefly a few literary characteristics of Palamas' dialogue that shed some light on education and scholarship during his time. Palamas wrote in the century directly preceding the development of printing. Hence, he is not able to pick up books at

random and thumb through them to find exact references and citations. Much work had to be done through memorization and it is impressive in this text how well Palamas knew his sourcs. A good bulk of the dialogue consists of quotations of earlier writers though there are times when Palamas is not quite certain where a citation comes from. For example, several times he quotes a writer and then says, "the same man says somewhere (else)" (X, XI). He knows the quote but is vague about where exactly it is located. Occasionally, his memory fails him and he wrongly cites a writer; so, at one point, he attributes a quote to Athanasius when, in fact, the writer was Maximus the Confessor (V). Toward the beginning of the dialogue he makes reference to Basil writing an apology against those who accused him of believing in three gods when he probably meant Gregory of Nyssa who wrote *About Not Saying that There Are Three Gods* (III).

There is also an abundant use of epithets attached to particular writers which is characteristic of an oral culture or cultures which depend heavily upon hearing and memory (one thinks immediately, for example, of Homer's use of epithets and stock descriptions). Hence, Basil is continually "the great Basil" (III, XI) or "the most accurate theologian of all" (X) or "the great and colorful Basil" (XLII); Maximus is "the greatest expert in divine things" (X) or "great in divine matters" (XIV) or "the divine Maximus" (XXI); Gregory of Nyssa is "the most brilliant star dealing with those who oppose themselves to the Spirit" (XVII); Athanasius is "the great Athanasius" (XX); John Damascene is "wise at divine matters" (XXI); Dionysius is "the revealer of God" (XXII) or "the God-revealer from the Areopagus" (LI); Kosmas is "the divine poet of the Church" (VIII); Metrophanes is "the divine singer" (XI). Rarely does a writer appear without some revealing epithet attached to his name that may be a leftover of the use of literary epithets to aid in memorization.

We also find in Palamas that, as a good Orthodox, he uses liturgical hymns from the Divine Liturgy to back up his statements. Thus, he supports his arguments first with church fathers (of the Orthodox tradition), then with illustrations from the liturgy, and occasionally citations from the New Testament. Palamas' Greek is rather convoluted and a bit thick, although he is much easier to read than Dionysius the Areopagite who

revelled in inventing new words. Palamas uses the Greek of the Church Fathers and, generally speaking, he is not particularly poetic. His style is rather dry and his sentences quite long. Nonetheless, he is mostly clear in expressing what he thinks. A few times he uses descriptions and metaphors taken from the world of nature which are distinctive in their clarity. For example, at one point, he tries to prove to the Barlaamite that the deifying grace of God (an example of God's energy or activity) exists independently of God but is not a creature. The fathers, he says, "believe that the grace of deification is enhypostatic, not in the sense that it is completely independent (authypostatic), but that it remains together with the persons in which it comes." He then uses an illustration drawn from meteorology: "It is not, like lightning and thunder, born at the moment of passing away, and abolished together with its manifestation in the objects" (XXVI). Later toward the conclusion of the dialogue he uses an extended metaphor from agriculture to show how what is most powerful is actually the most simple:

> But from agriculture, too, one can learn that bodies which have many powers are rather the more simple. For one does not put dung which is not perfectly mature upon the meadows; but when it is mature and after some time returns to the state of being absolutely simple, then the knowledgeable farmer puts it under vegetables and all kinds of plants, because it has good qualities for everything and can feed everything. Do you also see in the case of bodies that the most simple things are the most powerful? (LII)

Hence, in spite of God's immeasurable power, his essence remains simple.

Summary Remarks

As a result of Palamas' disputes with Barlaam, Palamite theology became normative for the Eastern Orthodox Church. It was not so much a matter of Palamas introducing original ideas into Orthodoxy. *That* would surely have been a most unorthodox way of dealing with Church truth. As a good Orthodox, Palamas relied on tradition, citing material particularly from the Cappadocian fathers, Pseudo-Dionysius and Maximus the Confessor. He was also a devoted man of the cloth as is evident from his insistence that prayer and contemplation be united with an active sacramental

and liturgical life. Intellection was fine, he might say, in agreement with Barlaam. But experience is better. The mystic vision involves the active experience of body and soul, allied with prayer; the passions are part of man's existence and must simply be directed toward virtue. This requires discipline. Prayer requires discipline. But for Gregory such discipline is never an individualistic affair: it only bears fruit within the active life of the community. What Palamas achieved was an articulation into doctrine of ideas already embedded within the rich theological, spiritual and monastic traditions of the East. By endorsing Palamas' ideas the Council of Constantinople in 1341 also spoke plainly in favor of monastic traditions and habits. In the Eastern Church monasticism is not opposed to ecclesiastical decisions. When Barlaam tangled with the so-called uneducated and illiterate monks he probably did not realize that he would be taking on the entire structure of the Orthodox Church. He also occupied a rather difficult position. Although claiming to be Orthodox and following his ancestors he did come from southern Italy and so, could not have been living in the thick of the Byzantine world. He was a man born with his feet in two different traditions, a philosopher-monk who had passionately imbibed the ideas of Platonism but who must have had much inner turmoil in satisfactorily assimilating Christianity with Greek philosophy. And it is surely unfortunate that his bedside manner, rather arrogant and impatient, did not help him when he tried to convince the Byzantines of his own Orthodoxy.

It seems that a good deal of the problem between these two men lies in the realm of hermeneutics. Each ardently read and quoted Pseudo-Dionysius, claiming that the other was wrong in his interpretation. But each also felt that the other sundered the unity of the Godhead. Each accused the other of succumbing to heresy via Messalianism or Arianism. Who was right? Whose interpretation was correct?

I think that the answer to this is that both men were right by adhering to their respective traditions and arguing consistently on the basis of that tradition. While both were Orthodox, Palamas was especially a churchman, an archbishop even, and he stood squarely within the mainstream of Byzantine Orthodoxy. Barlaam felt that the road to a knowledge of God lay in a strict adherence to secular education which provided the necessary prerequisite to theological and spiritual understanding. For Palamas, secular wisdom was acceptable as long as one dealt with it as one would with a snake: realize that it is full of poison, dissect it carefully, and take whatever

might be useful for more important work, i.e., one's attainment of virtue.[27] Barlaam's greatest problem was perhaps trying to convince mainstream Byzantine Orthodoxy that *his* interpretation of Orthodoxy was more accurate. The result was that his Byzantine colleagues, for the most part, considered him an outsider. Our own difficulties in assessing Barlaam are exacerbated by the fact that both the *Triads* and the *Dialogue* are the work of Palamas. Hence, his portrayal of his adversary, especially in the *Dialogue*, is his own. While it might have been a fairly accurate character presentation in some respects, his Barlaamite functions within the limits Palamas himself sets, limits that Barlaam or one of his followers might well have rejected or, at the very least, superceded. The fact that this is a literary creation, then, renders our own work more tricky.

Palamas' ideas, as crystallized in his *Triads* and developed further in his *Dialogue,* proved decisive for Orthodoxy. But what about the inner man? One does not detect in the writings of Palamas the sense of inner struggle between a classical heritage and Christian conviction that one feels in other Christian writers. For example, the 4th and 5th century philosopher-bishop Synesius of Cyrene wrote a letter explaining his difficulties regarding his imminent appointment as bishop of Ptolemais. In the letter he mentions a few reasons why he should not become bishop. His strongest argument stems from his inability to combine philosophical and Christian truths. He agrees to be bishop but makes clear his position: where possible, he will assimilate his philosophical heritage with the ideas he has learned from his conversion to Christianity. But if the two strands conflict, he says, he will opt for philosophy.[28] When one reads Synesius one feels an intense struggle between what one holds most dear from the classical world and what is accepted by Christianity. So, too, many centuries later in Peter Abelard, can one sense the conflict. Of course, Abelard's thoroughly Catholic medieval world was much different from Synesius' amalgam of Hellenism and Christianity in the fifth century; but Abelard had too much exposure to classical thought not to be deeply disturbed by it. His unfinished dialogic text "Dialogue of a Philosopher with a Jew, and a Christian" is a vivid witness to this.[29] The dialogue purports to take place in a dream in which a philosopher, a Christian and a Jew appeal to Abelard for help in deciding whose religious/philosophical tradition is to be rated most highly. First, the philosopher and the Jew converse and thereafter, the philosopher and the Christian. Since the work is incomplete (as dreams themselves are so often interrupted at crucial moments) we have no record

of Abelard's official "decision." It is quite clear from the dialogue, however, that the Christian was victorious. The Jew is given short shrift while the bulk of the text is centered on the Christian. And ardent Christian that Abelard was, we can hear how passionately he *becomes* the philosopher when arguing with the Jew. The dialogic struggle seems to mirror Abelard's own inner conflict between philosophical "truths" and the Christian "truths" of revelation. This sort of intense struggle is absent in Gregory Palamas. It is far more likely that Barlaam suffered from it though he is allowed so little opportunity to flex his own philosophical muscles either in the "dialogic" *Triads* or in the *Dialogue* under the guise of the Barlaamite. It is important, though, to keep in mind that the struggle between classical "truths" and Christian "truths" lurks beneath the surface of these dialogues; recognizing this will help, I think, in placing various arguments in a proper context.

In his work against Barlaam Palamas effected a shift away from Orthodoxy's classical tradition toward more dogmatically Christian channels. There is a great irony here. Palamas avails himself of Orthodox Christian writers who form such a significant part of tradition in the church. Yet most of those writers, especially the Cappadocian fathers and Pseudo-Dionysius, were greatly influenced themselves by classical concepts and categories. Their writings and vocabularies attest to the struggle for a harmonious blend of traditions. This mixture is the heritage of Palamas. Yet his own dissatisfaction with the philosophers and what he deemed to be shortcomings of the sages of old caused him to turn away from that classical tradition, although he uses the images and vocabulary of those very traditions in his arguments against philosophy. Indeed, his use of the dialogue form itself witnesses to the influence of a literary/philosophical tradition handed down from Plato, that an entire stream of Christian writers eagerly used in their polemics against non-Christians, particularly Jews.[30] Palamas came out of a world steeped in the thought and language of a tradition he rejected to a great extent. In addition, he felt that the discipline of theology and intellectual commitment were not divorced from one's active involvement in church life.

Although Palamas' *Dialogue* primarily discusses God's unity, it was the mystical vision of the monks that precipitated the original debate in his *Triads* and is reflected again in his *Dialogue*. The Orthodox in our *Dialogue* realizes how dreadfully serious the topic under examination is. "For our discussion deals with the superessentiality which lies beyond in hid-

den places" (XXXVII). His term, "superessentiality" is vintage Dionysius. How does one speak about things in hidden places where one has little business being, if any? The mystical experience does not rend God's nature asunder: it reveals how simple and uncomposite that nature is. We might indeed smile when we come to the Barlaamite's final words in the *Dialogue*, for the text identifies him as "The former Barlaamite." So, he has been converted. "What an evil (thing) jealousy is!" he exclaims (57). Yet, Palamas realized how important it was that peace be restored. Whether or not the problems have been satisfactorily or philosophically resolved, unity and peace are achieved. The formerly harsh tone of the Orthodox softens as he addresses the Barlaamite as *adelphe*, "brother" and welcomes him into the Orthodox community. The Orthodox closes the dialogue: "God gives the word according to His promise, my brother, to those who speak for Him. To Him alone be eternal glory. Amen!"

While Palamas emphasizes that the mystical vision reveals God's ultimate simplicity, it is clear that the mystical experience itself remains a complex and transcendental matter: the mystic can never separate himself from his tradition with the result that the experience is forever culturally and historically colored. But the historian can also sense the unity inherent in all mystical visions. One cannot fail but be struck by the underlying similarity of Palamas' insistence on faith to Plato's description of the ultimate stroke of intuition. In his *Triads*, Palamas pillories the merely theoretical man who does not seek knowledge through experience. "Such a man," he says, "impiously lays hands on the sacred and wickedly rends apart the holy, for he does not approach these things with that faith which alone can attain to the truth that lies above reason" (I.ii.12). For Palamas, reason can only do so much; truth lies above reason and requires an act of faith. *Mutatis mutandis* I think that Plato would have wholeheartedly agreed: discursive reasoning can lead us only to a certain point; to reach the full vision of the intelligible world something more is needed, a sort of leap of intuitive faith. And Plotinus, like Palamas, stresses in his *On the Three Primary Hypostases* the high birth and value of the soul and maintains that it is divine: "Since the soul is so honorable and divine a thing, be sure already that you can attain God by reason of its being of this kind, and with this as your motive ascend to him: in all certainty you will not look far" (V.1.3.1ff). He also speaks about the necessity of the soul to be "established in quietude" before its upward trek (V.1.2.14). One begins one's journey to the fatherland, the trip back to the One, by going into one's

self: "We must turn our power of apprehension inwards," he writes, "and make it attend to what is there...we must...keep the soul's power of apprehension pure and ready to hear the voices from on high" (V.1.12.15ff).[31]

Palamas drew upon a rich philosophical and theological tradition as spokesman for the Orthodox Church. As a devoted member of Orthodoxy and an active churchman, he would necessarily stress as authoritative Church tradition, liturgy, the sacraments, the writings of earlier church thinkers—sources a philosopher, who adhered to the process of intellection, might have difficulty in accepting without reservation as the final words. But Barlaam was also a monk and he, too, looked to certain traditional authorities for support. The tradition Palamas looked back to was one that reached through Dionysius and the Cappadocians, who, in their turn, had sifted through and contemplated the earlier Greek fathers and philosophers of antiquity. It was also a tradition that the great Western fifteenth century churchman Nicholas of Cusa absorbed as is evident from his use of negative theology and his "learned ignorance," a good Dionysian concept. In spite of historical, traditional and theological differences, however, these men sought, as surely as did Barlaam, how to express man's longing for the vision of God, how to return to our divine fatherland, and, by so doing, to become again, sons of God.

Notes

1. Fuller treatments of the life of Gregory Palamas may be found in Meyendorff's *A Study of Gregory Palamas* (New York: St Vladimir's Seminary Press, 1974) and V. Lossky, *The Vision of God* (New York: St Vladimir's Seminary Press, 1983). I present only the barest of outlines here.

2. Meyendorff, op. cit., 31-32.

3. Ibid.

4. Ibid., 42.

5. Ibid., 43.

6. *Divine Names,* ch. VII.3.872A. See *Pseudo-Dionysius. The Complete Works,* Coim Luibheid, trans. Classics of Western Spirituality (New York: Paulist Press, 1987), 108f.

7. Meyendorff, op. cit., 134.

8. For an extended discussion of the Jesus Prayer, see Irénée Hausherr, *The Name of Jesus* (Michigan: Cistercian Publications, Inc., 1978).

9. Vladimir Lossky; op. cit., 142.

10. *Gregory Palamas, The Triads,* Nicholas Gendle, trans. Classics of Western Spirituality (New York: Paulist Press, 1983); introductory information here is taken from John Meyendorff's introduction to the volume, p. 9. I will be basing my own discussion of the *Triads* on this translation.

11. (Toronto: Pontifical Institute of Medieval Studies, 1988).

12. See *Triads,* 118, n. *5*

13. *Mystical Theology* 1001A. This is where the phrase "cloud of unknowing" comes from that is so famous from the anonymous 14th century English writer whose text *A Book on Contemplation Called The Cloud of Unknowing in which Cloud a Soul is United with God* may be found in *The Cloud of Unknowing,* Clifton Walker, trans. (Penguin, 1961). See also the sixteenth century Spanish mystic St. John of the Cross, *Dark Night of the Soul,* B. Allison Peers, trans., 3rd ed. (New York: Image Books, 1959).

14. Quoted from Palamas' *Homilies 35,* PG. 151 (col. 433B), in Lossky, op. cit., 162. This interpretation is uncannily similar to rabbinic interpretations of the various lights that the Genesis account of creation describes. One legend tells how the light created on the first day was not the same as that created on the fourth day, in connection with the sun, moon and stars. Rather, "the light of the first day was of a sort that would have enabled man to see the world at a glance from one end to the other." In the coming world this light will be visible to the pious "in all its pristine glory." See Louis Ginzberg, *Legends of the Bible* (Philadelphia: Jewish Publication Society, 1956), 3.

15. Lossky, op. cit., 158.

16. *Maximus Confessor. Selected Writings,* George C. Berthold, trans. Classics of Western Spirituality (New York: Paulist Press, 1985), 23 (taken from "The Trial of Maximus").

17. See Sinkewicz, op. cit., Chapter 76, 170-173.

18. See Georgios I. Mantzaridis, *The Deification of Man. St. Gregory Palamas and the Orthodox Tradition,* Liadain Sherrard, trans. (New York: St Vladimir's Seminary Press, 1984), 107f.

19. Ibid., 102.

20. As in the translation of the text, Roman numerals indicate the chapter number of the text, in Christou's edition.

21. Palamas also uses this charge in the *Triads*. See above, p. 13.

22. See Lossky, op. cit., p. 158.

23. For a translation of this text, see *The Ante-Nicene Fathers,* vol. I (Michigan: Wm. B. Eerdmans Publishing Company, 1981), 194-270.

24. This image of the flame is remarkably similar to the image used by Plato in his Letter VII. See Sara Denning-Bolle, "Christian Dialogue as Apologetic: The Case of Justin Martyr Seen in Historical Context," *Bulletin of the John Rylands Library 69* (1987), 500f.

25. (Berkeley: University of California Press, 1975), 100.

26. For a discussion of the use of dialogue in Christian tradition, see Denning-Bolle, op. cit. and the bibliography cited there.

27. See *Triads* I.i.21.

28. Epistle 105. See Jay Bregman, *Synesius of Cyrene. Philosopher-Bishop* (Berkeley: University of California Press, 1982), 155f.

29. For a translation of this text see the volume by the same title, Pierre J. Payer, trans. (Toronto: Pontifical Institute of Medieval Studies, 1979).

30. See Denning-Bolle, op. cit.; A. Lukyn Williams, Adversus Judaeos: *A Bird's-Eye View of Christian Apologiae Until the Renaissance* (Cambridge, 1935). Of course, the dialogue form in Christian philosophical and theological works was not limited to non-Christian polemics. One thinks, for example, of *Augustine's Confessions, Boethius' Consolation of Philosophy,* or even the 12th century Aelredof *Rievaulx's Dialogue on the Soul* (C.H. Talbot, trans.; Kalamazoo: Cistercian Publications, 1981). The dialogue form was also used by Jewish writers for their own purposes; see, for example, Judah Halevi's dream dialogue, remarkably similar to Abelard's, written in the 12th century. Judah Halevi, *The Kuzari (Kitab al Khazari),* translated from the Arabic by Hartwig Hirschfeld, 1905, introduction by Henry S. Slonimsky (New York, 1964), and *Juda Hallévi, Le Kuzari. Apologie de Ia religion méprisée,* translated by Charles Touati (Collection "Les Dix Paroles"; Verdier; no date given for

publication but this translation became available after 1993). In this dialogue, set in the eighth century, the Kuzari king Bulun is converted to Judaism following a discussion between himself and four men: a philosopher, a Christian, a Muslim and a Jew.

31. Translation taken from A.H. Armstrong in the Loeb Series, *Plotinus* V Cambridge: Harvard University Press, 1984).

Selected Bibliography

Akindynos, Gregorios. *Gregorii Acindyni refutationes duae: operis Gregorii Palamae cui titulus dialogus inter orthodoxum et Barlaamitam/ Gregorii Acindyni; nunc primum editae curante Juan Nadal Canellas.* Turnhout: Brepols; Leuven: University Press, 1995. (Series: Corpus Christianorum. Series Graeca 31).

Anastasiou, Ioannes E. "The Social Teaching of Saint Gregory Palamas," *Greek Orthodox Theological Review* 32 (1987), 179-190.

Anastos, Thomas L. "Gregory Palamas' Radicalization of the Essence, Energies and Hypostasis Model of God," *Greek Orthodox Theological Review* 38 (1993), 335ff.

Christou, P., ed. *Gregoriou tou Palama suggrammata,* 3 vols. Thessaloniki, 1962-1970.

Clucas, Lowell. *The Hesychast Controversy in Byzantium in the Fourteenth Century: A Consideration of the Basic Evidence.* Dissertation. Ann Arbor, Michigan: University Microfilms International, 1975.

Contos, Leonidas. "The Essence-Energies Structure of Saint Gregory Palamas with a Brief Examination of its Patristic Foundation," *Greek Orthodox Theological Review* 12 (1967), 283-295.

Fahey, Michael A., Meyendorff, John. *Trinitarian Theology East and West: St. Thomas Aquinas-St. Gregory Palamas.* Brookline, Mass.: Holy Cross Orthodox Press, 1977. *Church History* 38 (1969),150-163.

Florovsky, Georges. "St. Gregory Palamas and the Tradition of the Fathers" in *Bible, Church, Tradition: An Eastern Orthodox View.* Massachusetts: Nordland Publishing Co., 1972, 105-120.

Geanakoplos, Deno. "Some Aspects of the Influence of the Byzantine Maximos the Confessor on the Theology of East and West," *Church History* 38(1969), 150-163.

Guillaumont, Antoine. "The Jesus Prayer among the Monks of Egypt," *Eastern Churches Review* 6 (1974), 66-71.

Habra, George. "The Sources of the Doctrine of Gregory Palamas on the Divine Energies," *The Eastern Churches Quarterly* 12 (1957-58), 244-252; 294-303; 338-347.

Hausherr, Irénée. *The Name of Jesus.* Kalamazoo: Cistercian Publications, Inc., 1978.

Kakridis, Ioannis. *Codex 88 des Klosters Decani und seine griechischen Vorlagen: ein Kapitel der serbisch-byzantinischen Literaturbeziehungen im 14.Jahrhundert.* Dissertation. München: O.Sagner, 1988. (Series: Slavistische Beiträge; Bd. 233).

Krivocheine, B. "St. Symeon the New Theologian and Early Christian Popular Piety," *Studia Patristica* 2 (1957), 485-494.

Leclerq, Jean, et. al. eds. *The Spirituality of the Middle Ages.* London: Burns and Oates, 1968. See especially, "Byzantine Spirituality," 547-590.

Lossky, Vladimir. *The Vision of God.* New York: St. Vladimir's Seminary Press, 1983.

____________. "Le problème de la 'vision face à face' et la tradition patristique de Byzance," *Studia Patristica* 2 (1957), 512-537.

McGinn, Bernard and Meyendorff, John, eds. *Christian Spirituality: Origins to the Twelfth Century.* New York: Crossroad, 1985.

Montzaridis. Georgios I. *The Deification of Man. St. Gregory Palamas and the Orthodox Tradition.* Liadain Sherrard, trans. New York: St. Vladimir's Seminary Press, 1984.

____________. "Gregory Palamas." *The Encyclopedia of Religion,* Mircea Eliade, ed. New York: Macmillan Publishing Company, 1987. Vol. 6, 131-133.

Maximus Confessor. *Selected Writings.* George C. Berthold, trans. New York: Paulist Press, 1985. Classics of Western Spirituality Series.

Meyendorff, John. *A Study of Gregory Palamas.* 2nd ed. New York: St. Vladimir's Seminary Press, 1974.

____________. *Saint Gregory Palamas and Orthodox Spirituality.* New York: St. Vladimir's Seminary Press, 1974.

____________., ed. and Introduction. *Gregory Palamas, The Triads.* Nicholas Gendle, trans. New York: Paulist Press, 1983. Classics of Western Spirituality Series.

Nicol, D. M. "The Byzantine Church and Hellenic Learning in the Fourteenth Century," *Studies in Church History* 5 (1969), 23-57.

Papametriou, George C. "The Human Body According to Saint Gregory Palamas." *Greek Orthodox Theological Review* 34 (1989), 1-9.

____________. *Introduction to Saint Gregory Palamas.* New York: Philosophical Library, 1973.

____________. *Maimonides and Palamas on God.* Brookline, Mass.: Holy Cross Orthodox Press, 1994.

Pseudo-Dionysius. *The Complete Works.* Colm Luibheid, trans. New York: Paulist Press, 1987. Classics of Western Spirituality Series.

Rogich, Daniel. "Homily 34 of Saint Gregory Palamas." *Greek Orthodox Theological Review* 33 (1988), 135-166.

Romanides, John. "Notes on the Palamite Controversy and Related Topics," *Greek Orthodox Theological Review* 6 (1960), 186-205.

____________. "Notes on the Palamite Controversy and Related Topics," *Greek Orthodox Theological Review* 9 (1963-64), 225-270.

Sherrard, Philip. *Athos, The Holy Mountain.* London: Sidgwick & Jackson, 1982.

Sinkewicz, Robert E. *The One Hundred and Fifty Chapters.* Toronto: Pontifical Institute of Medieval Studies, 1988.

___________. "A New Interpretation for the First Episode in the Controversy Between Barlaam the Calabrian and Gregory Palamas," *Journal of Theological Studies* 31 (1980), 489-500.

___________. "The Doctrine of the Knowledge of God in the Early Writings of Barlaam the Calabrian," *Mediaeval Studies* 44 (1982), 181-242.

Stiernon, Daniel. "Bulletin sur le palamisme," *Revue des études byzantines* 30 (1972), 231-241.

Weber, Nicholas Stephen. "Saint Gregory Palamas' Homily for Palm Sunday," *Greek Orthodox Theological Review* 34 (1989), 263-282.

SUMMARY OF INDIVIDUAL CHAPTERS

To aid the reader in following the rather complicated arguments of Palamas, I have provided short summaries of each chapter.

I. The text starts with the Orthodox asking: what are the charges? The Barlaamite: they are the same charges brought against the opposing party. The Orthodox: essence and activity are separate; therefore, they are open to charges of worshipping more than one deity. The Barlaamite: essence and activity are one; therefore, they argue for God's simplicity.

II. The Orthodox stresses that Barlaam has been refuted. He asks for true argumentation, not eristic discussion. The Barlaamite agrees.

III. The Barlaamite says that he learns his material from the saints. The Orthodox again brings in charges of heresies; he mentions Sabellius and Eunomius. He says that the Barlaamites might claim that they worship God as one but that they do not derive their arguments from Scripture.

IV. Physical things: the Orthodox says that things which *are* must possess physical things; otherwise, they have no being. To be = to possess physical things.

V. The Orthodox says that the attributes in God are there by nature. Everything in divine nature is uncreated. Things in God cannot be created because then one makes God a creature. There are also physical things in the divine nature. He argues that the Barlaamites say that the uncreated is nothing, not one, because they remove what is essential to the divine nature.

VI. The Barlaamite: the Barlaamites worship one uncreated divinity while the Orthodox worship two uncreated divinities. The Orthodox: he brings Mt. Thabor and the light of Mt. Thabor into the discussion: The Barlaamites say that it is created. The Synod (that condemned them) said it was uncreated.

VII. What is created divinity? The Barlaamite: it is divinized people. The Orthodox gives citations showing the greatness of divinity that gives the deifying gift. He wants to show that the Barlaamite makes God a creature by calling the divinity (the deification) created.

VIII. The Orthodox: he discusses the difference between the glory possessed by God and those who receive it from him. He hints that the light of Thabor was an activity distinct from the essence, although he does not use these terms.

IX. The Orthodox: he accuses the Barlaamite of ditheism since he makes God's divinity created. This demonstrates the difference between the Orthodox and the Barlaamite: divine grace is uncreated (Orthodox); divine grace is created (Barlaamite). The Barlaamites deny the saints' participation in God by claiming this.

X. The invisibility of uncreated divinity. The Barlaamite: the divinity is invisible, unintelligible and imparticipable; he quotes Maximus and Basil.

XI. The Orthodox argues that it is not only invisible but visible, not only unintelligible but also intelligible. Light is uncreated because the divinity is uncreated. It must be intelligible for the saints to participate mystically.

XII. If the Barlaamite also says that God's divinity is uncreated then he is caught in a contradiction: God is of more than one nature and he is created-uncreated. There is then the risk of worshipping two Gods, one with a created divinity and the other with an uncreated one. Yet, the Barlaamites say this (i.e., worshipping more than one God) about the Orthodox. The Orthodox cites Dionysius for the example of contradictions: God can be both unintelligible and intelligible.

XIII. The Barlaamite: he admits, then, to one divinity (but nothing more). He says that the soul is lifted up from the visible to the invisible, solitary, uncreated divinity. The Orthodox: he argues against going from effects to cause (i.e., creations to God's essence). God is visible through activities, not essence. Created things only show God's attributes, not his essence.

XIV. The Orthodox: he shows by example how God is revealed by his energies.

XV. The Barlaamite: he agrees that light is being, if uncreated.

XVI. The Barlaamite: he then enquires how the divinity of God is one and simple if it is unity because it is uncreated; how is it divided because it is visible; and all the other qualifications that the Orthodox gives that divinity? The Orthodox: he says that energy and uncreated being are inseparable. The distinction in the divinity is not contrary to its unity. The Barlaamite's mistake is that he misunderstood Maximus and he broke the divinity into created and uncreated (i.e., activity and essence).

XVII. Distinction in the divinity. The Orthodox: the essence exceeds all name, according to the Barlaamites. Divinity is not divine essence; it is God's power to see, to oversee everything. If divinity is called essence, that comes from its activity.

XVIII. This applies also to the divine names. The Orthodox: The Barlaamites say that divinity is created. The Orthodox calls for Dionysius' stress on God being above all names.

XIX. The Orthodox: a cause stands above caused thing. He says that the Barlaamite talks of two causes and two divinities.

XX. The Orthodox seems to argue that the being of God is above his divinity. Divinity = deification. Hence, divinity is God's power to see and is something that surrounds him. It is also the gift of deification.

XXI. The Barlaamite: since divinity is a participation and imitation, then it is created. The Orthodox: Dionysius called it an "inimitable imitation." This does not mean that it is created. Many things of God signify participation but participation does not mean a physical relationship. Because of participation, the saints become likenesses of God. He says that these activities of God cannot be created.

XXII. The Barlaamite again cites Dionysius. The Orthodox says that the Barlaamite has completely missed the point.

XXIII. The Orthodox: "Getting existence" signifies the coming into existence but not the *way* it does so. He points out the difference of terms and phrases in reference to God.

XXIV. The Orthodox: God cannot be a creature because he is participated in but he does not himself participate in anything. The powers of God are uncreated. He stresses reading the Fathers for authority.

XXV. The Orthodox: he discusses the oneness of trinity. He quotes Basil and says that creatures demonstrate God's powers but not the being itself.

XXVI. The Orthodox: the powers can exist enhypostatically but not as an independent being. This is also true for the light of deifying grace. He says that both God's essence and activity are called divinity, yet we worship one divinity. Divinity is one as a superessential nature.

XXVII. The Orthodox: one cannot separate God's essence from activities, making the latter creatures.

XXVIII. The Orthodox: he accuses the Barlaamites of using the political upheaval of the time to their advantage as others did in the past. He provides a history of such events.

XXIX. The Orthodox: the two natures of Christ do not indicate two divinities.

XXX. The Barlaamite: there is an opposition between: the deifying grace and activity are created and the uncreated deifying grace and activity are God's essence. The Orthodox: if activity in God is not different from the essence, then God has only act *or* essence but not both at the same time. The Barlaamite: God is active essence but no other activity other than essence; otherwise, he is composite.

XXXI. The Orthodox: he warns against separating activity from essence. Essence must have an activity. Is God active? If so, he must have activity. We only know that God *is* by his activities. If you deny his essential activity or *vice versa*, you take away from God, and are therefore an atheist. He cites Basil that no activity can exist independently.

XXXII. The Barlaamite: the saints also say that God's essence and activity are one. The Orthodox: he corrects this by saying that while saints call them one, they are the same and not the same in different manners. There is the problem of terms and word usage. We must distinguish between cause and effects.

XXXIII. The Orthodox: he explains what Gregory of Nyssa means by saying that there is no difference between uncreated and uncreated things.

XXXIV. The Barlaamite: there is still a problem with the citations that indicate that uncreated activity = divine essence. The Orthodox: those people deny divine activity to divine nature in any event. The Barlaamite: he cites John Damascene that the divine is simple and uncomposed. The Barlaamites say that whatever differs from the divine essence is created. The Orthodox introduces the difference between activity and essence in God.

XXXV. The Orthodox: The "heretics" have used Scriptural passages out of context. He cites several heresies. There is a long discussion on how God is simple though his essence and activity are not identical. Characteristics belong to God by nature but he is not composed. There is nothing about conditions in God or essential differences. The Fathers teach that simple essence has many uncreated activities. He tells the Barlaamite to place characteristics as qualities or "essences" but around the essence. Basil says that they are non-essential activities.

XXXVI. The Orthodox: if something has no beginning and is uncreated, it is not created nor is it essence. If something is not essence, how can it make distinctions in the essence? We do not know if the simple itself is the nature of God. Simplicity belongs to him as an activity since he can cause it in other things. The Son is a beginning but beginning is not his nature; in God beginning is an inborn activity.

XXXVII. The Orthodox: he stresses the need to determine word meanings. He points to the core of the discussion: superessentiality. Through his activity God makes himself known. He is one in essence and activity.

XXXVIII. The Barlaamite: according to Basil, everything said and thought about God has one meaning.

XXXIX. The Orthodox: he refers to the wiles of the evil one and the inability of some people to arrive at the right meaning. In the case of Basil, divine names do not signify the essence. Basil also says that if the divine names were referred to the essence, then God would be composed.

XL. The Orthodox: all divine names might signify different things but because they are referred to God, they have equal honor. They lead to one God, not many.

XLI. The Orthodox: he discusses Eunomius. The latter called the Son the activity of the Father, not identified with the essence. For Eunomius, activity was created and essence uncreated. Everything uncreated he called essence. Eunomius did not make a distinction between activity and essence but, instead, confused matters. The Orthodox insists that we know whatever we know God is by the common activity of the trinity.

XLII. The Barlaamite: he maintains that God can only be known from his creations and things like air, earth and sky are creations and activities. Uncreated activity is similar to essence and is unknowable. The so-called activity that is not similar to essence is created. The Orthodox wants to refute this. He cites Basil for ridiculing those who say that God's activities are created or that they are one with essence. They make God a creature by making the activity created. The essence of God is unknowable. Things like earth and air are known to us but not the essence of God, which is uncreated and unintelligible. The activities are manifold while essence is simple (Basil). The Orthodox cites yet another difference between the essence and activities. He concludes that those who equate essence with activity imply that essence is intelligible and participable.

XLIII. The Barlaamite: he confirms this. Participation would be both in the activity and essence. Otherwise, God would be divisible according to his activity but not participated in, according to the essence. The Orthodox: he brings in the Messalians (who say that one can participate in God's essence).

XLIV. The Orthodox: we participate in his activity and thereby do no outrage to his simplicity. If you participate in the activity but not the essence—does this divide the indivisible? Basil speaks of leading us up from our finite nature in a moderate and safe way.

XLV. The Orthodox: if God is contained in a moderate way he cannot be wholly contained. He goes on to show how what we experience can only be a part of the whole. The divine is divided in an undivided way and not the way bodies are. Those activities are not parts of God. God is wholly goodness, wholly wisdom, etc. While he is known through his activity he is also known as one and simple.

XLVI. Hence, we participate in God as a whole but that does not mean that we participate in his essence. If one participates in one activity, one participates in God as a whole.

XLVII. A discussion ensues on the difference between those things which participate only as sensible beings and those with perception.

XLVIII. The Orthodox continues. The person who participates in only one thing participates in the whole; it is not necessary to participate in all things. Why? Because the whole is undivided. If a person does not participate in the essence this does not mean that the divine has to undergo division. If a person received everything he might think that grace is nature. We participate moderately in the undivided grace. The activity is derived from the incorporeal essence.

XLIX. Activity can be divided.

L. The Barlaamite: if God has eternal essence and activity, how is he not composed? The Orthodox: the divine is one and simple in its essence. Activity is what it is for eternity.

LI. The powers referred to as activities. The Barlaamite gives an example of this.

LII. The Orthodox: the powers in a being do not necessarily make it a composite being. Otherwise, God would be the most composed of all.

LIII. If the more powerful is the more simple, than the most powerful is the most simple. Composition is derived in a certain sense from impotence.

LIV. The Orthodox: things with powers are not composed necessarily. The divine cannot acquire anything or put away anything because that would indicate change and, in turn, composition. Therefore, God is simple and almighty and is not composed because of his powers (activities).

LV. Every angel and any rational soul is simple but not simplicity; they are simple by participation. Only God is both genuinely simple and, because he gives part of himself through participation, he is simplicity itself. This holds true also for the divine names.

LVI. God was almighty before the creation as well as after it; hence, his essence is uncreated and so are his powers. The same may be said of the deifying power (called divinity by the saints) because it is also a power.

LVII. The Barlaamite: he is now identified as "the former Barlaamite." The Orthodox receives him into the community and stresses the importance of tradition. He ends the dialogue with "Amen!"

BILINGUAL TEXT

Dialogue between An Orthodox and a Barlaamite

By Saint Gregory Palamas

Gregory Palamas

Dialogue between an Orthodox and a Barlaamite which invalidates in detail the Barlaamite error.[1]

I. The Orthodox (hereafter abbreviated "O"). I would like to learn from you who investigate and give full credit to (the ideas) remaining from the heretic Barlaam (whose doctrine has been officially refuted by the synod) what the charges are which you recently brought against us again, basing yourself upon his teachings.

The Barlaamite (hereafter abbreviated "B"). I shall be very glad to speak about it. I also wish to hear how you can defend such obvious and admitted stupidities and how you yourselves also bring the same charges against us, who do not say anything of the kind. For we say that there is one uncreated being, the essence of God with three hypostases, and that all other beings other than that essence are created. But because you say that the uncreated beings are manifold, you clearly fall into the error of accepting a multiplicity of gods. And by saying that there are two divinities, one above and one below, one participable, the other imparticipable, one giving, the other given, and by saying that the essence and the activity of God differ from each other, you are earmarked as advocating two divinities. No such thing will befall us! We say that the activity of God is one and the same as His essence and does not differ from it; (hence) we honor His uncreated divinity and declare it one, simple, invisible, imparticipable and incomprehensible.

II. O. The Orthodox (pious) truth is really something difficult to ensnare and if you don't search for it like gold and silver (as the wise Solomon says) you will never get hold of it.[2] But if only for a little while I have listened to those fathers who, with the assistance of God and through the proper words, have removed the error of that Barlaam from the midst of the church of Christ, then, with confidence in God, the giver of

<ΓΡΗΓΟΡΙΟΥ ΤΟΥ ΠΑΛΑΜΑ>

ΔΙΑΛΕΞΙΣ ΟΡΘΟΔΟΞΟΥ ΜΕΤΑ ΒΑΡΛΑΑΜΙΤΟΥ ΚΑΤΑ ΜΕΡΟΣ ΑΝΑΣΚΕΥΑΖΟΥΣΑ ΤΗΝ ΒΑΡΛΑΑΜΙΤΙΔΑ ΠΛΑΝΗΝ

I. ΟΡΘΟΔΟΞΟΣ. Μαθεῖν ἐβουλόμην παρ' ὑμῶν τῶν ζητούντων καὶ ἐπεκδικούντων τὰ λείψανα τοῦ συνοδικῶς ἐξεληλεγμένου κακοδόξου Βαρλαάμ, τίνα ἐστὶν ἃ κατ' ἐκεῖνον ἡμῖν αὖθις ἀρτίως ἐγκαλεῖτε.
ΒΑΡΛΑΑΜΙΤΗΣ. Λέξω καὶ μάλα ἄσμενος. Ἐπὶ κἀμοι πυθέσθαι πόθος, τίς ὑμῖν ἀπολογία γένοιτ' ἂν ἐφ' οὕτω φανεροῖς καὶ ἀνωμολογημένοις ἀτοπήμασι, πῶς δ' ἄρα καὶ αὐτοὶ τὰ αὐτὰ ἡμῖν ἀντεγκαλεῖτε μηδὲν τοιοῦτον λέγουσιν· ἡμεῖς γὰρ ἓν ἄκτιστόν φαμεν, τὴν τρισυπόστατον οὐσίαν τοῦ θεοῦ, τὰ δὲ παρ' αὐτὴν ἅπαντα κτιστά. Ὑμεῖς δὲ πολλὰ τὰ ἄκτιστα λέγοντες πολυθεΐᾳ περιπίπτετε σαφῶς· δύο τε θεότητας λέγοντες καὶ τὴν μὲν ὑπερκειμένην τὴν δὲ ὑφειμένην, καὶ τὴν μὲν μεθεκτήν, τὴν δὲ ἀμέθεκτον, καὶ τὴν μὲν χορηγοῦσαν, τὴν δὲ χορηγουμένην, τήν τε οὐσίαν καὶ τὴν τοῦ θεοῦ ἐνέργειαν διαφέρειν λέγοντες ἀλλήλων, δύο θεοὺς πρεσβεύοντες ἐλέγχεσθε. Ἡμῖν δὲ οὐδὲν τοιοῦτο προσπεσεῖται· τὴν μὲν ἐνέργειαν ἓν καὶ ταὐτὸ καὶ ἀδιάφορον λέγουσι τῇ οὐσίᾳ τοῦ θεοῦ, θεότητα δὲ ἄκτιστον σέβουσί τε καὶ κηρύττουσι μίαν, ἁπλῆν, ἀόρατον, ἀμέθεκτον, ἀπερινόητον.
II. ΟΡΘΟΔ. Ὄντως ἡ κατ' εὐσέβειαν ἀλήθεια δυσθήρατον χρῆμα· κἂν μὴ ὡς τὸ χρυσίον καὶ τὸ ἀργύριον ἐκζητήσῃς, κατὰ Σολομῶντα φάναι τὸν σοφόν, οὐ μήποτε πορίσῃ ταύτην. Ἐγὼ δ' εἰ καὶ πρὸς ὀλίγον ὡμιληκὼς τυγχάνω τοῖς πατράσιν ἐκείνοις, οἳ θεοῦ συναιρομένου διὰ τῶν οἰκείων λόγων τὴν τοῦ Βαρλαὰμ ἐκείνου πλάνην ἐκ μέσου πεποιήκεσαν τῆς ἐκκλησίας

truth Himself, I shall brace myself for the defense of those people and for the refutation of your opposition, since you brag endlessly about (your) piety and, consequently, try to drag the masses along. But, in fact, you lead them astray from the orthodox (pious) truth in an unheard of manner! I have only one condition: that you wish to listen and speak for truth, not for the sake of argumentation.

B. We shall converse in that fashion as it is fitting when we speak about the truth in God, convinced that truth itself is looking down upon us.

III. O. Very well, then. Those doctrines in which you proudly think that you alone, apart from us, unfailingly believe--did you learn them from yourselves or did the saints teach them to you?

B. The saints. For, if you wish, also from the things they said, I'll provide you with a lot of evidence which agrees with my words in all respects.

O. I don't think in *all* respects. In fact, wouldn't every heretic claim that the saints before him agree with him? And how many testimonies, to the extent that the Father and the Son are one, would Sabellius[3], in your opinion, be able to produce from the Holy Scriptures? Hence, he said that people who did not share his opinion believed in the multiplicity of gods. And how many testimonies could Eunomius[4] provide that the uncreated and incomparable is one? Therefore, he called those who do not hold the same opinion "believers in three gods," which induced the great Basil[5] to write an apology against those who charged him with tritheism. But they were convicted of lying about the saints and denying the unity of God Himself. For even they said that God, who is above all things, is one, but not in the manner He revealed Himself in many ways through the prophets, nor in the way the Father made Himself known by the Son at a later stage and in a clearer fashion, nor in the way He made Himself manifest by the witnesses of orthodox faith to all the ends of the world. In that way, then, I myself also hope in a moment, when God gives me "the word in opening my mouth,"[6] to establish clearly that you, even if you stubbornly maintain that you alone --apart from us-- accept the oneness of the uncreated and of the divinity, don't say so because you are

τοῦ Χριστοῦ, ἀλλ᾽ αὐτῷ τῷ τῆς ἀληθείας χορηγῷ θεῷ θαρρήσας, πρός τε τὴν ὑπὲρ ἐκείνων ἀπολογίαν ἀποδύσομαι καὶ πρὸς ἔλεγχον τῆς ὑμῶν ἀντιλογίας, τῶν ἄμετρα μὲν ἐπ᾽ εὐσεβείᾳ καυχωμένων καὶ τοὺς πολλοὺς ἐντεῦθεν συναρπάζειν πειρωμένων, οὐ μετρίως δὲ τῆς κατ᾽ εὐσέβειαν ἀληθείας ἀποβουκολουμένων, μόνον εἰ μὴ πρὸς ἔριν, ἀλλὰ πρὸς ἀλήθειαν ἀκούειν τε καὶ λέγειν προαιρῇ.

ΒΑΡΛ. Οὕτω διαλεξόμεθα, ὡς ὑπὲρ τῆς ἐν θεῷ ἀληθείας διαλεγόμενοι καὶ ὡς αὐτῆς τῆς αὐτοαληθείας ἐφορώσης.

III. ΟΡΘΟΔ. Ὑπέρευγε· ταῦτα τοίνυν, ἐφ᾽ οἷς ὡς μόνοι πλὴν ἡμῶν ἀσφαλῶς δοξάζοντες μέγα τι φρονεῖτε, παρ᾽ ὑμῶν αὐτῶν ἔγνωτε ἢ παρὰ τῶν ἁγίων ἐδιδάχθητε;

ΒΑΡΛ. Παρὰ τῶν ἁγίων· καὶ γὰρ εἰ βούλει, καὶ ἀπὸ τῶν ἐκείνοις εἰρημένων πλῆθός σοι προήσομαι μαρτυριῶν κατὰ πάνθ᾽ ὁμολόγων τοῖς ἐμοῖς.

ΟΡΘΟΔ. Οὐκ ἔγωγε οἶμαι κατὰ πάντα. Τί δέ, οὐχὶ καὶ πᾶς κακόδοξος συμφθεγγομένους φαίη ἂν ἑαυτῷ τοὺς πρὸ αὐτοῦ ἁγίους; Τὸν δὲ Σαβέλλιον πόσας οἴει μαρτυρίας ἀπὸ τῶν ἱερῶν γραφῶν ἔχειν προενέγκασθαι ὅτι ἕν ἐστιν ὁ πατὴρ καὶ ὁ υἱός; Διὸ καὶ πολυθέους τοὺς μὴ κατ᾽ αὐτὸν φρονοῦντας ἔλεγε. Πόσας δ᾽ αὖθις τὸν Εὐνόμιον ὅτι ἕν ἐστι τὸ ἄκτιστον καὶ ἀσύγκριτον; Διὸ καὶ τριθεΐτας ἐκάλει τοὺς μὴ ὡς αὐτὸς δοξάζοντας, ὡς καὶ τὸν μέγαν Βασίλειον ἀπολογίαν συγγράψασθαι πρὸς τοὺς τριθεΐαν αὐτοῦ κατηγοροῦντας. Ἀλλ᾽ ἐξηλέγχθησαν τῶν ἁγίων καταψευδόμενοι καὶ αὐτὸν τὸν ἕνα θεὸν ἀρνούμενοι. Ἕνα μὲν γὰρ κἀκεῖνοι τὸν ἐπὶ πάντων ἔλεγον θεόν, ἀλλ᾽ οὐχ ὡς διὰ τῶν προφητῶν αὐτὸς ἑαυτὸν πολυτρόπως ἀπεκάλυψεν, οὐδ᾽ ὡς διὰ τοῦ υἱοῦ ὁ πατὴρ ὕστερον ἐμφανέστερον ἐγνώρισεν, οὐδ᾽ ὡς διὰ τῶν τῆς εὐσεβείας κηρύκων τοῖς πέρασι πᾶσιν ἐφανέρωσεν. Οὕτω τοίνυν καὶ αὐτὸς ἀρτίως τοῦ θεοῦ <διδόντος λόγον ἐν ἀνοίξει τοῦ στόματός μου>, τρανῶς ἐλπίζω παραστήσειν ὡς, εἰ καὶ ἓν ἄκτιστον καὶ μίαν θεότητα μόνοι πλὴν ἡμῶν λέγειν ἰσχυρίζεσθε, ἀλλ᾽ οὐχ

initiated in and are instructed by the Holy Writ--as is the case with us.[7] That is why you do not proclaim the oneness of the uncreated and of the divinity in the true sense. You do not (even) notice that you are rolling headlong down the slope of polytheism. But, thanks to His great gift, we are the ones who truly and unfailingly honor one divinity and the one uncreated God.

IV. For tell me, in all of nature,[8] are there not physical things, in some more, in some less?

B. So it would seem.

O. Are there also, then, in the divine nature some physical things or not?

B. Perhaps there cannot be. First, because it transcends all natures; second, since one nature partakes of more, the other of less, it would not be improbable that there would be absolutely nothing in the divine nature. Only when you can demonstrate that one of the saints clearly says that the divine nature has physical things, then I'll accept it.

O. He who says that the divine nature does not possess physical things does not make it transcend all nature, but demonstrates that it has no being whatsoever. For that which has absolutely no physical things is not in a transcendental way, but is absolutely not. And how could it be characterized as being at all, if it has none of the things which characterize it, i.e., show it? But because you want to hear that from the fathers--though it is already quite clear since they acknowledge it all explicitly-- I will make it obvious to you by way of a common doctrine, lest we spoil our time in things which everybody acknowledges. We are taught, then, that our Lord Jesus Christ has two natures and two physical wills, one belonging to the human nature, the other to the divine.

B. I agree now; but are the physical things with God different from nature?

O. Of course.

B. What's the difference?

ὡς ὑπὸ τῆς θείας μεμυήμεθα γραφῆς. Διὸ οὐδὲ ἓν ἄκτιστον καὶ μίαν θεότητά φατε κυρίως, ἀλλὰ κατὰ κρημνοῦ πολυθεΐας κυβιστῶντες οὐκ αἰσθάνεσθε. Οἱ δ' ἀληθῶς καὶ ἀσφαλῶς μίαν θεότητα καὶ ἕνα σέβοντες ἄκτιστον θεὸν ἡμεῖς ἐσμεν κατὰ τὴν ἐκείνου μεγαλοδωρεάν.

IV. Εἰπὲ γάρ μοι· οὐ πάσῃ φύσει πρόσεστι καὶ φυσικά, τῇ μὲν πλείω τῇ δὲ ἐλάττω;

ΒΑΡΛ. Ἔοικεν.

ΟΡΘΟΔ. Πρόσεστιν οὖν καὶ τῇ θείᾳ φύσει φυσικά τινα ἢ οὔ;

ΒΑΡΛ. Ἴσως οὐ προσείη ἄν· τοῦτο μὲν ὡς πασῶν ὑπερεξῃρημένῃ, τοῦτο δ' εἴπερ ἡ μὲν πλειόνων, ἡ δὲ ἐλαττόνων εὐμοιρεῖ, οὐκ ἀπεικότως ἂν εἴη τῇ θείᾳ φύσει μηδαμῶς προσεῖναι. Πλὴν ἄλλ' εἴ τινα τῶν ἁγίων ἔχεις δεῖξαι φανερῶς λέγοντα φυσικὰ τὴν θείαν ἔχειν φύσιν, δέχομαι.

ΟΡΘΟΔ. Ὁ μὴ λέγων φυσικὰ τὴν θείαν ἔχειν φύσιν οὐχ ὑπεραίρει ταύτην πάσης φύσεως, ἀλλὰ μηδαμῇ μηδαμῶς οὖσαν ἀποφαίνει· τὸ γὰρ μὴ ἔχον ὅλως φυσικὰ οὐχ ὑπεροχικῶς ἐστιν, ἀλλ' οὐδαμῶς. Πόθεν δ' ἂν καὶ χαρακτηρισθείη ὅλως εἶναι, μηδὲν ἔχον τῶν χαρακτηριζόντων, δηλαδὴ δεικνύντων; Ἀλλ' ἐπεὶ παρὰ τῶν πατέρων τοῦτο καίτοι φανερὸν ὄν, ὅμως θέλεις διδαχθῆναι, πάντων τοῦτο διαρρήδην ἀνομολογούντων, ἵνα μὴ τρίβωμεν τὸν χρόνον ἐν τοῖς ἀνωμολογημένοις, ἐκ κοινοῦ τοῦτο παραστήσω δόγματος. Δύο γὰρ φύσεις καὶ δύο φυσικὰ θελήματα τὸν κύριον ἡμῶν Ἰησοῦν Χριστὸν ἔχειν διδασκόμεθα· τὸ μὲν τῆς ἀνθρωπείας φύσεως, τὸ δὲ τῆς θείας.

ΒΑΡΛ. Συντίθεμαι νῦν, ἀλλ' ἔχει τινὰ διαφορὰν τῆς φύσεως τὰ φυσικὰ ἐπὶ θεοῦ;

ΟΡΘΟΔ. Καὶ πάνυ γε.

ΒΑΡΛ. Τίνα ταύτην;

ΟΡΘΟΔ. Ὅτι τὸ φυσικὸν θέλημα τῆς φύσεώς ἐστι, καὶ ἐκ τῆς φύσεως καὶ περὶ τὴν φύσιν θεωρεῖται, τὴν φύσιν ἀρχὴν ἔχον καὶ οἷόν τινα ῥίζαν καὶ αἰτίαν, ὅθεν

O. That the physical will belongs to nature, we conclude from nature and in the context of nature, since the will has nature as its beginning and, as it were, as a root and cause from which it proceeds. But nature does not belong to the physical will or otherwise we could speculate about it as if the will were its cause and as if it came forth from it. One could talk about many other things in which physical things differ from nature. But, for now, this will be enough.

V. B. Then, is only the will present in the divine nature in a physical way or other things as well?

O. A great many. For God has (His) foreknowledge in a physical way and that is different from His will. For He knows everything beforehand, but He doesn't "will" all things that happen. He also has compassion and judgment which differ from each other and from those things; and simply put, to speak with the great Athanasius, "all the things which God has, He has by nature and not as acquired."[9] Of all these things we know that they are uncreated. For according to the expert in divine things, Maximus, "there is nothing uncreated in the human nature nor anything created in the divine nature."[10] And when you bring charges against us on account of these things, either you think that they are created or that they do not exist at all. If they are created, you make God a creature. For according to the divine John Damascene, "the physical things must correspond to the natures."[11] And if you say that there are no physical things, you take away the divine nature. For the same expert Maximus asks "how there can be a God or a man when the physical will and the essential activity is taken away?"[12] Hence, you don't say that the uncreated is one, but nothing. But we say, appropriately, that the divine nature itself is one, which, by showing those physical things, reveals its real character through them.

VI. B. Don't you explicitly say that there are two uncreated divinities? We, on the other hand, assert that there is only one uncreated divinity.

O. At first, we didn't want to speak or write about these things, but we were forced by you to write an apology because you were so eager to criticize us. With God's wise help we will therefore also speak about divinity. But first, we must clarify this. Since you call the un-

πρόεισιν. Οὐχ ἡ φύσις δὲ τοῦ φυσικοῦ θελήματος ἢ περὶ αὐτὸ θεωρηθείη ἂν αἰτίαν τοῦθ᾽ ἑαυτῆς ἔχουσα καὶ προϊοῦσα παρ᾽ αὐτοῦ. Πολλὰ δ᾽ ἂν φαίη τις καὶ ἕτερα, καθ᾽ ἃ διενήνοχε τῆς φύσεως τὰ φυσικά· νῦν δὲ ἡμῖν καὶ τὰ εἰρημένα ἀποχρήσει.

V. ΒΑΡΛ. Τὸ θέλημα δ᾽ ἄρα μόνον ἢ καὶ ἕτερα φυσικῶς πρόσεστι τῇ θείᾳ φύσει;

ΟΡΘΟΔ. Πλεῖστα· τήν τε γὰρ πρόγνωσιν φυσικῶς ἔχει ὁ θεός, ἕτερον οὖσαν παρὰ τὴν θέλησιν αὐτοῦ. Προγινώσκει μὲν γὰρ ἅπαντα, θέλει δὲ οὐχ ἅπανθ᾽ ὅσα γίνεται· τόν τε ἔλεον καὶ τὴν κρίσιν, ἀλλήλων τε κἀκείνων διαφέροντα, καὶ ἁπλῶς, ἵνα κατὰ τὸν μέγαν Ἀθανάσιον εἴπω, <πάντα ὅσα ἔχει ὁ θεὸς φύσει ἔχει καὶ οὐκ ἐπίκτητα>. Ταῦτα τοίνυν ἡμεῖς ἅπαντ᾽ ἴσμεν ὄντα ἄκτιστα· κατὰ γὰρ τὸν σοφὸν τὰ θεῖα Μάξιμον, <οὐ πρόσεστιν οὔτε τῇ ἀνθρωπίνῃ φύσει τι ἄκτιστον οὔτε τῇ θείᾳ φύσει τι κτιστόν>. Ὑμεῖς δὲ διὰ ταῦθ᾽ ἡμῶν κατηγοροῦντες ἢ κτιστὰ ταῦτ᾽ οἴεσθε ἢ μηδαμῶς εἶναι. Καὶ εἰ μὲν κτιστά, κτίσμα τὸν θεὸν ποιεῖτε· κατὰ γὰρ τὸν ἐκ Δαμασκοῦ θεῖον Ἰωάννην, <δεῖ κατάλληλα ταῖς φύσεσιν εἶναι τὰ φυσικά>. Εἰ δὲ μὴ εἶναι φυσικά φατε, τὴν θείαν φύσιν ἀναιρεῖτε· κατὰ γὰρ τὸν σοφὸν αὖθις Μάξιμον, <τοῦ φυσικοῦ θελήματος καὶ τῆς οὐσιώδους ἐνεργείας ἀναιρουμένης, πῶς θεὸς ἢ ἄνθρωπος ἔσται>; Ὥστε οὐχ ἓν ὑμεῖς λέγετε τὸ ἄκτιστον, ἀλλὰ οὐδέν. Ἡμεῖς δὲ ἓν κυρίως λέγομεν αὐτὴν τὴν θείαν φύσιν, ἣ τοιαῦτα φυσικὰ προϊσχομένη δι᾽ αὐτῶν τοιαύτη δείκνυται.

VI. ΒΑΡΛ. Δύο δὲ θεότητας ἀκτίστους οὐ διαρρήδην λέγετε; Ἀλλ᾽ ἡμεῖς μίαν ἄκτιστον θεότητά φαμεν.

ΟΡΘΟΔ. Ἡμεῖς περὶ τοιούτων λέγειν ἢ γράφειν τὴν ἀρχὴν οὐκ ἐβουλήθημεν, ὑφ᾽ ὑμῶν δὲ κατηγορεῖν ἐσπουδακότων ἀναγκαίως πρὸς ἀπολογίαν ἥκομεν. Τοῦ θεοῦ τοίνυν συνετίζοντος ἐροῦμεν καὶ περὶ θεότητος. Ἀλλ᾽ ἐκεῖνο γενέσθω πρῶτον φανερόν, ὡς ἐπειδήπερ ὑμεῖς ἓν οὕτω τὸ ἄκτιστόν φατε, οὐ τινὰ μὲν ἐπεκδικεῖτε, τινὰ δ᾽ οὔ, τῶν ὑπὸ τοῦ Βαρλαὰμ ἐκείνου

created in that sense one, you do not give credit to some of the things that Barlaam expressed so badly about God, and to some others not, but to all things. For that light with which the Lord shone upon the mountain and with which He illuminated the disciples you deem created and therefore the synod excommunicated you.[13] For the synod proclaimed that, according to the Scriptures, that light was uncreated and, besides that, showed that since the divine nature is completely invisible and imparticipable, it transcends that vision. It excommunicated and publicly renounced those who do not share that opinion and cut them off completely from the perfect congregation of the Christians, if they would not repent. Although, in that respect, you still share the same opinion as Barlaam, and are subjected to the same accusations, you have just now deceptively pretended to obey the Church and the overseers of the Church and, openly, you have slyly discarded Barlaam; in fact, you house his heresy (alas!) in your soul and try to win over the people to that belief in a scandalous manner.

VII. But since you also accuse us of saying that there are two uncreated divinities (whereas you say that there is one uncreated divinity), may I ask: the one whom you call the created divinity: whose divinity is it?

B. We call it the divinity of people who have partaken of divinization.

O. And if it is the divinity of people who have partaken, how much more is it the divinity of Him who gives part? For God has created us for that purpose, he[14] says, to make us partake in His own divinity and for that purpose He came on earth. And, as the divine Gregory of Nyssa says to Harmonius, Christ put on our nature for the reason that "He received the rejected into sonship and the enemies of God into partnership with His divinity."[15] And again, "the purity which we see in Christ and in the person who has part in Him is by nature one. But Christ is the source and he who takes part draws the water."[16] And again, "Christ will bring each one to union with the divinity, if he carries nothing unworthy of the kinship with the divine."[17] For the divinity of him who has truly been divinized belongs to God to whom he has been united and by whom he has been divinized in grace; he has not thrown away his own nature

κακῶς εἰρημένων περὶ τοῦ θεοῦ, ἀλλ' ἅπαντα· καὶ τὸ φῶς γὰρ ἐκεῖνο, καθ' ὃ λάμψας ὁ κύριος ἐπ' ὄρους περιηύγασε τοὺς μαθητὰς κτιστὸν ἡγεῖσθε, καὶ τῷ συνοδικῷ ὑπόκεισθε ἀφορισμῷ· τοῦτο γὰρ τὸ φῶς ἡ σύνοδος ἐγγράφως ἄκτιστον ἐκήρυξε, καὶ τὴν θείαν φύσιν ὡς ἀόρατον παντάπασι καὶ ἀμέθεκτον ὑπερκεῖσθαι τῆς θέας ἐκείνης προσαπεφήνατο, καὶ τοὺς μὴ οὕτω φρονοῦντας ἀφώρισε καὶ ἀπεκήρυξε καὶ τοῦ τῶν χριστιανῶν τελέως, εἰ μὴ μεταμεληθεῖεν, ἐξέκοψε πληρώματος. Ὑμεῖς οὖν τὴν αὐτὴν κἀν τούτῳ δόξαν ἔτ' ἔχοντες τῷ Βαρλαὰμ καὶ ταῖς αὐταῖς ὑποκείμενοι εὐθύναις, πρὸς ἐξαπάτην ἔναγχος τὴν πρὸς τὴν ἐκκλησίαν καὶ τοὺς τῆς ἐκκλησίας προεστῶτας ὑπεκρίθητε ὑπακοήν, καὶ τὸν Βαρλαὰμ παρρησίᾳ δολίως ἀπεβάλεσθε, τὴν ἐκείνου φεῦ κακοδοξίαν οἰκουροῦσαν ἔχοντες ἐν τῇ ψυχῇ καὶ πρὸς αὐτὴν κακούργως τοὺς πολλοὺς σφετεριζόμενοι.

VII. Ἀλλ' ἐπεὶ καὶ δύο θεότητας ἀκτίστους λεγόντων ἡμῶν κατηγορεῖτε, μίαν δὲ ὑμεῖς ἄκτιστόν φατε, ἣν λέγετε κτιστὴν θεότητα, τίνος ἐστὶ θεότης;

ΒΑΡΛ. Τῶν ἀνθρώπων ταύτην φαμὲν τῶν θεώσεως μετειληφότων.

ΟΡΘΟΔ. Καὶ εἰ τῶν μετειληφότων, πόσῳ μᾶλλον τοῦ μεταδιδόντος· εἰς τοῦτο γάρ φησι πεποίηκεν ἡμᾶς ὁ θεός, ἵνα κοινωνοὺς ἡμᾶς ποιήσῃ τῆς οἰκείας θεότητος, καὶ εἰς τοῦτο ἐπεδήμησε τῇ γῇ. Καὶ καθάπερ πρὸς Ἁρμόνιόν φησιν ὁ Νύσσης θεῖος Γρηγόριος, τούτου χάριν ὁ Χριστὸς τὴν ἡμετέραν ἀνελάβετο φύσιν, <ἵνα προσδέξηται τοὺς ἀποκηρύκτους εἰς υἱοθεσίαν καὶ τοὺς ἐχθροὺς τοῦ θεοῦ εἰς τὴν τῆς θεότητος αὐτοῦ μετουσίαν>. Καὶ πάλιν· <μία τῇ φύσει ἡ καθαρότης, ἥ τε ἐν τῷ Χριστῷ καὶ ἡ ἐν τῷ μετέχοντι θεωρουμένη. Ἀλλ' ὁ μὲν πηγάζει, ὁ δὲ μετέχων ἀρύεται>. Καὶ πάλιν· <ἕκαστον προσάξει τῇ συναφείᾳ τῆς θεότητος ὁ Χριστός, εἰ μηδὲν ἐπάγοιτο τῆς πρὸς τὸ θεῖον συμφυΐας ἀνάξιον>. Ἡ γοῦν θεότης τοῦ πρὸς ἀλήθειαν τεθεωμένου τοῦ θεοῦ ἐστιν, ᾧπερ ἥνωται καὶ παρ' οὗ κατὰ χάριν

but by that grace he has transcended nature. By calling that divinity created, you make God a creature.

VIII. Concerning the glory which appeared on Thabor, the divine Damascene says: "From the divinity the glory came forth physically and was also joined to the body by the sameness of the substance."[18] That human part of the Lord possessed that glory completely and did not dimly partake in it. But the participation of the others is different; it is as if they draw (water from Him) as from a cistern: "from His fullness we have all received," he says.[19] And "the righteous will shine like the sun"[20] (which is the same as saying that Christ shone on the mountain) when He will appear in His future unspeakable revelation,[21] of which He showed a preview by a dim light on Thabor[22] where, in fact, in a mystical way He unfolded the future. That that light does not simply belong to the venerable body, but is the brightness of the divinity, is demonstrated not only by the other theologians but also by Kosmas, the divine poet of the Church. He sang about it in his verses for Christ: "You made the nature which was obscured in Adam shine forth again by transforming it into Your glory and brightness of the divinity."[23] And that we must believe that that divinity also belongs to the Father and the Spirit is taught to us not only by the other theologians but by Damascene as well, a poet of the Church no less divine than Kosmas. He sings of it: "Come hither, believe me, my people, let us climb the holy mountain and contemplate with our mind the immaterial divinity of the Father and the Spirit which shines forth in the only-begotten Son."[24]

IX. Since, then, that divinity also belongs to God, which you call created, *you* are truly the ones who claim that there are two divinities of God; you assert that they differ so much from each other that it will never be possible that they come together as one, as Arius and Eunomius say, who contend that the Son is also God, but created. You utter slander and lies about us by proclaiming about us exactly what you yourselves wrongly believe. The real difference with us is clearly this: we

τεθέωται, τὴν οἰκείαν φύσιν οὐκ ἀποβαλὼν καὶ ὑπὲρ φύσιν κατὰ τὴν χάριν γεγονώς· ἣν ὑμεῖς λέγοντες κτιστὴν κτίσμα τὸν θεὸν ποιεῖτε.

VIII. Περὶ δὲ τῆς ἐν Θαβὼρ ἐπιφανείσης δόξης, φησὶ Δαμασκηνὸς ὁ θεῖος· <ἐκ τῆς θεότητος ἡ δόξα φυσικῶς προϊοῦσα κοινὴ καὶ τοῦ σώματος διὰ τὴν τῆς ὑποστάσεως ἐγίνετο ταυτότητα>. Τὸ μὲν οὖν δεσποτικὸν ἐκεῖνο πρόσλημμα πᾶσαν εἶχε ταύτην, ἀλλ᾽ οὐκ ἀμυδρῶς αὐτῆς μετεῖχε. Τῶν δ᾽ ἄλλων ὡς ἀπὸ δεξαμενῆς ἀρυομένων ἡ μέθεξίς ἐστιν· <ἐκ γὰρ τοῦ πληρώματος αὐτοῦ>, φησίν, <ἡμεῖς πάντες ἐλάβομεν>. Καὶ <λάμψουσιν οἱ δίκαιοι ὡς ὁ ἥλιος>, ταὐτὸ δ᾽ εἰπεῖν ὡς ὁ Χριστὸς ἔλαμψεν ἐπ᾽ ὄρους, ὅταν ἐκεῖνος ἐκφανῇ κατὰ τὴν μέλλουσαν ἄφραστον ἐκείνην ἔκφανσιν, ἧς τὸ προοίμιον ἀμυδρᾶς αὐγῆς ἐν Θαβὼρ ὑπέδειξεν, ἔργῳ μυσταγωγῶν τὸ μέλλον. Ὅτι γε μὴν τοῦτο φῶς οὐ τοῦ προσκυνητοῦ σώματος ἁπλῶς, ἀλλὰ τῆς θεότητός ἐστι λαμπρότης, πρὸς τοῖς ἄλλοις θεολόγοις καὶ ὁ τῆς ἐκκλησίας ἔνθους μελῳδὸς παρίστησι Κοσμᾶς, τῷ Χριστῷ ψάλλων ἐπ᾽ αὐτῆς· <τὴν ἀμαυρωθεῖσαν ἐν Ἀδὰμ φύσιν ἀπαστράψαι πάλιν πεποίηκας, μεταστοιχειώσας αὐτὴν εἰς τὴν σὴν τῆς θεότητος δόξαν τε καὶ λαμπρότητα>. Ὅτι δὲ καὶ τοῦ πατρὸς καὶ τοῦ πνεύματος ταύτην εἶναι δεῖ δοξάζειν τὴν θεότητα, πρὸς τοῖς ἄλλοις θεολόγοις καὶ ὁ τῆς ἐκκλησίας μηδὲν ἧττον τοῦ προτέρου θεῖος ᾠδικὸς Δαμασκηνὸς προτρέπεται ψάλλων ἐπ᾽ αὐτῆς· <δεῦτέ μοι πείθεσθε λαοί, ἀναβάντες εἰς τὸ ὄρος τὸ ἅγιον ἐποπτεύσωμεν νοῒ θεότητα ἄϋλον πατρὸς καὶ πνεύματος ἐν υἱῷ μονογενεῖ ἀπαστράπτουσαν>.

IX. Ἐπεὶ τοίνυν τοῦ θεοῦ ἐστι θεότης καὶ ἣν ὑμεῖς λέγετε κτιστὴν, ὑμεῖς ἐστε κυρίως οἱ λέγοντες δύο εἶναι τοῦ θεοῦ θεότητας, οἱ τοσοῦτο διαφέρειν λέγοντες ἀλλήλων, ὡς μηδ᾽ εἰς μίαν εἶναί ποτε ταύτας συνελθεῖν, καθάπερ Ἄρειός τε καὶ Εὐνόμιος, οἱ καὶ τὸν υἱὸν θεὸν λέγοντες ἀλλὰ κτιστόν. Συκοφαντοῦντες οὖν καὶ καταψευδόμενοι ἡμῶν, τοῦθ᾽ ὃ κακῶς ὑμεῖς φρονεῖτε,

say that the divine grace is uncreated while you call it created. Since, then, the Lord has come on earth and has made those who, according to the Scriptures, were worthy of it, partakers in His own divinity, you who say that that grace of the divinity which was added to the saints is created, either deny the participation and union of the saints with God, or you think that God's divinity (in which they partake out of grace), is created; in this manner you again make God a creature.[25]

X. Come on, then; that one divinity which you call uncreated: do you also call it invisible or not?

B. Not only invisible, but also unintelligible and imparticipable. For Maximus, the greatest expert in divine things, says: "God is One, because divinity is one. Unity, without beginning, simple, transcending being, without parts and undivided,"[26] neither intelligible nor visible nor participable.

O. Well said; for it will soon be demonstrated that you quote the saint's word deprived of the most important (arguments). Let it be for the moment. Do you think, however, that all the saints hold that opinion and teach it?

B. Without a doubt.

O. At least Basil, the most accurate theologian of all, says so in many places and always holds to this idea; again, the same man says somewhere: "The Beauty of the truly almighty, namely God, is His intelligible and visible divinity; for that is really beautiful which surpasses all human apperception and power and which is only fathomable by thinking."[27] Do you not think that he says that to the same God belongs not only the completely unintelligible divinity but also the intelligible? And not only the intelligible but also the visible? For further on he writes: "Peter and the sons of thunder saw His beauty on the mountain which surpassed the brilliance of the sun and they were deemed worthy of perceiving with their eyes the previews of His glorious appearance."[28]

καθ' ἡμῶν περιαγγέλλετε. Ἡ δὲ πρὸς ἡμᾶς ἀληθὴς διαφορὰ τοῦτό ἐστι σαφῶς· ὅτι τὴν θείαν χάριν ἡμεῖς μὲν ἄκτιστον, ὑμεῖς δὲ κτιστήν φατε. Τοῦ κυρίου τοίνυν ἐλθόντος ἐπὶ γῆς καὶ κοινωνοὺς πεποιηκότος τοὺς ἀξίους κατὰ τὰς γραφὰς τῆς οἰκείας θεότητος, ὑμεῖς οἱ κτιστὴν λέγοντες τὴν προσγεγενημένην ταύτην τοῖς ἁγίοις χάριν τῆς θεότητος, ἢ τὴν πρὸς τὸν θεὸν τῶν ἁγίων κοινωνίαν καὶ ἕνωσιν ἀρνεῖσθε, ἢ καὶ τὴν τοῦ θεοῦ θεότητα, ἧς κεκοινωνήκασιν οὗτοι κατὰ χάριν οἴεσθε κτιστήν, καὶ οὕτω πάλιν κτίσμα τὸν θεὸν ποιεῖτε.

Χ. Φέρε δὴ τὴν μίαν ἐκείνην, ἣν ἄκτιστον λέγετε θεότητα, καὶ ἀόρατον λέγετε ἢ οὔ;

ΒΑΡΛ. Οὐκ ἀόρατον μόνον, ἀλλὰ καὶ ἀπερινόητον καὶ ἀμέθεκτον· φησὶ γὰρ ὁ σοφὸς εἴπερ τις τὰ θεῖα Μάξιμος· <εἷς θεός, ὅτι μία θεότης· μονὰς ἄναρχος καὶ ἁπλῆ καὶ ὑπερούσιος καὶ ἀμερὴς καὶ ἀδιαίρετος>, οὔτε νοητὴ οὔτε ὁρατὴ οὔτε μεθεκτή.

ΟΡΘΟΔ. Εὖγε· τὸ μὲν γὰρ περιῃρημένην τῶν καιριωτάτων προάγειν ὑμᾶς τὴν τοῦ ἁγίου ταύτην ῥῆσιν, ἔπειτα δειχθήσεται. Τὸ δὲ νῦν εἶναι κείσθω. Δοκεῖ δέ σοι φρονεῖν οὕτω καὶ διδάσκειν πάντας τοὺς ἁγίους;

ΒΑΡΛ. Καὶ πάνυ μὲν οὖν.

ΟΡΘΟΔ. Ὁ γοῦν ἀκριβὴς εἴπερ τις ἐν θεηγορίᾳ Βασίλειος τοῦθ' οὕτω πολλαχοῦ λέγων καὶ ἀεὶ φρονῶν, καὶ αὖθις ἔστιν οὗ φάσκων ὁ αὐτός, <κάλλος> τοῦ ὄντος δυνατοῦ, δηλονότι τοῦ θεοῦ, <ἡ νοητὴ αὐτοῦ καὶ θεωρητὴ θεότης· ἐκεῖνο γὰρ ὄντως καλόν, τὸ κατάληψιν πᾶσαν ἀνθρωπίνην καὶ δύναμιν ὑπερβαῖνον καὶ διανοίᾳ μόνῃ περιληπτόν>, οὐ δοκεῖ σοι τοῦ αὐτοῦ θεοῦ λέγειν εἶναι μὴ μόνον τὴν παντάπασιν ἀπερινόητον ἀλλὰ καὶ τὴν νοητὴν θεότητα; Καὶ μὴ νοητὴν μόνον, ἀλλὰ καὶ θεωρητήν; Ἐπεὶ καὶ γράφων ἐφεξῆς φησίν· <εἶδον δὲ αὐτοῦ τὸ κάλλος Πέτρος καὶ οἱ υἱοὶ τῆς βροντῆς ἐν τῷ ὄρει ὑπερλάμπον τὴν τοῦ ἡλίου λαμπρότητα, καὶ τὰ

XI. B. And where does the great Basil say this?

O. In his ethical writings where he explains the 44th Psalm of David. And let the great theologian Gregory, who agrees with him, also be a witness. For he, too, honors the one invisible and unintelligible divinity of the sacred trinity and he says somewhere, "the divinity shown on the mountain to the disciples, almost more concrete than even a vision, was light."[29] Do you see that he also knows that the divinity of God is not only invisible but visible as well? That that divinity is also uncreated, since the light in agreement with that divinity is also uncreated? That is also the opinion of father Chrysostom who called it a beam of the divinity: "For the Lord appeared, brighter than Himself, when His divinity showed its beams."[30] And the divine interpreter Symeon says that the best theologian of all, John, "saw the divinity of the Word itself naked on the mountain."[31] But when he also relates the principles of the divine (Nicean) fathers in a nutshell, he says: "Since every argument goes into the heart by way of the presentation of some perceptible things, the blessed light of the divinity illuminates it then when it is completely empty of everything and loses all those forms,"[32] because that brightness shines into the pure mind deprived of all concepts. And that that light is not only visible, but is also partaken of by all those who are truly initiated, is proven by the man who says that "God is the reward of virtue and He is ablaze with the purest light on that day when He becomes Son, a day which is not interrupted by darkness. For another sun makes that day, the one which pours forth the true light. That sun puts the light in those who are worthy of it forever and without interruption and it makes those who partake of that light other suns."[33] For the righteous will shine like the sun, he says.[34] Hence, the divine singer Metrophanes says in his songs: "Deem us worthy, good Lord, to enjoy the brightness of the three-

προοίμια τῆς ἐνδόξου αὐτοῦ παρουσίας ὀφθαλμοῖς λαβεῖν κατηξιώθησαν>.

XI. ΒΑΡΛ. Καὶ ποῦ τοῦτό φησιν ὁ μέγας Βασίλειος;

ΟΡΘΟΔ. Ἐν τοῖς ἠθικοῖς λόγοις, τὸν δαυϊτικὸν τεσσαρακοστὸν τέταρτον διασαφῶν ψαλμόν. Παρίτω δὲ τούτῳ συμφθεγγόμενος ὁ μέγας ἐν θεολογίᾳ Γρηγόριος· σέβων γὰρ καὶ οὗτος μίαν τῆς σεπτῆς τριάδος ἀόρατόν τε καὶ ἀπερινόητον θεότητα, εἶτα ὁ αὐτὸς ἔστιν οὗ φησι· <φῶς ἡ παραδειχθεῖσα θεότης ἐπὶ τοῦ ὄρους τοῖς μαθηταῖς, μικροῦ στερροτέρα καὶ ὄψεως>. Ὁρᾷς ὅτι καὶ οὗτος οὐ μόνον ἀόρατον οἶδε τοῦ θεοῦ θεότητα, ἀλλὰ καὶ ὁρατήν; Ἄκτιστον καὶ ταύτην οὖσαν, ἐπειδήπερ καὶ τὸ κατὰ ταύτην φῶς; Ταῦτ᾽ ἄρα καὶ ὁ Χρυσόστομος πατὴρ ἀκτῖνα τοῦτο προσεῖπε τῆς θεότητος· <λαμπρότερος γάρ> φησίν, <ἑαυτοῦ ἐφαίνετο ὁ κύριος τῆς θεότητος παραδειξάσης τὰς ἀκτῖνας αὐτῆς>. Συμεὼν δὲ ὁ ἔνθεος μεταφραστὴς τὸν τῶν θεολόγων ἐξοχώτατον Ἰωάννην, <αὐτήν>, φησί, <τὴν τοῦ λόγου θεότητα παραγυμνωθεῖσαν> ἐπ᾽ ὄρους <ἰδεῖν>. Ἀλλὰ καὶ τὰ τῶν θεοφόρων πατέρων ἀπαγγέλλων κεφαλαιωδῶς, <ἐπειδή>, φησί, <πᾶς λογισμὸς διὰ φαντασίας αἰσθητῶν τινων εἰσέρχεται ἐν τῇ καρδίᾳ, τότε αὐγάζει αὐτὴν τὸ μακάριον φῶς τῆς θεότητος, ὅταν πάντῃ εὐκαιρήσῃ ἀπὸ πάντων καὶ ἀσχημάτιστος ἐκ τούτων γένηται>, εἴπερ ἡ λαμπρότης ἐκείνη κατὰ στέρησιν πάντων νοημάτων παραφαίνεται τῷ καθαρῷ νοΐ. Ὅτι δὲ μὴ μόνον ὁρᾶται, ἀλλὰ καὶ μετέχεται τουτὶ τὸ φῶς ὑπὸ τῶν ὡς ἀληθῶς ἐποπτευόντων, δείκνυσιν ὁ λέγων, <ἆθλον ἀρετῆς θεὸν γενέσθαι καὶ τῷ ἀκραιφνεστάτῳ φωτὶ καταστράπτεσθαι τῆς ἡμέρας ἐκείνης υἱὸν γενόμενον, ἣ μὴ διακόπτεται ζόφῳ· ἄλλος γὰρ ταύτην ποιεῖ ἥλιος, ὁ τὸ ἀληθινόν φῶς ἀπαστράπτων. Ὅς διηνεκὲς καὶ ἀδιάδοχον τοῖς ἀξίοις τὸ φῶς ἐμποιεῖ, καὶ αὐτοὺς τοὺς μετέχοντας τοῦ φωτὸς ἐκείνου ἄλλους ἡλίους ἀπεργαζόμενος>· <λάμψουσι γάρ>, φησί, <καὶ οἱ δίκαιοι ὡς ὁ ἥλιος>. Διὸ ᾄδων Μητροφάνης ὁ θεῖος ᾠδικὸς <τρισσοφαοῦς>, φησίν,

fold light and the unitary lightning of the divinity."[35] And again: "You, the essentially invisible word, have been seen as a man, calling people to participation in your divinity."[36] Do you see clearly that not only the completely invisible and unintelligible and imparticipable divinity, but also the divinity which is visible and intelligible and participable for only the saints in a mystical way, belongs to God? You, then, who say that that divinity and brightness of God which surpasses our intellect (for if it is participated in and seen and thought, then it reveals itself only in a mystical way, deprived of all concepts, as you have heard, by its utmost purity, to the heart of the saints which has neither form nor figure) is created--do you not clearly make God a creature?

XII. But since you also say that the divinity of the same God is uncreated, your God has more than one nature and is, so to speak, created-uncreated, composed of two most contrary things, a created and an uncreated divinity. Or, if you don't dare to say that, because it is really impossible that the same God has a created and an uncreated divinity, then you risk worshipping two Gods who are evidently opposite to each other, one with a created divinity, the other with an uncreated one. You then, who clearly suffer from the most despicable disease of believing in two Gods--and the synod has found you out this year!-- spread that lie about us and all the saints who, through thick and thin, confess that God is one. For that sometimes the same God is seen and thought and participated in and other times He is invisible and unintelligible and imparticipable and that we can call Him in all simplicity both wholly intelligible and unintelligible, the great Dionysius the Areopagite has taught us, too. But until today we have not yet heard that the same God is both created and uncreated because He has admittedly a created and an uncreated divinity.

XIII. B. We conclude from all these facts that there is one divinity.

<αἴγλης, ἀγαθέ, καὶ ἑνιαίας ἀστραπῆς θεότητος ἀπολαῦσαι καταξίωσον ἡμᾶς >. Καὶ πάλιν· <ὁ κατ᾽ οὐσίαν ἀθεώρητος λόγος ἄνθρωπος ὤφθης, τὸν ἄνθρωπον ἀνακαλούμενος πρὸς μετουσίαν τῆς σῆς θεότητος>. Ὁρᾷς σαφῶς ὡς οὐ μόνον ἡ παντάπασιν ἀόρατος καὶ ἀπερινόητος καὶ ἀμέθεκτος θεότης, ἀλλὰ καὶ ἡ τοῖς ἁγίοις μόνοις ἀπορρήτως ὁρατὴ καὶ νοητὴ καὶ μεθεκτὴ θεότης τοῦ θεοῦ ἐστιν; Ὑμεῖς οὖν οἱ τὴν ὑπὲρ νοῦν ταύτην τοῦ θεοῦ θεότητά τε καὶ λαμπρότητα - ἐι γὰρ μετέχεταί τε καὶ ὁρᾶται καὶ νοεῖται, ἀλλὰ κατὰ στέρησιν πάντων τῶν νοημάτων, ὡς ἀκήκοας, ὑπ᾽ ἄκρας καθαρότητος ἀσχηματίστῳ καὶ ἀνειδέῳ γεγονυίᾳ τῇ καρδίᾳ τῶν ἁγίων ἀπορρήτως ἀναφαίνεται - ὑμεῖς οὖν οἱ ταύτην λέγοντες κτιστὴν οὐχὶ κτίσμα τὸν θεὸν ποιεῖτε φανερῶς;

XII. Ἀλλ᾽ ἐπεὶ καὶ ἄκτιστον λέγετε τοῦ αὐτοῦ θεότητα, σύνθετος ὑμῖν ἐστιν ὁ θεὸς καί, ἵν᾽ οὕτως εἴπω, κτιστοάκτιστος, ἐκ δύο τῶν ἐναντιωτάτων, κτιστῆς καὶ ἀκτίστου συγκείμενος θεότητος· ἢ εἰ μὴ τοῦτ᾽ ἀνέχεσθε λέγειν, ὡς καὶ ἀδυνάτου ὄντος τὸν αὐτὸν θεὸν κτιστὴν ἔχειν καὶ ἄκτιστον θεότητα, δύο θεοὺς σαφῶς ἐναντίως πρὸς ἀλλήλους ἔχοντας κινδυνεύετε πρεσβεύειν, τὸν μὲν ἄκτιστον, τὸν δὲ κτιστὴν κεκτημένον θεότητα. Ὑμεῖς οὖν ὄντες οἱ διθεΐαν αἰσχίστην περιφανῶς νενοσηκότες, ὡς κἀπὶ τῆς συνόδου τῆτες ἐφωράθητε, ἡμῶν καὶ τῶν ἁγίων πάντων ἕνα διὰ πάντων κηρυττόντων τὸν θεὸν τοῦτο καταψεύδεσθε· τὸν γὰρ αὐτὸν θεὸν ἔστι μὲν ὡς ὁρᾶσθαι καὶ νοεῖσθαι καὶ μετέχεσθαι, ἔστι δ᾽ ὡς ἀόρατον εἶναι καὶ ἀμέθεκτον καὶ ἀπερινόητον, καὶ ἁπλῶς εἰπεῖν παννόητόν τε καὶ ἀνεννόητον, καὶ ὁ μέγας Διονύσιος ἐθεολόγησε· τὸν αὐτὸν δ᾽ εἶναι κτιστόν τε καὶ ἄκτιστον θεόν, ὡς κτιστήν τε καὶ ἄκτιστον ἔχοντα θεότητα, οὐδέπω καὶ τήμερον ἀκηκόαμεν.

XIII. ΒΑΡΛ. Ἡμεῖς ἐκ πάντων τούτων μίαν εἶναι συνάγομεν θεότητα.

O. Well, see to it (then), that that does not become your foundation for wrongly concluding that God has one divinity or for lawlessly making two of them, one of which is treated irreverently by everybody, because they understand the unity of the divinity in the wrong way. There are also people who fall into these two opposite impieties because of the assumption that there is one. If, on account of that, you say that there is one, do you (then) believe that it is the same as and not different from the visible and intelligible divinity of the great Basil, that completely invisible and unimaginable divinity, and do you conclude in that way that there is one, or do you assert that that one divinity is composed of a created and an uncreated divinity?

B. Come on, don't think that we're *that* stupid! No, we raise the thinking part of our soul from the visible divinity up to the completely invisible and solitary uncreated divinity, and so we revere the one uncreated divinity, the essence of God itself.

XIV. O. Now the argument has already denounced you beautifully in just a few words! For look, you clearly say that the glory and divinity of Christ, which were seen on the mountain, are created. You are both truly proven to fall into the traps which opened themselves a short while ago and you continually prove to be guilty of the written accusations directed against Barlaam. To proceed from the creations to the essence of God, and to perceive the uncreated essence from the visible creatures, is part of the misleading doctrine of Eunomius.[37] Hence, both things necessarily have as a result that there is a diversity (of divinities) both by concluding impiously (in your fashion) (that there is one divinity) and by atheistically cutting up the one divinity of God. Therefore, the divine bishop of Nyssa says: "The essentially invisible God becomes visible by His energies. He is not visible in His essence, but in some of His characteristics."[38] "None of the divine characteristics is acquired, even if they are not His essence."[39] In his books against Eunomius, the great Basil runs completely counter to you who hold to the doctrine of Barlaam; setting forth Eunomius' written doctrines, who says: "By seeing the created things, a person can be brought from them to the essences, discovering the Son as

ΟΡΘΟΔ. Ἀλλ' ὅρα μὴ τοῦθ' ὑμῖν ἀφορμὴ γίνεται τοῦ κακῶς τὴν μίαν τοῦ θεοῦ θεότητα συνάγειν ἢ διχοτομεῖν ἀθέσμως, ὧν θάτερον πᾶς τις δυσσεβεῖ, κακῶς ἐκδεχόμενος τὸ ἑνιαῖον τῆς θεότητος. Εἰσὶ δ' οἳ καὶ ἀμφοτέραις ἐκ τοῦ μίαν δῆθεν λέγειν περιπίπτουσι ταῖς ἐκ διαμέτρου δυσσεβείαις ταύταις. Μίαν οὖν ὑμεῖς ἐκ τούτων λέγοντες, ἆρα ταὐτὸ καὶ ἀδιάφορόν φατε τῇ κατὰ τὸν μέγαν Βασίλειον ὁρατῇ καὶ νοητῇ, τὴν παντάπασιν ἀόρατόν τε καὶ ἀπερινόητον θεότητα, καὶ οὕτως ἐκ τούτων συνάγετε τὴν μίαν, ἢ τὴν μίαν ταύτην ἐκ κτιστῆς καὶ ἀκτίστου φατὲ συντεθειμένην εἶναι;

ΒΑΡΛ. Ἄπαγε, μὴ οὕτως ἡμᾶς ἀνοηταίνειν νόμιζε. Ἀλλ' ἐκ τῆς ὁρατῆς εἰς τὴν παντάπασιν ἀόρατον καὶ μόνην ἄκτιστον θεότητα τὸ νοερὸν τῆς ψυχῆς ἀναβιβάζομεν, καὶ οὕτω μίαν ἄκτιστον θεότητα πρεσβεύομεν, αὐτὴν τὴν οὐσίαν τοῦ θεοῦ.

XIV. ΟΡΘΟΔ. Καλῶς ἄρ' ὑμᾶς φθάσας διὰ βραχέων ἐστηλίτευσεν ὁ λόγος· ἰδοῦ γὰρ σαφῶς κτιστήν φατε τὴν ἐκφανεῖσαν ἐπ' ὄρους τοῦ Χριστοῦ δόξαν καὶ θεότητα. Καὶ ἀληθῶς, οἷς προαναπέφηνε περιπίπτοντες ἐλέγχεσθε, καὶ ταῖς κατὰ τοῦ Βαρλαὰμ ἐγγράφοις ἀποκηρύξεσιν ἔνοχοι διατελοῦντες δείκνυσθε. Τό γε μὴν ἐκ τῶν κτισμάτων ἐπὶ τὴν οὐσίαν τοῦ θεοῦ ἀνάγεσθαι καὶ ἐκ τῶν ὁρατῶν κτισμάτων τὴν ἄκτιστον οὐσίαν καθορᾶν τῆς Εὐνομίου ἐστὶ παραφορᾶς. Ὅθεν ἐξ ἀνάγκης ἀμφότερα πολυειδῶς συμβαίνει, καὶ τὸ δυσσεβῶς συνάγειν καὶ τὸ ἀθέως κατατέμνειν τὴν μίαν τοῦ θεοῦ θεότητα. Διό φησιν ὁ Νύσσης θεῖος πρόεδρος· <ὁ ἀόρατος τῇ οὐσίᾳ ὁρατὸς ταῖς ἐνεργείαις γίνεται· οὐ κατὰ τὴν οὐσίαν, ἀλλ' ἔν τισι τοῖς περὶ αὐτὸν ἰδιώμασι καθορώμενος>. <Οὐδὲν δὲ ἐπίκτητον τῶν θείων ἰδιωμάτων, εἰ καὶ μὴ ταῦτα ἡ οὐσία ἐστίν>. Ὁ δὲ μέγας Βασίλειος ὑμῖν ἄντικρυς τοῖς τὰ τοῦ Βαρλαὰμ φρονοῦσιν ἐν τοῖς *Πρὸς Εὐνόμιον* ἀντιφθεγγόμενος τἀκείνου προθεὶς γράφοντος, εἴπερ ἐκ τῶν δημιουργημάτων σκοπούμενός τις ἐκ τούτων εἰς τὰς οὐσίας ἀνάγοιτο, τοῦ μὲν ἀγεννήτου τὸν υἱὸν εὑρίσκων

a creature of the unborn and the Spirit as a creature of the only begotten Son," he says: "I do not see how it is possible to arrive by reasoning to the essences from the created things; for the created things show His power and wisdom and craft, but not the essence itself. Nor do they necessarily demonstrate all the power itself of the Creator, because it is possible that the craftsman does not put all his strength into his energies, but often uses the weaker energies in the works of his craft. And even if he would put all his power into his work, even so it would be possible to measure his strength in his works but not to understand what his essence is."[40] That is exactly what the divine Paul says: "Ever since the creation of the world His eternal power and divine nature, invisible though they are, have been understood and seen through the things He has made."[41] And Maximus, great in divine matters, says this in his exegesis: "The seeds of the beings, which have been preliminarily performed in God before all ages, are invisible, as He knows Himself; (the) divine men are accustomed to call them good wills and they are perceived by the mind from the created things. For all the creatures of God which are contemplated and known by us according to nature with due insight, reveal to us, in a hidden way, the seeds according to which they have come into being, and they show forth along with themselves the divine purpose in each created thing. Hence, "the heavens declare the glory of God; and the firmament proclaims the work of His hands."[42] "The providence which holds the beings together and the energy which deifies the foreseen things in accordance with it are an eternal power and divinity."[43] Have you now also learned from Paul that the deification is the divinity of God and is eternal?

XV. B. To tell you the truth and to conceal nothing, we heard that you cite something the great Dionysius said, on account of which we could even speak against you. But a short time ago you showed that all the saints were in agreement with you. Know, then, that we say that that light is essence, if indeed it is uncreated.

ποίημα, τοῦ δὲ μονογενοῦς τὸν παράκλητον, <πῶς δυνατόν>, φησίν, <ἐκ τῶν δημιουργημάτων τὰς οὐσίας ἀναλογίζεσθαι ἐγὼ μὲν οὐχ ὁρῶ· δυνάμεως γὰρ καὶ σοφίας καὶ τέχνης, οὐχὶ δὲ τῆς οὐσίας αὐτῆς ἐνδεικτικά ἐστι τὰ ποιήματα. Καὶ οὐδὲ αὐτὴν πᾶσαν τοῦ δημιουργοῦ τὴν δύναμιν ἀναγκαίως παρίστησιν, ἐνδεχομένου ποτὲ τὸν τεχνίτην μὴ πᾶσαν ἑαυτοῦ τὴν ἰσχὺν ἐναποθέσθαι ταῖς ἐνεργείαις, ἀλλ' ὑφειμένοις πολλάκις ἐπὶ τῶν ἔργων τῆς τέχνης τοῖς τόνοις χρήσασθαι. Εἰ δὲ καὶ ὅλην τὴν δύναμιν ἐπὶ τὸ ἔργον ἀνακινήσειε, καὶ οὕτως ἂν ὑπάρχοι τὴν ἰσχὺν αὐτοῦ διὰ τῶν ἔργων ἀναμετρεῖσθαι, οὐχὶ δὲ τὴν οὐσίαν, ἥτις ποτέ ἐστι καταλαμβάνεσθαι>. Τοῦτ' αὐτὸ καὶ ὁ θεσπέσιος διδάσκει Παῦλος· <τὰ ἀόρατα>, γράφων, <τοῦ θεοῦ ἀπὸ κτίσεως κόσμου τοῖς ποιήμασι νοούμενα καθορᾶται, ἥ τε ἀΐδιος αὐτοῦ δύναμις καὶ θειότης>. Ἐπεὶ καὶ ὁ πολὺς τὰ θεῖα Μάξιμος τοῦτ' ἐξηγούμενός φησιν· <οἱ τῶν ὄντων λόγοι προκαταρτισθέντες τῶν αἰώνων ἐν τῷ θεῷ, καθὼς οἶδεν αὐτός, ἀόρατοι ὄντες, οὓς καὶ ἀγαθὰ θελήματα καλεῖν τοῖς θείοις ἐστὶν ἔθος ἀνδράσιν, ἀπὸ τῶν ποιημάτων νοούμενοι καθορῶνται. Πάντα γὰρ τὰ ποιήματα τοῦ θεοῦ κατὰ φύσιν μετὰ τῆς δεούσης ἐπιστήμης γνωστικῶς ὑφ' ἡμῶν θεωρούμενα, τοὺς καθ' οὓς γεγένηνται λόγους κρυφίως ἡμῖν ἀπαγγέλλουσι, καὶ τὸν ἐφ' ἑκάστῳ ποιήματι θεῖον σκοπὸν ἑαυτοῖς συνεκφαίνουσι· καθὸ καὶ 'οἱ οὐρανοὶ διηγοῦνται δόξαν θεοῦ, καὶ τὸ στερέωμα τὴν τῶν χειρῶν ἀναγγέλλει ποίησιν'. Ἀΐδιος δὲ δύναμίς ἐστι καὶ θειότης ἡ συνεκτικὴ τῶν ὄντων πρόνοια καὶ ἡ κατ' αὐτὴν ἐκθεωτικὴ τῶν προνοουμένων ἐνέργεια>. Μανθάνεις καὶ παρὰ Παύλου τοῦ θεοῦ θειότητα καὶ ἀΐδιον οὖσαν τὴν θέωσιν;

XV. ΒΑΡΛ. Ἵν' ἐξείπω τἀληθὲς μηδὲν ὑποστειλάμενος, ἡμεῖς τοῦ μεγάλου Διονυσίου ῥῆσιν ἠκούομεν ὑμᾶς προβαλλομένους, ἀφ' ἧς καὶ ἀντιλέγειν εἴχομεν. Σὺ δὲ πάντας τοὺς ἁγίους ἀρτίως ὑμῖν ἔδειξας ὁμολογοῦντας.

O. But even from that point of view you still fall into the trap of the most impious atheism and ditheism.

B. How? In what manner?

O. Since you showed before that there is one uncreated divinity, the altogether invisible essence of God (wrongly interpreting the words of the fathers by taking away all physical aspects of it); and since you also demonstrated that, on account of that, the light of the Lord's transformation, because it was visible to those who were deemed worthy of it, is created, whereas you now say that that is essence: either you continue to say that creature and essence of God are the same--for you assert that what was first a creature is now essence, which is altogether impious--or you say that there are two essences of God and two divinities: that which you formerly maintained in earnest to be invisible and that light which was seen by the eyes of the apostles, which you now strongly assert to be essence, if indeed it is uncreated.[44]

XVI. B. It now occurs to me very clearly how puzzling it is that, while the saints (as we said before) maintain that the divinity of God is visible and invisible, together we can all revere one divinity, as something we agree upon and which the same saints handed down. For even if it is a unity according to its uncreated character, then it appears to be divided according to its visibility (whatever that may be), and to its invisibility, and to all the other qualifications you too give it. How, then, is it one and simple?

O. Obviously, my friend, the uncreated essence and the uncreated energy are inseparable from each other. For neither of them is ever seen separate from the other. And so there is in essence and energy one uncreated divinity of the Father, the Son and the Holy Spirit. That was also the opinion of Maximus, wise in divine matters, when he wrote, "One divinity without beginning, simple, super-essential, without parts and indivisible."[45] He added: "For the Father and the Son and the Holy Spirit are the divinity. And there is one God, the Father and the Son and the Holy Spirit. For one and the same are the essence and the energy and the

Ἴσθι γε μὴν ὡς οὐσίαν τοῦτ᾽ εἶναι λέγομεν ἡμεῖς τὸ φῶς, εἴπερ ἄκτιστόν ἐστιν.
ΟΡΘΟΔ. Ἀλλὰ κἀντεῦθεν οὐδὲν ἧττον ἀθεΐᾳ τε καὶ διθεΐᾳ περιπίπτετε δυσσεβεστάτῃ.
ΒΑΡΛ. Πῶς καὶ τίνα τρόπον;
ΟΡΘΟΔ. Ἐπεὶ φθάσαντες ἀπεφήνασθε μίαν ἄκτιστον εἶναι θεότητα, τὴν παντάπασιν ἀόρατον οὐσίαν τοῦ θεοῦ, κακῶς ἐκδεξάμενοι τὰς πατερικὰς φωνάς, καὶ περιελόντες ταύτης ἅπαν φυσικόν, κἀντεῦθεν καὶ τὸ φῶς τῆς τοῦ κυρίου μεταμορφώσεως, ἅτε τοῖς ἠξιωμένοις ὁραθέν, εἶναι κτιστὸν συναπεφήνασθε, νῦν οὐσίαν εἶναι τοῦτο λέγοντες, ἢ τὸ αὐτὸ διατελεῖν φατε κτίσμα τε καὶ οὐσίαν τοῦ θεοῦ - ὃ γὰρ κτίσμα πρότερον, νῦν οὐσίαν εἶναι ἰσχυρίζεσθε, παντάπασιν ἀθέως - ἢ δύο λέγετε οὐσίας τοῦ θεοῦ καὶ δύο θεότητας· ἣν πρότερον ἀόρατον ὑπάρχειν διετείνασθε, καὶ τὸ ἑωραμένον τοῦτο τοῖς ὀφθαλμοῖς τῶν ἀποστόλων φῶς, ὃ νῦν οὐσίαν εἶναι διαβεβαιοῦσθε, εἴπερ ἄκτιστον.
XVI. ΒΑΡΛ. Ἔμοιγε νῦν ἐκεῖνο λίαν ἔπεισι θαυμάζειν, πῶς τῶν ἁγίων ὡς προαναπέφηνεν ὁρατὴν καὶ ἀόρατον λεγόντων τοῦ θεοῦ θεότητα, προσκυνεῖν θεότητα μίαν κοινῇ πάντες ἀνωμολογημένον ἔχομεν καὶ ὑπὸ τῶν αὐτῶν ἁγίων παραδεδομένον. Εἰ γὰρ καὶ κατὰ τὸ ἄκτιστον ἥνωται, ἀλλὰ κατὰ τὸ ὁρατὸν ὁπηδήποτε καὶ ἀόρατον καὶ τἆλλ᾽ ὅσα καὶ ὑμεῖς φατε διῃρημένη φαίνεται. Πῶς οὖν μία καὶ ἁπλῆ;
ΟΡΘΟΔ. Αὐτόθεν, ὦ βέλτιστε, τὸ πρὸς ἀλλήλας ἀχώριστον ἔχουσιν ἡ ἄκτιστος οὐσία καὶ ἡ ἄκτιστος ἐνέργεια· οὐ γὰρ ὦπταί ποτέ τις αὐτῶν τῆς ἑτέρας ἔρημος. Καὶ οὕτως ἐν οὐσίᾳ καὶ ἐνεργείᾳ μία ἐστιν ἄκτιστος θεότης, τοῦ πατρὸς καὶ τοῦ υἱοῦ καὶ τοῦ ἁγίου πνεύματος. Ταῦτ᾽ ἄρα καὶ ὁ σοφὸς τὰ θεῖα Μάξιμος εἰπών, ὅτι <μία θεότης ἄναρχος καὶ ἁπλῆ καὶ ὑπερούσιος καὶ ἀμερὴς καὶ ἀδιαίρετος>, ἐπήνεγκε· <πατὴρ γὰρ καὶ υἱὸς καὶ ἅγιον πνεῦμα ἡ θεότης. Καὶ εἷς θεός, ὁ πατὴρ καὶ ὁ υἱὸς καὶ τὸ πνεῦμα τὸ ἅγιον· μία γὰρ καὶ ἡ αὐτὴ οὐσία καὶ δύναμις καὶ ἐνέργεια

power of the Father and the Son and the Holy Spirit."[46] That one divinity and the one God, "who is invisible by His essence becomes visible by His energies, when He is seen in some of the characteristic features around Him,"[47] according to Gregory of Nyssa, the speaker from God; and, according to the blessed Cyril, none of the divine characteristics is acquired.[48] Hence, what you yourself initially cited as evidence from the divine Maximus, even if he did not literally write it down in that way, could be a pious thought. For the distinction in the divinity is not contrary to its unity.[49] But you did not understand that and you broke apart the one divinity into a created and an uncreated one, in a most impious manner, just as Arius had done. For that man had also broken up the One God into a created and an uncreated one, because he had not understood the pious distinction according to the divine hypostases.

XVII. Well, then, now we must talk more to you about the distinction in the divinity. Later on, with God's help, we will also show that that divinity is one and simple and undivided and does not abandon the supernatural simplicity on account of the pious distinction according to the activities. Tell me now: does God's essence have a name?

B. All the theologians agreed that the essence of God is without a name and exceeds all names.

O. True. For the great Dionysius the Areopagite called the name of essence itself the surname of the power of God which makes essence, because that supra-essentiality does not possess a name of its own.[50] But since divinity is not the name of the divine essence, then what does it belong to and what does that name mean? However, let's stop asking each other questions about them, and let us both rather be instructed by the saints. Gregory of Nyssa, the most brilliant star dealing with those who oppose themselves to the Spirit, says: "They say that divinity reveals (divine) nature. But we know that the divine nature has no name which signifies it. But if something is said about it either by human convention or by the divine Scriptures, it signifies something about that which surrounds divinity. But the divine nature itself remains unspoken and unuttered; it exceeds all possibility of being revealed by name.

πατρός, υἱοῦ καὶ πνεύματος>. Ἡ δὲ μία αὕτη θεότης καὶ ὁ εἷς θεός, <ἀόρατος ὢν τῇ οὐσίᾳ ὁρατὸς ταῖς ἐνεργείαις γίνεται, ἐν τισι τοῖς περὶ αὐτὸν ἰδιώμασι καθορώμενος> κατὰ τὸν Νύσσης θεορρήμονα Γρηγόριον, <οὐδὲν δὲ τῶν θείων ἰδιωμάτων ἐπίκτητον> κατὰ τὸν μακάριον Κύριλλον. Διὸ καὶ ὃ τὴν ἀρχὴν ὡς τοῦ θείου προήνεγκας αὐτὸς Μαξίμου, εἰ καὶ μὴ οὕτως ἐπὶ λέξεως ἐκεῖνος ἔγραψεν, ἀλλ' εὖ ἂν ἔχοι εὐσεβῶς νοούμενον· οὐ γὰρ ἐναντιοῦται τῷ ἑνιαίῳ τὸ διακεκριμένον τῆς θεότητος. Ὑμεῖς δὲ τοῦτο μὴ συνέντες εἰς κτιστὴν καὶ ἄκτιστον δυσσεβέστατα διερρήξατε τὴν μίαν θεότητα κατὰ μίμησιν Ἀρείου· καὶ οὗτος γὰρ μὴ συνεὶς τὴν κατὰ τὰς θείας ὑποστάσεις εὐσεβῆ διάκρισιν εἰς κτιστὸν καὶ ἄκτιστον τὸν ἕνα κατέτεμε θεόν.

XVII. Φέρε δέ σοι νῦν ἔτι περὶ τοῦ διακεκριμένου τῆς θεότητος ῥητέον. Ὕστερον δὲ καὶ ὅτι μία καὶ ἁπλῆ καὶ ἀμερὴς θεότης μὴ ἐκστᾶσα τῆς ὑπερφυοῦς ἁπλότητος διὰ τὴν κατὰ τὰς ἐνέργείας εὐσεβῆ διάκρισιν σὺν θεῷ δειχθήσεται. Λέγε μοι τοίνυν· ἔστιν ὄνομα τῇ οὐσίᾳ τοῦ θεοῦ;

ΒΑΡΛ. Τοῦτο συμφώνως πάντες ἔφησαν οἱ θεολόγοι ἀνώνυμον καὶ ὑπερώνυμον εἶναι τὴν οὐσίαν τοῦ θεοῦ.

ΟΡΘΟΔ. Ἀληθές· καὶ αὐτὸ γὰρ τὸ τῆς οὐσίας ὄνομα τῆς οὐσιοποιοῦ τοῦ θεοῦ δυνάμεως ἐπωνυμίαν ὁ ἐξ Ἀρείου Πάγου μέγας ἔφη Διονύσιος, ὡς τῆς ὑπερουσιότητος ἐκείνης προσηγορίαν ἰδίαν οὐδαμῶς ἐχούσης. Ἀλλ' ἐπεὶ τῆς θείας οὐσίας ἡ θεότης ὄνομα οὐκ ἔστι, τίνος ἄρ' ἔστι καὶ τί ποτε σημαίνει τοὔνομα; Μᾶλλον δὲ καὶ περὶ τούτων ἀφέμενοι τοῦ πυνθάνεσθαι ἀλλήλων, ἀμφότεροι παρὰ τῶν ἁγίων διδαχθῶμεν. Φησὶ τοίνυν Γρηγόριος ὁ Νύσσης φανότατος φωστὴρ περὶ τῶν πνευματομάχων, ὅτι <φασὶ φύσεως εἶναι σημαντικὴν τὴν θεότητα. Ἡμεῖς δ' ἴσμεν ὅτι ἡ θεία φύσις ὄνομα σημαντικὸν οὐκ ἔχει· ἀλλ' εἴ τι καὶ λέγεται εἴτε παρὰ τῆς ἀνθρωπίνης συνηθείας εἴτε παρὰ τῆς θείας γραφῆς, τῶν περὶ αὐτήν τι ἀποσημαίνει· αὐτὴ δὲ ἡ θεία φύσις ἄφραστός τε καὶ ἀνεκφώνητος μένει, ὑπερβαίνουσα πᾶσαν τὴν διὰ φωνῆς

So the name divinity shows not the nature of the Spirit, but the power of seeing."[51] Divinity, therefore, is really God's power of seeing: it knows everything, it oversees everything, and foresees everything.[52] The essence of God is also called divinity, but it gets that name with reason from its appropriate activity, as the same man says elsewhere. Therefore, the most theological of the two Gregories says: "Let yourself be illuminated by one light according to the aspect of the essence, i.e., of the divinity."[53]

XVIII. You would be able to find the same thing with the other divine names as well. Hence, Dionysius, who described these names most excellently, says at the beginning of his praise of the divine appellation of being: "Our discourse does not promise to express the absolutely super-essential goodness and essence and life and wisdom of the absolutely super-essential divinity, which has its foundation beyond all goodness and divinity and essence and life and wisdom, in a secret place as the Scriptures say. But it sings of the providence which is revealed to us and which produces good things, the all-transcending goodness and cause of all good things, both being and life and wisdom, and that which causes essence and life and which gives wisdom, to all those who partake of being and life and spirit and reason and sense perception."[54] You, then, who say that one divinity is created, since you could not call created that being which transcends all possibility of being called by a human name because it is established in a secret place, you call the divinity of God itself--which gets that name genuinely from the fathers, namely His power of seeing and of deification and His providence which is revealed to us and which produces good things--(you) very impiously (call that) created! And you evilly attack us who piously proclaim that that divinity is uncreated! For we don't say that some divinities produce these and others those and that there are higher and lower beings, but that of the one God are all the good manifestations and processions and the appellations of God which are piously celebrated. He is above all name and all manifestation and all hymn which is sung by holy angels and men.

σημασίαν. Οὐκοῦν οὐ τὴν φύσιν τοῦ πνεύματος, ἀλλὰ τὴν θεατικὴν δύναμιν ἡ τῆς θεότητος προσηγορία παρίστησι>. Θεότης οὖν κυρίως ἡ τοῦ θεοῦ θεατικὴ δύναμις, τό τε πάντ᾽ εἰδέναι καὶ τὸ πάντα ἐφορᾶν προνοούμενον ἁπάντων. Λέγεται δὲ θεότης καὶ ἡ οὐσία τοῦ θεοῦ, ἀλλὰ κατ᾽ αἰτίαν ἀπὸ τῆς οἰκείας ἐνεργείας ὀνομαζομένη, καθάπερ ὁ αὐτὸς ἀλλαχοῦ παρίστησι. Διὸ καὶ Γρηγορίων ὁ θεολογικώτατός φησιν· < ἑνὶ φωτὶ περιαστράφθητε κατὰ τὸν τῆς οὐσίας λόγον εἴτουν θεότητος>.

XVIII. Τὸ αὐτὸ δ᾽ ἂν εὕροις καὶ ἐπὶ τῶν ἄλλων θείων ὀνομάτων. Διὸ καὶ Διονύσιος ὁ τούτων ἐξόχως ὑμνῳδὸς ἀρχόμενος τὴν τοῦ ὄντος θεωνυμίαν ἐξυμνεῖν, <οὐκ ἐκφράσαι>, φησίν, < ὁ λόγος τὴν αὐτοϋπερούσιον ἀγαθότητα καὶ οὐσίαν καὶ ζωὴν καὶ σοφίαν τῆς αὐτοϋπερουσίου θεότητος ἐπαγγέλλεται, τὴν ὑπὲρ πᾶσαν ἀγαθότητα καὶ θεότητα καὶ οὐσίαν καὶ ζωὴν καὶ σοφίαν ἐν ἀποκρύφοις, ὥς τὰ λόγιά φησιν, ὑπεριδρυμένην· ἀλλὰ τὴν ἐκπεφασμένην ἀγαθοποιὸν πρόνοιαν ὑπεροχικῶς ἀγαθότητα καὶ πάντων ἀγαθῶν αἰτίαν ὑμνεῖ, καὶ ὂν καὶ ζωὴν καὶ σοφίαν, τὴν οὐσιοποιὸν καὶ ζωοποιὸν καὶ σοφοδότιν αἰτίαν, τῶν οὐσίας καὶ ζωῆς καὶ νοῦ καὶ λόγου καὶ αἰσθήσεως μετειληφότων>. Ὑμεῖς οὖν οἱ τὴν ἑτέραν λέγοντες κτιστήν, ἐπεὶ τὴν οὐσίαν οὐκ ἂν εἴποιτε, τὴν καὶ πᾶσαν φωνῆς σημασίαν ὑπερβαίνουσαν ὡς ἐν ἀποκρύφοις ὑπεριδρυμένην, οὐκοῦν αὐτὴν τὴν κυρίως κατὰ τοὺς πατέρας λεγομένην τοῦ θεοῦ θεότητα, δηλαδὴ τὴν θεατικὴν καὶ θεοποιὸν δύναμιν αὐτοῦ καὶ τὴν ἐκπεφασμένην ἀγαθοποιὸν πρόνοιαν κτιστὴν λίαν δυσσεβῶς φατε, καὶ ἡμῖν τοῖς εὐσεβῶς ἄκτιστον κηρύττουσιν αὐτὴν ἐπανίστασθε κακῶς· οὐ γὰρ ἄλλων ἄλλας παρακτικὰς θεότητας ἤτοι οὐσίας λέγομεν ἡμεῖς ὑπερεχούσας καὶ ὑφειμένας, ἀλλ᾽ ἑνὸς θεοῦ τὰς ὅλας ἀγαθὰς ἐκφάνσεις καὶ προόδους καὶ τὰς εὐσεβῶς ἐξυμνουμένας θεωνυμίας, τοῦ ὄντος ὑπὲρ πᾶν ὄνομα

XIX. B. Show me this: how, with you too, can the different divinities be one?

O. Let me refute one absurd thesis which exceeds all others in its absurdity even before I prove that there is one God; I leave out the other crazy traps you risk falling into by not theologizing according to the Scriptures and even by speaking counter to those who do theologize according to them.

B. Which one?

O. Doesn't all cause as such stand above the caused thing? And isn't it true that that which as such does not stand above a thing cannot be the cause of it?

B. That's true. For "the Father is greater than the Son because He is the cause" whereas in all other respects He deserves the same honor; so says Gregory, the father of theology.[55]

O. Not only Gregory, my friend, but the great Basil also says: "The Son is second in rank to the Father because He is begotten by Him. And in honor, because He (the Father) is the beginning and the cause by being His Father and because the way and the access to the Father is through Him. But in nature He is not second, because the divinity in both of them is one."[56] Since, then, that which does not stand above is not a cause, and since the divinity of God is not only called by the fathers invisible and without a name and imparticipable but also having a name and participated in and visible, you, accusing us because we say that one (divinity) (namely, the essence of God) just because it is a cause and a giver, stands above the unspeakable grace which proceeds out of it and above the so-called power of seeing--we share this opinion with the fathers--you do not refer the gift of deification to that cause. Therefore, you speak about two causes and two divinities which completely differ from each other and you make two beginnings and you fall into the trap of truly the most impious ditheism!

XX. B. And which father has said that the uncreated essence stands above the uncreated grace? For you have introduced them as saying that

καὶ πᾶσαν ἔκφανσιν καὶ πάντα ὕμνον ὑπ᾽ ἀγγέλων ἁγίων καὶ ἀνθρώπων προσαγόμενον.

XIX. ΒΑΡΛ. Ἐκεῖνό μοι δεῖξον· πῶς μία καὶ παρ᾽ ὑμῖν αἱ διάφοροι θεότητες;

ΟΡΘΟΔ. Ἔτι πρὸ τῆς τοῦ ἑνιαίου ἀποδείξεως τἄλλα παρεὶς τῶν ἀτοπημάτων, οἷς περιπίπτειν κινδυνεύετε μὴ κατὰ τὰς γραφὰς θεολογοῦντες, ἀλλὰ καὶ τοῖς κατ᾽ αὐτὰς θεολογοῦσιν ἀντιλέγοντες, μίαν μηδεμίαν ὑπερβολὴν ἐλλείπουσαν ἐξελέγξω ἀτοπίαν.

ΒΑΡΛ. Τίνα ταύτην;

ΟΡΘΟΔ. Οὐ πᾶν τὸ αἴτιον καθὸ αἴτιον τοῦ αἰτιατοῦ ὑπερκεῖται, καὶ τὸ μὴ κατὰ τοῦτο ὑπερκείμενον οὐδ᾽ αἴτιον αὐτοῦ δύναιτ᾽ ἂν ὑπάρχειν;

ΒΑΡΛ. Οὕτως ἔχει. Καὶ γὰρ καὶ <ὁ πατὴρ τοῦ υἱοῦ μείζων τῷ αἰτίῳ>, τἄλλα πάνθ᾽ ὁμότιμος ὑπάρχων, καθάπερ καὶ Γρηγόριός φησιν ὁ τῆς θεολογίας ἐπώνυμος.

ΟΡΘΟΔ. Οὐ Γρηγόριος μόνον, ὦ ᾿γαθέ, ἀλλὰ καὶ Βασίλειος ὁ μέγας, <τάξει μέν>, φησί, <δεύτερος ὁ υἱὸς τοῦ πατρός, ὅτι ἀπ᾽ ἐκείνου· καὶ ἀξιώματι, ὅτι ἀρχὴ καὶ αἰτία, τῷ εἶναι πατέρα αὐτοῦ, καὶ ὅτι δι᾽ αὐτοῦ ἡ πρόσοδος καὶ προσαγωγὴ πρὸς τὸν πατέρα· φύσει δὲ οὐκέτι δεύτερος, ὅτι ἡ θεότης ἐν ἑκατέρῳ μία>. Ἐπεὶ τοίνυν τὸ μὴ ὑπερκείμενον οὐδ᾽ αἴτιον, οὐκ ἀόρατος δὲ μόνον καὶ ἀνώνυμος καὶ ἀμέθεκτος, ἀλλὰ καὶ ὀνομαζομένη καὶ μετεχομένη καὶ ὁρατὴ θεότης τοῦ θεοῦ τοῖς πατράσιν εἴρηται, κατηγοροῦντες ἡμῶν ὅτι τὴν ἑτέραν, ἤτοι τὴν οὐσίαν τοῦ θεοῦ, ὡς αἰτίαν τε καὶ χορηγὸν ὑπερκεῖσθαι τῆς ἐξ αὐτῆς χορηγουμένης ἀπορρήτου χάριτος καὶ τῆς ὀνομαζομένης θεατικῆς δυνάμεως - καὶ τοῦτο κατὰ τοὺς πατέρας λέγομεν - , ὑμεῖς οὐκ εἰς αἰτίαν ταύτην ἀνάγετε τὸ δῶρον τὸ θεοποιόν. Τοιγαροῦν δύο λέγετε τὰ αἴτια καὶ δύο θεότητας ἀλλήλων ἀντιδιῃρημένας, καὶ δύο ἀρχὰς ποιεῖτε καὶ διθεΐᾳ ὡς ἀληθῶς ἀσεβεστάτῃ περιπίπτετε.

XX. ΒΑΡΛ. Καὶ τίς τῶν πατέρων ὑπερκεῖσθαι τῆς ἀκτίστου χάριτος τὴν ἄκτιστον οὐσίαν ἔφη; Δύο γὰρ

they are two, but not yet that one stands above and the other below.

O. One must carefully listen to the words that were spoken if one wants to arrive at their truth. Now you don't seem to understand the power of what I just said. A little while ago we introduced the great Dionysius and the divine Gregory of Nyssa, saying that the essence of God is without a name because it is above all names and transcends all manner of signification by words. They also say that everything that is said about God denotes something that surrounds that essence and that the word "divinity" does not signify genuinely its nature but the power of God to see. That also the essence of God which is above all names is called divinity but not with the genuine name. That which is above all names stands in fact above all that which is named, and the essence is higher than all the things around it. Therefore the great Athanasius says: "Being God is second to His nature."[57] And again Gregory: "If the judgments of God cannot be discerned and the ways are not searched out and the promise of good things transcends all conjecture founded upon queries, how much more is the divine above and higher than all the things that are thought around it, on account of its unnamable and unapproachable character."[58] And the great Basil says: "Which are the activities of the Spirit? Unnamable due to their greatness and innumerable because of (their) multitude. For how can we think what is above the ages, and which were His activities before the intelligible creation, how many are the graces which flow from Him to the creation, and what is the power in relation to the coming ages? Hence, even if you think something above the ages, even that is lower than the Spirit."[59] Would, then, the essence of God--which is above all names, unutterable, around which are the powers and activities which are before all ages, which has its name "divinity" from its proper activity--(would that) not be above the divinity, namely the power of seeing which is before all ages and the activity of God who knows everything before its birth of which the great Basil has said that it is below the Spirit while the great Athanasius (called it) second to the nature, the divinity which rightly has that name, being around the divine nature, as Gregory of Nyssa has revealed?

λέγοντας αὐτοὺς παρήγαγες, ὑπερκειμένην δὲ καὶ ὑφειμένην οὔπω.

ΟΡΘΟΔ. Συνετῶς δεῖ κατακούειν τῶν λεγομένων, εἰ βούλεταί τις ἐφικνεῖσθαι τῆς ἐν τούτοις ἀληθείας. Σύ δ' οὐκ ἐπιγνόντι ἔοικας τὴν δύναμιν τῶν εἰρημένων ἄρτι. Ἀλλὰ καὶ μικρὸν ἀνωτέρω προηγάγομεν τὸν μέγαν Διονύσιον καὶ τὸν Νύσσης θεῖον Γρηγόριον λέγοντας τὴν μὲν οὐσίαν τοῦ θεοῦ ἀνώνυμον, ὡς ὑπερώνυμον καὶ πᾶσαν τὴν διὰ φωνῆς σημασίαν ὑπερβαίνουσαν, πάντα δὲ τὰ λεγόμενα ἐπὶ θεοῦ τῶν περὶ αὐτήν τι ἀποσημαίνειν, καὶ τὸ τῆς θεότητος ὄνομα οὐ τὴν φύσιν, ἀλλὰ τὴν θεατικὴν τοῦ θεοῦ κυρίως δύναμιν δηλοῦν. Λέγεσθαι δὲ καὶ τὴν ὑπερώνυμον οὐσίαν τοῦ θεοῦ θεότητα, ἀλλ' οὐ κυριωνύμως. Τοῦ γοῦν ὀνομαζομένου τὸ ὑπερώνυμον ὑπέρκειται, καὶ ἡ οὐσία τῶν περὶ αὐτὴν ἁπάντων ὑπερτέρα. Διὸ καὶ ὁ μέγας Ἀθανάσιος, <τὸ θεὸς εἶναι>, φησί, <δεύτερόν ἐστι τῆς φύσεως>. Καὶ ὁ Νύσσης αὖθις· <εἰ τὰ κρίματα τοῦ θεοῦ ἐξερευνηθῆναι οὐ δύναται καὶ αἱ ὁδοὶ οὐκ ἐξιχνιάζονται καὶ ἡ τῶν ἀγαθῶν ἐπαγγελία πάσης ὑπέρκειται τῆς ἀπὸ στοχασμῶν εἰκασίας, πόσῳ μᾶλλον κατὰ τὸ ἄφραστον καὶ ἀπροσπέλαστον ἄνω καὶ ὑψηλότερόν ἐστιν αὐτὸ τὸ θεῖον τῶν περὶ αὐτὸ νοουμένων>. Ὁ δὲ μέγας Βασίλειος, <αἱ δὲ ἐνέργειαι>, φησί, <τοῦ πνεύματος τίνες; Ἄρρητοι μὲν διὰ τὸ μέγεθος, ἀνεξαρίθμητοι δὲ διὰ τὸ πλῆθος. Πῶς γὰρ νοήσωμεν τὰ τῶν αἰώνων ἐπέκεινα, τίνες ἦσαν αὐτοῦ πρὸ τῆς νοητῆς κτίσεως ἐνέργειαι, πόσαι δὲ αἱ ἀπ' αὐτοῦ περὶ τὴν κτίσιν χάριτες, τίς δὲ ἡ πρὸς τοὺς αἰῶνας τοὺς ἐπερχομένους δύναμις; Ὥστε κἂν τι νοήσῃς τῶν αἰώνων ἐπέκεινα, καὶ τοῦτό ἐστι τοῦ πνεύματος κατωτέρω>. Τῆς οὖν θεότητος, δηλαδὴ τῆς προαιωνίου θεατικῆς δυνάμεως καὶ ἐνεργείας τοῦ τὰ πάντα εἰδότος πρὸ γενέσεως θεοῦ, ἣν κατωτέρω μὲν τοῦ πνεύματος ὁ μέγας εἴρηκε Βασίλειος, δευτέραν δὲ τῆς φύσεως ὁ μέγας Ἀθανάσιος, τῆς κυρίως θεότητος προσαγορευομένης, τῆς περὶ τὴν θείαν φύσιν οὔσης, ὡς ὁ Νύσσης

We must also call upon the great Dionysius. For he says more clearly than the others that both the deification is the divinity of God and the essence which is above it, firmly and, at the same time, clearly and wisely and piously. For in the *Divine Names* he says: "We call divinity in the sense of really origin, God and cause, the one and only origin and cause of everything, above all origin and essence, but in a derivative sense, the power flowing from the imparticipable God, the divinization itself through which those things which partake of it are divine and are said to be divine."[60] And writing *To Gaius* how God is above the Godhead and the principle of goodness he says: "This is possible if we think of the divinity as the gift which makes us God and good according to which we become God and good. For if that is the beginning of becoming God for those who become God, then God who is above all beginning is also above the divinity which gets its name in that sense."[61]

XXI. B. But he says there that that divinity is a participation and an imitation; hence, we call it created.

O. He called it an inimitable imitation. Hence, it is no more an imitation than a non-imitation. Therefore, it is not created on account of that. Many things of God signify participation. For the kingdom of God itself, which has also been promised to us, is a participation, while being uncreated. For the divine Maximus says: "The kingdom of God is above the ages; for it is improper that the kingdom of God has had a beginning or would have been preceded by ages. And we trust that that is the inheritance of the saved."[62] But Damascene, wise at divine matters, also taught us that many things which are said about God signify participation. But no sensible person would call any of them created. And when you hear the word "participation" in those cases, don't think that that is a physical relationship of those who are in possession (of the divine). No, it is a supernatural partaking through the spirit. Hence, he

ἀπεφήνατο Γρηγόριος, ταύτης οὖν ἡ οὐσία τοῦ θεοῦ ἡ ὑπερώνυμος, ἡ ἀνεκφώνητος, περὶ ἣν αἱ προαιώνιαί εἰσι δυνάμεις καὶ ἐνέργειαι, θεότης ἀπὸ τῆς οἰκείας ἐνεργείας καὶ αὕτη ὀνομαζομένη, πῶς οὐκ ἂν ὑπερκειμένη εἴη; Δεῖ δὲ καὶ τὸν μέγαν Διονύσιον προαγαγεῖν· οὗτος γὰρ τῶν ἄλλων ἐμφανέστερον καὶ τὴν θέωσιν λέγει τοῦ θεοῦ θεότητα καὶ ταύτης ὑπερκειμένην τὴν οὐσίαν, ἀσφαλῶς ἅμα καὶ σαφῶς καὶ σοφῶς καὶ εὐσεβῶς· ἐν γὰρ τῷ *Περὶ θείων ὀνομάτων,* <θεότητα>, φησί, <φαμὲν ἀρχικῶς μὲν καὶ θεϊκῶς καὶ αἰτιατικῶς τὴν μίαν πάντων ὑπεράρχιον καὶ ὑπερούσιον ἀρχὴν καὶ αἰτίαν, μεθεκτῶς δὲ τὴν ἐκδιδομένην ἐκ θεοῦ τοῦ ἀμεθέκτου δύναμιν, τὴν αὐτοθέωσιν, ἧς τὰ μετέχοντα ἔνθεά ἐστί τε καὶ λέγεται>. Γράφων δὲ *Πρὸς Γάϊον,* πῶς ὑπὲρ θεαρχίαν καὶ ἀγαθαρχίαν ὁ θεός ἐστιν, <εἰ θεότητα>, φησί, <νοήσαις τὸ θεοποιὸν καὶ ἀγαθοποιὸν δῶρον, καθ᾽ ὃ θεούμεθα καὶ ἀγαθυνόμεθα· καὶ γὰρ εἰ τοῦτό ἐστιν ἀρχὴ τοῦ θεοῦσθαι τοῖς θεουμένοις, ὁ πάσης ἀρχῆς ὑπεράρχιος καὶ τῆς οὕτω λεγομένης θεότητός ἐστιν ἐπέκεινα>.

XXI. ΒΑΡΛ. Ἀλλὰ ταύτην τὴν θεότητα σχέσιν οὗτος καὶ μίμησιν ἐκεῖ φησι· διὸ ἡμεῖς ταύτην λέγομεν κτιστήν.

ΟΡΘΟΔ. <Ἀμίμητον μίμημα> ταύτην ὠνόμασεν. Ὥστ᾽ οὐ μᾶλλον μίμησις ἢ ἀμιμησία. Οὔκουν κτιστή γε παρὰ τοῦτο. Σχέσιν δὲ δηλοῖ πολλὰ τῶν τοῦ θεοῦ· καὶ αὐτὴ γὰρ ἡ τοῦ θεοῦ βασιλεία, ἥτις καὶ ἡμῖν ἐπήγγελται, σχέσις τίς ἐστιν ἄκτιστος οὖσα. Φησὶ γὰρ ὁ θεῖος Μάξιμος, ὡς <ἔστι τι πρᾶγμα ὑπὲρ αἰῶνας ἡ τοῦ θεοῦ βασιλεία· οὐ γὰρ θέμις ἦρχθαι ἢ φθάνεσθαι ὑπὸ αἰώνων τὴν τοῦ θεοῦ βασιλείαν. Ταύτην δὲ πιστεύομεν εἶναι τὴν τῶν σωζομένων κληρονομίαν>. Ἀλλὰ καὶ ὁ τὰ θεῖα σοφὸς Δαμασκηνὸς πολλὰ τῶν ἐπὶ θεοῦ λεγομένων σχέσιν δηλοῦν ἐδίδαξεν· ὧν οὐδὲν ἂν φαίη τις κτιστὸν νοῦν ἔχων. Σχέσιν δ᾽ ἀκούων ἐπὶ τῶν τοιούτων μὴ φυσικὴν εὐμοιρηκότων οἰκειότητα νομίσῃς, ἀλλὰ τὴν διὰ τοῦ πνεύματος ὑπερφυεστάτην

himself added that that belongs to people who take part in it, but not to those who are by nature disposed to do that. For through that kind of participation in the spirit the saints become an imitation and a likeness of God in a supernatural way. According to the divine Maximus, "they become living images of Christ and, in agreement with the grace, the same as Him rather than a likeness."[63] That participation is therefore also supernatural. Hence, you will find that in the fathers the grace of deification is called imparticipable because it has no power whatsoever in nature.[64] And how could the Godhead, the source of goodness, the deification, the deification itself, the divinity of God, the divinity itself, be numbered among created things?

XXII. B. I know, too, that Dionysius the Areopagite, the revealer of God, praised the divinity in those terms and called it divine power and providence. But I also know that he said that God gives existence to it and not only to that but also to life itself and similar things. Hence, when the divine Timothy made enquiries about it, he writes to him: "And what," you say, "is meant when we say that being itself or life itself and so many other things *are* in an absolute and primary sense and posit that they have gotten their existence from God in the first place."[65] By saying that those things were created by God of which he says that they got their existence from God and of which he makes God the giver of existence--do we not have the same opinion as that great man in that respect?

O. Not in the least! For you missed his trustworthy and divine insight to the utmost degree!

XXIII. B. How? In what manner?

O. Because "getting existence" (from God) signifies only the coming into existence (of those things) but not the *way* they came into existence. Hence, those things could both be said concerning what exists created by God and what exists uncreated by God. So, Basil the Great, writing his *Refutations,* used about both things the expression, "For he who has begotten the drops of dew[66] did not cause the drops and the Son to come into existence in the same way."[67] He used the expression also in connection with the uncreated things alone: "For he speaks about the breath of the mouth of God,[68] in order that you do not think that it is something

μέθεξιν. Διὸ καὶ αὐτὸς ἐπήγαγε τῶν μετεχόντων εἶναι ταύτην, ἀλλ᾽ οὐχὶ τῶν πρὸς ταύτην πεφυκότων. Καὶ γὰρ διὰ τῆς τοιαύτης ἐν πνεύματι μεθέξεως μίμημα καὶ ὁμοίωμα τοῦ θεοῦ γίνονται οἱ ἅγιοι ὑπερφυές· κατὰ δὲ τὸν θεῖον Μάξιμον εἰπεῖν, <εἰκόνες ζῶσαι Χριστοῦ, καὶ ταὐτὸν αὐτῷ μᾶλλον κατὰ τὴν χάριν ἢ ἀφομοίωμα>. Ὑπερφυὴς ἄρα καὶ ἡ σχέσις αὕτη. Διὸ καὶ ἄσχετον εὑρήσεις παρὰ τῶν πατέρων τὴν τῆς θεώσεως ὠνομασμένην χάριν, ὡς μὴ ἔχουσαν τὴν οἱανοῦν ἐν τῇ φύσει δύναμιν. Πῶς δ᾽ ἄρα καὶ ἡ θεαρχία, ἡ ἀγαθαρχία, ἡ θέωσις, ἡ αὐτοθέωσις, ἡ τοῦ θεοῦ θεότης, ἡ αὐτοθεότης τοῖς κτιστοῖς συναριθμοῖτο ἄν;

XXII. ΒΑΡΛ. Οἶδα κἀγὼ τὸν ἐξ Ἀρείου Πάγου θεοφάντορα τοιούτοις ἐξυμνοῦντα προσρήμασιν αὐτὴν, καὶ θείαν δύναμιν καὶ πρόνοιαν καλοῦντα ταύτην. Ἀλλ᾽ οἶδα καὶ ὑποστάτην αὐτῆς εἰρηκότα τὸν θεὸν, καὶ οὐ μόνον ταύτης, ἀλλὰ καὶ τῆς αὐτοζωῆς καὶ τῶν παραπλησίων. Διὸ καὶ ὡς τοῦ θείου πυνθανομένου Τιμοθέου γράφει πρὸς αὐτόν· <τί δὲ φῂς, τὸ αὐτοεῖναι λέγομεν ἢ τὴν αὐτοζωήν, καὶ ὅσα ἄλλα ἀπολύτως καὶ ἀρχικῶς εἶναι, καὶ ἐκ θεοῦ πρώτως ὑφεστηκέναι τιθέμεθα>. Λέγοντες οὖν ἡμεῖς ἐκτίσθαι πρὸς θεοῦ, ἅπερ οὗτος ὑφεστηκέναι φησὶν ἐκ τοῦ θεοῦ, καὶ ὧν ὑποστάτην τίθεται θεόν, ἆρ᾽ οὐ ταὐτὰ τῷ μεγάλῳ φρονοῦμεν κατὰ τοῦτο;

ΟΡΘΟΔ. Ἥκιστα· διαπεπτώκατε γὰρ τῆς ἀσφαλοῦς ἐκείνου καὶ θείας διανοίας ἐς τὰ μάλιστα.

XXIII. ΒΑΡΛ. Πῶς καὶ τίνα τρόπον;

ΟΡΘΟΔ. Ὅτι τὸ ὑφεστηκέναι τὴν ὕπαρξιν δηλοῖ μόνον, ἀλλ᾽ οὐχὶ καὶ τὸν τρόπον τῆς ὑπάρξεως. Ταῦτ᾽ ἄρα καὶ ἐπὶ τῶν κτιστῶς ὄντων καὶ ἐπὶ τῶν ἀκτίστως ἐκ θεοῦ ῥηθείη ἄν. Ἔνθεν τοι καὶ Βασίλειος ὁ μέγας ἐπ᾽ ἀμφοτέρων ἐχρήσατο τῇ λέξει γράφων ἐν τοῖς *Ἀντιρρητικοῖς* <ὁ γὰρ τετοκὼς βώλους δρόσου οὐχ ὁμοίως τάς τε βώλους καὶ τὸν υἱὸν ὑπεστήσατο>. Κέχρηται δὲ ταύτῃ κἀπὶ τῶν ἀκτίστων μόνων· <᾽πνεῦμα γάρ φησι στόματος θεοῦ᾽, ἵνα μὴ τῶν ἔξωθέν τι καὶ τῶν κτισμάτων αὐτὸ κρίνῃς, ἀλλ᾽ ὡς ἐκ θεοῦ τὴν ὑπόστασιν

external and belonging to created things, but that you believe that it got its existence from God."[69] And elsewhere again, theologizing in a divine way about the same breath, he says: "It has this sign of the specific character concerning its existence, that it is known through the Son and has come into existence by God."[70] And in many places in his own works, the theologian Gregory also calls the being of the Son before all ages a '(coming into) existence.'[71] Those persons, then, who reveal that those divine powers are created for no other reason than because the cause of everything has also given existence to those things--would they perhaps prove to us that on account of that kind of language both the Son and the Spirit are created? And they could not even be aware of the point that nothing of what had been brought forward by God out of not-being could be in an absolute and primary sense, a characteristic which that great man ascribed to the divine powers.

XXIV. But none of the things that *are* and *live* in a created way could possibly be called being itself or life itself. For each one of them is and lives by participation. And how can that which partakes of life be life itself? And how can that which is participated in but does not participate in something else be a creature, since all creatures possess their being by participation? And the following point is even greater proof that those powers of God are uncreated, namely, that the same man calls them "in a transcendental way not being." For after having referred to the "forces to foresee (things) which are springing forth from God the imparticipable" he added: "If the beings are participating in them in a manner which befits them, they are being and living and divine and are called so."[72] Since those powers are in every respect above the beings, the things which are participated in have never started with being, according to the divine Maximus. For he says: "All the participating beings had a beginning of being because they were not participations. And saying "things which are participated in" is the same as saying "those participations and powers."[73] According to the same man, however, "God is infinite times above even all the things that are participated in."[74] And when you make enquiries you will see the great difference in the things which partake in them; one will know that difference in a trustworthy manner by reading the works which are newly published by our fathers.

ἔχον δοξάζῃς>. Ἀλλαχοῦ δ' αὖθις περὶ τοῦ αὐτοῦ πνεύματος θεολογῶν ἐνθέως, <τοῦτο>, φησί, <τῆς κατὰ τὴν ὑπόστασιν ἰδιότητος σημεῖον ἔχει, τὸ διὰ τοῦ υἱοῦ γνωρίζεσθαι καὶ ἐκ τοῦ πατρὸς ὑφεστάναι>. Πολλαχοῦ δὲ τῶν οἰκείων λόγων καὶ Γρηγόριος ὁ θεολόγος ὑπόστασιν ὀνομάζει τὴν τοῦ υἱοῦ προαιώνιον ὕπαρξιν. Οἱ τοίνυν δι' οὐδὲν ἕτερον τὰς θείας ἐκείνας δυνάμεις κτιστὰς εἶναι ἀποφαινόμενοι, ἢ ὅτι καὶ τούτων ὑποστάτις ἐστὶν ἡ πάντων αἰτία, τάχ' ἂν ἡμῖν διὰ τὰ τοιαῦτα προσρήματα καὶ τὸν υἱὸν καὶ τὸ πνεῦμα κτιστὸν ἀποδείξαιεν; Καὶ οὐδ' ἐκεῖνο συνιδεῖν ἐδυνήθησαν, ὡς τῶν ὑπὸ θεοῦ ἐκ μὴ ὄντων προηγμένων οὐδὲν ἀπολύτως καὶ ἀρχικῶς εἶναι δύναιτ' ἄν, ὃ ταῖς θείαις δυνάμεσιν ὁ μέγας ἐκεῖνος προσεμαρτύρησεν.

XXIV. Ἀλλ' οὐδὲ <αὐτοεῖναι> ἢ <αὐτοζωὴ> κληθείη πώποτ' ἄν τι τῶν κτιστῶς ὄντων τε καὶ ζώντων· μεθέξει γὰρ τούτων ἕκαστον ἔστι τε καὶ ζῇ. Πῶς οὖν αὐτοζωὴ ἔσται τὸ ζωῆς μετέχον; Πῶς δὲ τὸ μετεχόμενον ἀλλ' οὐ μετέχον ἄλλου κτίσμα, τῶν κτισμάτων πάντων μετοχῇ τὸ εἶναι σχόντων; Τὸ δ' ἔτι μεῖζον εἰς ἀπόδειξιν ὡς ἄκτιστοί εἰσιν αἱ δυνάμεις ἐκεῖναι τοῦ θεοῦ, ὅτι καὶ καθ' ὑπεροχὴν μὴ οὔσας ὁ αὐτὸς προσείρηκεν αὐτάς. Εἰπὼν γὰρ <τὰς ἐκδιδομένας ἐκ θεοῦ τοῦ ἀμεθέκτου προνοητικὰς δυνάμεις>, ἐπήγαγεν· <ὧν τὰ ὄντα οἰκείως ἑαυτοῖς μετέχοντα καὶ ὄντα καὶ ζῶντα καὶ ἔνθεα καὶ ἔστι καὶ λέγεται>. Πάντως ὡς τῶν δυνάμεων ἐκείνων οὐσῶν ὑπὲρ τὰ ὄντα· <πάντων γὰρ τῶν μετεχόντων, ὡς μὴ μετοχῶν ὄντων, ἀρχὴν τοῦ εἶναι σχόντων, τὰ μεθεκτὰ> - ταὐτὸ δ' εἰπεῖν αἱ μετοχαὶ καὶ αἱ δυνάμεις αὗται - οὐδέποτε τοῦ εἶναι ἤρξαντο κατὰ τὸν θεῖον Μάξιμον. Καίτοι κατὰ τὸν αὐτὸν <καὶ τῶν μεθεκτῶν πάντων ἀπειράκις ἀπείρως ὁ θεὸς ὑπερεξῄρηται>. Πολλὴν δ' ἂν ἴδοις ἐξετάζων τὴν διαφορὰν ἐν τοῖς μετέχουσιν αὐτῶν, ἣν εἴσεταί τις ἀσφαλῶς τοῖς ἀρτίως ἐξενηνεγμένοις τοῖς ἡμετέροις πατράσιν ἐντυχὼν συγγράμμασιν.

XXV. B. I would like you to make that clearer to me. When, as has been revealed, our holy fathers speak in that way about two different divinities, how do we say that they worship one divinity in the holy trinity?

O. We should now try to make it clear to you that there are also some fools who contend that the deifying gift of the spirit is created. But since you set out to demand a reason for the Oneness of the divinity, my friend, one divinity belongs to the three persons and no one who has chosen to live piously has ever spoken differently. And you can learn clearly, wisely, and briefly from the great Basil how the threefold character of it is not in conflict with its unity. For writing to the doctor Eustathius, he first gives the definition that the name "divinity" provides genuine proof of an overseeing or active power, and that with good reason the essence of God is also called divinity. After having shown so clearly the difference between essence and activity, he then says: "But either you call the nature of God divinity, and then the nature of the three is one; or you call the activity divinity, and then the activity of the three persons is one."[75] So we venerate one divinity with three hypostases but not as if it would be devoid of grace and power and activity, so that that which does not proceed from God is the same as and similar to that which proceeds from God and that which manifests itself is the same as that which remains hidden. For such is the talk of idiots. And just as we say that power and wisdom are common to the Father, the Son and the Spirit, and contend also that the Son is the power and the wisdom of the Father[76], but existing independently, and nevertheless venerate wisdom and power as one in the highest and venerate trinity--for the enhypostatic[77] power and wisdom of God is one; and when you speak about the common power and wisdom of the three hypostases, that one is also one--in the same way we honor the divinity of the three (hypostases) as one. For which one you speak about, the three have only one. The essence is existing independently and is, in all respects, unthinkable; but the power which is around it in a physical way and which is understood by us according to our faculties on the basis of the creatures and which is named

XXV. ΒΑΡΛ. Ἐκεῖνό μοι ἀξιῶ σαφήνισον· πῶς δύο θεοτήτων διαφόρων οὕτω παρὰ τῶν ἁγίων, καθάπερ ἀνεφάνη, λεγομένων μίαν φαμὲν ἐπὶ τῆς ἁγίας τριάδος προσκυνεῖν θεότητα;
ΟΡΘΟΔ. Ἔδει μέν σοι παραστῆσαι νῦν ὡς καὶ λατινόφρονές εἰσιν οἱ τὴν θεοποιὸν δωρεὰν τοῦ πνεύματος λέγοντες κτιστήν. Ἐπεὶ δ' ἐπίκεισαι τοῦ μοναδικοῦ τῆς θεότητος τὸν λόγον ἀπαιτῶν, μία τῶν τριῶν προσώπων, ὦ τάν, ὑπάρχει ἡ θεότης, καὶ οὐδείς ποτ' ἄλλως εἶπε ζῆν εὐσεβῶς προῃρημένος. Ὅπως δὲ τῷ ἑνιαίῳ τὸ διακεκριμένον ταύτης οὐ προσίσταται, σαφῶς καὶ σοφῶς καὶ συντόμως παρὰ τοῦ μεγάλου Βασιλείου μάθοις ἄν. Οὗτος γὰρ πρὸς τὸν ἰατρὸν Εὐστάθιον γράφων, προδιορισάμενος ὡς κυρίως μὲν ἐποπτικῆς ἢ ἐνεργητικῆς δυνάμεως ἔνδειξιν ἡ τῆς θεότητος προσηγορία φέρει, κατ' αἰτίαν δὲ λέγεται καὶ ἡ οὐσία τοῦ θεοῦ θεότης, καὶ τρανῶς πρότερον οὕτω δείξας τὸ διάφορον τῆς οὐσίας καὶ τῆς ἐνεργείας, εἶτά φησιν· <ἀλλ' εἴτε τὴν φύσιν τοῦ θεοῦ φαίη τις θεότητα, μία τῶν τριῶν ἡ φύσις· εἴτε τὴν ἐνέργειαν ὀνομάσει τις θεότητα, μία τῶν τριῶν προσώπων ἡ ἐνέργεια>. Οὕτω μίαν θεότητα προσκυνοῦμεν τρισυπόστατον, ἀλλ' οὐχ ὡς χάριτος καὶ δυνάμεως καὶ ἐνεργείας ἄμοιρον, ὡς εἶναι ταὐτὸν καὶ ἀπαράλλακτον τῇ προόδῳ τοῦ θεοῦ τὸ ἀνεκφοίτητον καὶ τῇ κρυφιότητι τὸ ἐκφανές· τοῦτο γὰρ παραφρονούντων λέγειν. Ὥσπερ δὲ δύναμιν καὶ σοφίαν κοινὴν πατρός, υἱοῦ καὶ πνεύματός φαμεν, λέγομεν δὲ καὶ δύναμιν καὶ σοφίαν τοῦ πατρὸς τὸν υἱόν, ἀλλὰ αὐθυπόστατον, μίαν δ' ὅμως σέβομεν ἐπὶ τῆς ἀνωτάτω καὶ προσκυνητῆς τριάδος σοφίαν καὶ δύναμιν - ἥ τε γὰρ ἐνυπόστατος τοῦ θεοῦ δύναμίς τε καὶ σοφία μία, εἴτε τὴν κοινὴν εἴποι τις τῶν τριῶν ὑποστάσεων, μία καὶ αὐτή ἐστιν -, οὕτω καὶ θεότητα τῶν τριῶν μίαν προσκυνοῦμεν. Ἣν γὰρ ἂν εἴποις, μία τῶν τριῶν ἐστιν· ἡ μὲν οὐσία αὐθύπαρκτός τε καὶ παντάπασιν ἀπερινόητος, ἡ δὲ δύναμις περὶ αὐτὴν οὖσα φυσικῶς καὶ νοουμένη παρ' ἡμῶν κατὰ τὸ ἐγχωροῦν ἀπὸ τῶν

and praised appropriately on the basis of those things which are created from non-beings and which are composed and improved in agreement with that (essence), as foreseeing, creative and theurgic, is contemplating and directing everything. "For," the great Basil says, "the creatures demonstrate the power and wisdom and skill, but not the essence itself."[78]

XXVI. B. But you say that also that common theurgic power and grace are enhypostatic.

O. But not in the sense of independent. Come on! In that respect too we once again follow the fathers. For they say that the light of the deifying grace is enhypostatic, but not in the sense you wrongly understand it. But since "enhypostatic" has many meanings, just as "anhypostatic", they believe that the grace of deification is enhypostatic, not in the sense that it is completely independent (authypostatic), but that it remains together with the persons in which it comes; it is not, like lightning and thunder, born at the moment of passing away, and abolished together with its manifestation in the objects.[79] "For," he (Basil) says, "the light works in those for whom it shines, continuously and uninterruptedly." But let us add a few words more to the unicity of the divinity. What do you think? Is the Spirit, one part of the trinity, not to be venerated by us? But we also call the grace of the Spirit which is a common characteristic of the Father, the Son and the Spirit, "spirit". And God Himself too, who is worshipped in the trinity, is spirit. Will we, on that account, be hindered from worshipping one spirit? And will someone because of that accuse us of saying that there are many spirits to be venerated?

XXVII. B. Not at all.

O. So then we know that both God's essence and His activity are called divinity and nevertheless we are worshippers of one divinity. For Isaiah also said there are seven spirits which another prophet (Zechariah) called the seven eyes of God.[80] And the divine Maximus says that these exist in a physical way in God the Son and Word of God.[81] Just as the seven spirits do not take away the oneness of the spirit-- for they are the emanations and manifestations and powers and activities of the one holy

ποιημάτων, λεγομένη τε καὶ ὑμνουμένη καταλλήλως ἐκ τῶν προηγμένων ἐκ μὴ ὄντων, καὶ συνεστηκότων καὶ βελτιουμένων κατ᾽ αὐτὴν, ὡς προνοητική, δημιουργική τε καὶ θεουργική, θεωρός τε καὶ ἔφορος ἁπάντων· <δυνάμεως γάρ>, φησὶν ὁ μέγας Βασίλειος, <καὶ σοφίας καὶ τέχνης, ἀλλ᾽ οὐχὶ τῆς οὐσίας αὐτῆς ἐνδεικτικά ἐστι τὰ ποιήματα>.

XXVI. ΒΑΡΛ. Ἀλλ᾽ ὑμεῖς καὶ τὴν κοινὴν ταύτην θεουργικὴν δύναμιν καὶ χάριν ἐνυπόστατόν φατε.

ΟΡΘΟΔ. Ἀλλ᾽ οὐχ ὡς αὐθυπόστατον· ἄπαγε. Καὶ κατὰ τοῦτο μέντοι τοῖς πατράσιν ἑπόμενοι· τὸ γὰρ φῶς τῆς θεοποιοῦ χάριτος ἐνυπόστατον ἐκεῖνοι λέγουσιν, ἀλλ᾽ οὐχ ὡς ὑμεῖς κακῶς νοεῖτε. Ἀλλ᾽ ἐπεὶ τὸ ἐνυπόστατον πολυσήμαντός ἐστι φωνή, καθάπερ καὶ τὸ ἀνυπόστατον, οὐχ ὡς αὐθυπόστατον ἐνυπόστατόν φασι τὴν τῆς θεώσεως χάριν, ἀλλ᾽ ὡς παραμένουσαν οἷς ἂν ἐγγένηται, καὶ μὴ καθάπερ ἀστραπῆς τε καὶ βροντῆς φύσις γινομένην ἐν τῷ φθείρεσθαι, καὶ τῇ φανερώσει παρ᾽ αὐτὰ συνδιαλυομένην· <οἷς γὰρ ἄν>, φησίν, <ἐπιλάμψῃ, διηνεκὲς καὶ ἀδιάδοχον τὸ φῶς ἐμποιεῖ>. Ἀλλὰ γὰρ τῷ ἑνιαίῳ τῆς θεότητος ἔτι προσδιατρίψωμεν. Τί γάρ, οὐ πνεῦμα ἡμῖν σεπτόν ἐστι τὸ τῆς τριάδος ἕν; Ἀλλὰ πνεῦμά φαμεν καὶ τὴν χάριν τοῦ πνεύματος, ἥτις κοινή ἐστι πατρός, υἱοῦ καὶ πνεύματος. Πνεῦμα δέ ἐστι καὶ αὐτὸς ὁ ἐν τριάδι προσκυνούμενος θεός. Ἆρ᾽ οὖν παρὰ τοῦτο κωλυθησόμεθα ἓν πνεῦμα προσκυνεῖν καὶ κατηγορήσει τις ἡμῶν ὡς προσκυνητὰ πολλὰ πνεύματα λεγόντων;

ΒΑΡΛ. Οὐδαμῶς.

XXVII. ΟΡΘΟΔ. Οὕτω τοίνυν θεότητα εἰδότες λεγομένην καὶ τὴν τοῦ θεοῦ οὐσίαν καὶ τὴν τοῦ θεοῦ ἐνέργειαν μιᾶς οὐδὲν ἧττον θεότητός ἐσμεν θεραπευταί. Καὶ πνεύματα γὰρ ἑπτὰ ὁ Ἠσαΐας εἶπεν, ἃ καὶ ὀφθαλμοὺς θεοῦ ἑπτὰ ἕτερος προφήτης. Ταῦτα δὲ φυσικῶς ἐνεῖναί φησιν ὁ θεῖος Μάξιμος ὡς θεῷ τῷ υἱῷ καὶ λόγῳ τοῦ θεοῦ. Καθάπερ οὖν τὰ ἑπτὰ πνεύματα τὸ μοναδικὸν τοῦ πνεύματος οὐκ ἀναιρεῖ - πρόοδοι γάρ εἰσι καὶ

spirit--so the oneness of the divinity is not annihilated by its manifoldness. For the divinity of the three hypostases is one, namely a superessential nature and essence, simple, invisible, imparticipable, in all respects unthinkable. And if another activity is called divinity by the saints, either one, or two, or more--for being everywhere gets its name divinity (*theotes*) from running (*thein*) and, so to speak, going everywhere.[82] And being nowhere gets its name divinity *(theotes)* from running (*thein*), or, as it were, fleeing from everywhere; and God's brilliance (which the apostles also saw on the mountain and in which not only do the saints partake now by way of a foretaste but also in future times in a more perfect manner) is called divinity (*theotes*), because of its *aithein*, i.e., to shine. Likewise the power of purification is derived from *aithein*, i.e., to burn and destroy all evil. So, too, knowing everything is in agreement with the fact that God (*theos*) beholds (*theasthai*) everything before it is born[83]; and providence is derived from overseeing[84] and, in addition, deification is derived from overseeing. All these things, then, are emanations and manifestations and powers and activities of that one divinity; they are with that divinity in a physical and inseparable fashion. The person who separates them from it and drags them down to make them creatures also drags the divinity down along with them; or rather he himself has lost the reverence for it just as that Barlaam who has (alas!) done that and suffered from it and just like you who followed him and used him as your teacher in divine matters.

XXVIII. B. And what is the reason that some of those allotted to the church of Christ and who have devoted themselves to speaking scientifically neither spoke against him earlier nor now (speak) against us?

O. Stupidity and madness, wicked parents of even more wicked heresies! For when a person who is not familiar with some divine things not only does not in the least believe those who know, but also opposes himself to them, he leads first himself astray and then all those who follow him. And there are more of them lately, since "all of them are seeking their own interests, not those of Jesus Christ"[85]. And what they have in their power, either words or axioms, even if these happen to be

ἐκφάνσεις καὶ δυνάμεις καὶ ἐνέργειαι τοῦ ἑνὸς ἁγίου πνεύματος -, οὕτω καὶ τῷ διῃρημένῳ τῆς θεότητος τὸ μοναδικὸν αὐτῆς οὐκ ἀναιρεῖται· μία γάρ ἐστι τῶν τριῶν ὑποστάσεων θεότης, ἤτοι φύσις καὶ οὐσία ὑπερούσιος, ἁπλῆ, ἀόρατος, ἀμέθεκτος, παντάπασιν ἀπερινόητος. Εἰ δέ τις ἄλλη τῶν ἐνεργειῶν παρὰ τῶν ἁγίων λέγοιτο θεότης, εἴτε μία εἴτε δύο εἴτε πλείους - καὶ γὰρ καὶ τὸ πανταχοῦ εἶναι ἀπὸ τοῦ θεῖν καὶ οἱονεὶ φθάνειν πανταχόσε θεότητα ἔχει τὴν ἐπωνυμίαν· καὶ τὸ μηδαμοῦ εἶναι ἀπὸ τοῦ θέοντα, ὥσπερ διαφεύγειν πανταχόθεν· ἥ τε τοῦ θεοῦ λαμπρότης, ἣν καὶ οἱ ἀπόστολοι ἐπὶ τοῦ ὄρους εἶδον, ἧς καὶ νῦν ὡς ἐν ἀρραβῶνος μέρει κἀπὶ τοῦ μέλλοντος αἰῶνος οἱ ἅγιοι τελεώτερον μεθέξουσι, θεότης λέγεται ἀπὸ τοῦ αἴθειν, δηλονότι λάμπειν· καὶ ἡ καθαρτικὴ δύναμις ἀπὸ τοῦ αἴθειν, τουτέστι καίειν τε καὶ ἀναλίσκειν πᾶσαν μοχθηρίαν· τό τε γινώσκειν ἅπαντα παρὰ τὸ θεᾶσθαι πάντα τὸν θεὸν πρὶν γενέσεως αὐτῶν· καὶ τὸ προνοεῖν ἀπὸ τοῦ ἐφορᾶν, καὶ πρὸς τούτοις τὸ θεοποιεῖν -, ταῦτα τοίνυν ἅπαντα πρόοδοί εἰσι καὶ ἐκφάνσεις καὶ δυνάμεις καὶ ἐνέργειαι τῆς μιᾶς θεότητος ἐκείνης, φυσικῶς προσοῦσαι ταύτῃ καὶ ἀναφαιρέτως. Ἅς ὁ ἀφελὼν ἐκείνης καὶ εἰς κτίσμα κατασπάσας κἀκείνην συγκατέσπασε, μᾶλλον δὲ αὐτὸς τὸ πρὸς ἐκείνην σέβας ἐζημίωται κατὰ τὸν τοῦθ᾽ οὕτω, φεῦ, πεποιηκότα τε καὶ πεπονθότα Βαρλαάμ, καὶ ὑμᾶς τοὺς αὐτῷ φοιτήσαντας κἀπὶ τῶν θείων αὐτῷ κεχρημένους διδασκάλῳ.

XXVIII. ΒΑΡΛ. Καὶ πῶς ἔνιοι τῶν κεκληρωμένων τῇ ἐκκλησίᾳ τοῦ Χριστοῦ, τῶν τε ἐσχολακότων περὶ λόγους, οὔτ᾽ ἐκείνῳ πρῴην οὔθ᾽ ἡμῖν ἀρτίως ἀντιλέγουσιν;

ΟΡΘΟΔ. Ἄνοια καὶ ἀπόνοια, πονηροὶ γεννήτορες πονηροτέρων αἱρέσεων· ὅταν γάρ τις ἔνια τῶν θείων ἀγνοῶν, ἔπειτ᾽ οὐ μόνον ἥκιστα πείθηται τοῖς εἰδόσιν, ἀλλὰ καὶ τούτοις ἐπανιστάμενος ᾖ, πλανᾷ μὲν πρῶτον ἑαυτὸν αὐτός, ἔπειτα τοὺς ἑπομένους πάντας. Πλείους δ᾽ ἄρ᾽ ἀρτίως, ἐπεὶ <πάντες σχεδὸν τὰ ἑαυτῶν ζητοῦσιν, οὐ τὰ τοῦ Χριστοῦ Ἰησοῦ>. Καὶ τὰ ἀνὰ χεῖρας σφίσιν,

sacred, they make it a means to earn money (with) and a basis to acquire glory among people. Who of them cares for those sorts of things? The more so since the party which you, because you do not derive your power from the truth, have given such a predominate place in your own company, is clothed with the name of power and the garbage of richness and according to Sirach (8:2), is able to "make you feel its weight," especially at a time of political upheaval which you have accepted as a gift of Hermes, just as the people who suffered once from the disease of the impious (*dyssebes*) Severus (Greek: Seberos) and the unhappy (*dystyches*) Eutyches.[86] For when Basiliscus,[87] the brother of Zeno's mother-in-law Verina, had rebelled against Zeno and when the situation was extremely confused because the emperor at that time had almost without any effort conceded his power to his general (Basiliscus), they seized the opportunity to discredit the divine council of Chalcedon (451) and to persuade the church to make an official notice to the effect that with the utmost authority the Document of the holy Pope Leo of the old Rome[88] which the synod of Chalcedon and, before that, the synod of Ephesus (431) had accepted as the canon for piousness, should be condemned. These synods both belong to the seven (councils); one accomplished the place of the triad, the other the place of the tetras in them.[89] Another effect of the notice was that the writings of the divine Cyril[90] and all the things which had been confirmed by them concerning the dogmas which had been accepted according to those synods, should be burned wherever they were found. And the pretext was the same as you used a little while ago: for the words of the saints are enough, it says, and people should not make or add new doctrines examining what is not comprehensible to the crowd. Have you not also taken the same pains as they have at the upheaval of these days? However, the truth will soon reappear with peace and speak freely and, with God's help, so will reason as well. For it is God himself who ordains victories for Jacob.[91]

B. Who doesn't desire peace and truth? So don't falsely accuse us of rejoicing in turmoil. But tell me this: is it not unseemly even to hear that some people revere two divinities?

εἴτε λόγοι εἴτε ἀξιώματα, κἂν ἱερὰ τυγχάνῃ, πορισμὸν βίου καὶ τῆς παρ᾽ ἀνθρώπων δόξης ἀφορμὰς ποιοῦνται. Τίνι δὴ τούτων μέλει τῶν τοιούτων; Καὶ ταῦτα τῆς ἣν ὑμεῖς, ἅτε μὴ παρὰ τῆς ἀληθείας ἔχοντες τὸ δύνασθαι, τῆς ἑαυτῶν συμμορίας προεστήσασθε ὄνομά τε δυναστείας καὶ συρφετὸν πλούτου περιβεβλημένης, καὶ κατὰ τὸν Σιρὰχ ἑτοίμης οὔσης <ἀνθιστάναι τὴν ὁλκήν>, καὶ μάλιστα κατὰ τὸν τῆς πολιτικῆς συγχύσεως καιρόν, ὃν ὡς ἕρμαιον ὑμεῖς εὕρεσθε, καθάπερ οἱ τὰ Σεβήρου ποτὲ τοῦ δυσσεβοῦς καὶ Εὐτυχοῦς τοῦ δυστυχοῦς νοσοῦντες. Οὗτοι γὰρ ἐπαναστάντος Ζήνωνι Βασιλίσκου τοῦ τῆς πενθερᾶς αὐτῷ Βερίνης ἀδελφοῦ, καὶ τῶν πραγμάτων ἐς τὰ μάλιστα συγκεχυμένων, ἅτε τοῦ βασιλέως τηνικαῦτα τῆς ἀρχῆς ὑπεκστάντος τῷ τυράννῳ σχεδὸν ἀκονιτί, καιροῦ λαβόμενοι, τὴν ἐν Χαλχηδόνι θείαν σύνοδον ἀνασκευάζουσι καὶ πρόγραμμα γενέσθαι πείθουσιν, ἐγκελευόμενον μεθ᾽ ὅτι πλείστης ἐξουσίας ἀναθεματίζεσθαι μὲν τὸν *Τόμον* τοῦ τῆς πρεσβυτέρας Ῥώμης ἐν ἁγίοις Λέοντος, ὃν ὡς κανόνα εὐσεβείας ἥ τε κατὰ Χαλκηδόνα καὶ ἡ πρὸ αὐτῆς ἐν Ἐφέσῳ σύνοδος ἐδέξατο, ἀμφότεραι οὖσαι τῶν ἑπτά, καὶ ἡ μὲν τὸν τῆς τριάδος, ἡ δὲ τὸν τῆς τετράδος ἐκπληροῦσα τόπον ἐν αὐταῖς, τά τε συγγεγραμμένα Κυρίλλῳ τῷ θείῳ καὶ δι᾽ αὐτῶν κεκυρωμένα περὶ τῶν κατ᾽ αὐτὰς κεκινημένων κατακαίεσθαι οὗ ἂν εὑρεθῶσιν. Ἡ δὲ πρόφασις ἥτις καὶ ὑμῖν ἀρτίως· ἱκανὰ γάρ φησι τὰ τῶν ἁγίων καὶ οὐ δεῖ καινὰ δογματίζειν καὶ προσδιατάττεσθαι, διερευνωμένους τὰ μὴ χωρητὰ τοῖς πλείοσιν. Ἆρ᾽ οὐχὶ καὶ ὑμεῖς τὴν αὐτὴν ἐκείνοις ἐπὶ τῆς νυνὶ συγχύσεως ἀνελάβεσθε σπουδήν; Ἀλλὰ γὰρ ἐπανήξει ταχέως καὶ παρρησιάσεται, σὺν θεῷ δ᾽ ὁ λόγος, μετὰ τῆς εἰρήνης καὶ ἡ ἀλήθεια· καὶ γὰρ αὐτός ἐστιν ὁ θεὸς <ὁ ἐντελλόμενος τὰς σωτηρίας Ἰακώβ>.

ΒΑΡΛ. Εἰρήνης καὶ ἀληθείας τίς οὐκ ἐφίεται; Μὴ τοίνυν ἡμῶν ὡς ἐπιχαιρόντων ταῖς ταραχαῖς καταψεύδου.

XXIX. Τοῦτο δέ μοι φράσον· οὐχὶ καὶ ἀκοῦσαι ἀπρεπὲς δύο τινὰς θεότητας πρεσβεύειν;

XXIX. O. Who is it who says so? For not even they who speak about spirit and the hypostasis itself and the grace of the spirit, but also they who call the activities of the spirit the seven spirits, revere two or more spirits. In the same way the theologians who have even called the deifying grace of God and some of the other activities of God, divinity--and we the people who agree with those saints: we do not revere two or more divinities but one, to which belong the grace and the activities. And if the accusers of people who think and speak piously take that message to the crowd, must we then, on account of that, abstain from our reliable agreement with the honorable fathers? Come on! The Monophysites also falsely accused those who said that there were two natures in Christ of revering two sons of God. Sabellius, Arius, Aëtius,[92] Eunomius and their followers brought the charge of tritheism against those who proclaimed not only that the Son was truly God but also in the same way the Spirit of God. People who were wrong in both respects (i.e., concerning the Son and the Spirit) mockingly called those who were right with respect to the Son alone, ditheists. And then? Have some of those who clung to the pious dogma at various times refrained from saying that God incarnate had two natures and others, that both the Son and the Spirit of God were an uncreated God lest they were accused of ditheism or tritheism by those who have evil thoughts? Not at all! In the same way we would never shrink from the consensus with the fathers because of the quibblings of some people these days, so that we would not call both the deifying grace and the activity of God an uncreated divinity, as the fathers did. The more so since so many and such wicked heresies became strong because that doctrine was rejected.

XXX. B. But those who do not believe that that divinity is uncreated--for it seems to me, to tell the truth, when I listen to your words, that you speak the truth--namely they who say that the deifying grace and activity is created, contend that the uncreated grace and activity is the same as God's essence and does not differ from it. Hence, when asked by some people whether they say that God's grace is created, they subject those

ΟΡΘΟΔ. Καὶ τίς ὃς τοῦτο λέγει; Οὐδὲ γὰρ οἱ πνεῦμα λέγοντες καὶ τὴν ὑπόστασιν αὐτὴν καὶ τὴν χάριν τοῦ πνεύματος, ἀλλὰ καὶ τὰς ἐνεργείας τοῦ πνεύματος ἑπτὰ καλοῦντες πνεύματα, δύο ἢ πολλὰ πνεύματα πρεσβεύουσιν. Οὕτως οὐδ' οἱ θεότητα προσειρηκότες καὶ τὴν τοῦ θεοῦ θεοποιὸν χάριν θεολόγοι, καὶ τῶν ἄλλων ἐνίας τῶν τοῦ θεοῦ ἐνεργειῶν, καὶ οἱ τοῖς ἁγίοις ἐκείνοις ἡμεῖς ὁμολογοῦντες, δύο ἢ πολλὰς θεότητας πρεσβεύομεν, ἀλλὰ μίαν ἧς ἡ χάρις καὶ αἱ ἐνέργειαι. Εἰ δ' οἱ κατήγοροι τῶν εὐσεβῶς καὶ φρονούντων καὶ λεγόντων τοῦτο τοῖς πλήθεσι περιαγγέλλουσιν, ἀποσταῖμεν διὰ τοῦθ' ἡμεῖς τῆς πρὸς τοὺς σεπτοὺς πατέρας ἀσφαλοῦς ὁμολογίας; Ἄπαγε· καὶ οἱ μονοφυσῖται γὰρ τοὺς δύο φύσεις λέγοντας ἐπὶ Χριστοῦ δύο σέβειν τοῦ θεοῦ υἱοὺς ἐσυκοφάντουν. Σαβέλλιός τε καὶ Ἄρειος, Ἀέτιός τε καὶ Εὐνόμιος καὶ ὅσοι κατ' αὐτοὺς τριθεΐαν ἐνεκάλουν τοῖς καὶ τὸν υἱὸν θεὸν ἀληθινὸν κηρύττουσιν, ὡσδαύτως καὶ τὸ πνεῦμα τοῦ θεοῦ. Διθεΐτας δὲ σκώπτοντες ὠνόμαζον τοὺς περὶ τὸν υἱὸν μόνον ὑγιαίνοντας οἱ κατ' ἄμφω νοσοῦντες. Τί οὖν; Ἆρα παρῃτήσαντο τῶν τοῦ εὐσεβοῦς ἐν διαφόροις καιροῖς δόγματος ἀντεχομένων, οἱ μὲν λέγειν δύο φύσεις τοῦ ἐνανθρωπήσαντος θεοῦ, οἱ δὲ θεὸν ἄκτιστον τὸν υἱόν τε καὶ τὸ πνεῦμα τοῦ θεοῦ, ὡς ἂν μὴ διθεΐαν ἢ τριθεΐαν ἐγκληθῶσι παρὰ τῶν κακῶς φρονούντων; Οὐμενουν. Οὕτως οὐδ' ἡμεῖς ἂν ἐκσταίημέν ποτε τῆς πρὸς τοὺς πατέρας συμφωνίας διὰ τὰς ἐνίων τῶν νῦν ἐρεσχελίας, ὡς μὴ καὶ τὴν θεοποιὸν τοῦ θεοῦ χάριν καὶ ἐνέργειαν ἄκτιστον κατ' αὐτοὺς θεότητα καλεῖν. Καὶ ταῦτα τοσούτων καὶ οὕτω πονηρῶν αἱρέσεων ἐκ τῆς πρὸς αὐτὴν ἀθετήσεως κρατυνομένων.

XXX. ΒΑΡΛ. Ἀλλ' οἱ μὴ πειθόμενοι ταύτην ἄκτιστον ὑπάρχειν - ἐμοὶ γάρ, ἵνα τἀληθῆ λέγω, τῶν σῶν ἀκούσαντι λόγων δοκεῖς λέγειν ἀληθῆ -, φασὶ τοίνυν οἱ κτιστὴν λέγοντες τὴν θεοποιὸν χάριν καὶ ἐνέργειαν, ὡς ἡ μὲν ἄκτιστος χάρις καὶ ἐνέργεια ταὐτόν ἐστι καὶ ἀδιάφορον τῇ οὐσίᾳ τοῦ θεοῦ. Διὸ καὶ ὑπ' ἐνίων ἐρωτώμενοι, εἰ κτιστήν

who deem it created to the ban (*anathema*) having in mind that grace which is the same as the essence of God and which does not differ from it; but the grace, whatever, or activity which differs in whatever way from the essence of God, they call a creature and then say that the person who does not agree with this makes God composed of divine essence and activity.

O. Those who say that in God the activity is not different from His essence contend that He does not have essence and activity but only activity or only essence. For if there is no difference whatsoever between those things, why do they say that God not only has this but that as well unless they say that those things belong to God as empty names which have nothing to do with real things? In this way, they lead their followers astray by this tautology, pretending that they accept both ideas, whereas in fact they themselves believe that God is essence without activity or activity without essence.

B. They claim that God is active essence but that he has no other activity besides His essence lest He be a composite being.

XXXI. O. Take caution that they do not bestow upon God "active" as an empty sound of a word, while they contrive precisely by that fact to lead astray those who are in dialogue with them. For the divine Maximus says: "Just as it is impossible to be without being, so is it not possible to be active without activity."[93]Hence, by taking away the divine activity and by fusing it with essence by saying that the activity does not differ from that essence, they have made God an essence without activity. And not only that, but they have also completely annihilated God's being itself and they have become atheists in the universe [a world without god]; for the same Maximus says:"When the divine and human activity is taken away, there is no God, nor man."[94]For it is absolutely necessary that the person who says that the activity in God is not different from his essence falls into the trap of atheism. For we know that God *is* only from His proper activities. Hence, for him who destroys God's activities and does not admit that they differ from His essence, the necessary consequence is that he does not know that God

φασι τὴν χάριν τοῦ θεοῦ, καὶ ἀναθέματι καθυποβάλλουσι τοὺς φάσκοντας αὐτὴν κτιστὴν, ἐκείνην ἐπὶ νοῦν ἔχοντες τὴν ταὐτὸν οὖσαν καὶ ἀδιάφορον τῇ οὐσίᾳ τοῦ θεοῦ, ἥτις δ᾽ ἂν ἔιη χάρις ἢ ἐνέργεια διαφέρουσα καθ᾽ οἱονδήποτε τρόπον τῆς οὐσίας τοῦ θεοῦ, κτίσμα ταύτην λέγουσι, τὸν δὲ μὴ οὕτω λέγοντα σύνθετόν φασι τὸν θεὸν ποιεῖν ἐξ οὐσίας τε καὶ ἐνεργείας θείας.

ΟΡΘΟΔ. Οἱ λέγοντες ἐπὶ θεοῦ ἀδιάφορον τῇ οὐσίᾳ τὴν ἐνέργειαν οὐκ οὐσίαν φασὶν αὐτὸν ἔχειν καὶ ἐνέργειαν, ἀλλ᾽ ἐνέργειαν μόνην ἢ οὐσίαν μόνην. Εἰ γὰρ μὴ ἔχει ταῦθ᾽ ἡντινοῦν διαφοράν, πῶς τοῦτό τε κἀκεῖνο λέγουσιν ἔχειν τὸν θεὸν, εἰ μὴ ἄρα ὀνόματα κενὰ προσεῖναι τῷ θεῷ ταυτί φασιν, ἄμοιρα πραγμάτων; Οὐκοῦν τῇ ταυτολογίᾳ τοὺς ἀκροωμένους ὡς ἀμφότερα δοξάζοντες παρακρουόμενοι, ἐπ᾽ ἀληθείας τὸν θεὸν αὐτοὶ δοξάζουσιν οὐσίαν ἀνενέργητον ἢ ἐνέργειαν ἀνούσιον.

ΒΑΡΛ. Οὐσίαν ἐνεργῆ φασιν εἶναι τὸν θεόν, ἐνέργειαν δὲ μὴ ἔχειν ἄλλην παρὰ τὴν οὐσίαν, ἵνα μὴ σύνθετος εἴη.

XXXI. ΟΡΘΟΔ. Σκέψαι δὴ μὴ ψιλὸν ἦχον ῥήματος χαρίζωνται αὐτῷ τὸ ἐνεργὲς κλέπτειν κἀν τούτῳ τοὺς προσδιαλεγομένους μηχανώμενοι· φησὶ γὰρ ὁ θεῖος Μάξιμος, <ὡς οὐκ ἔστιν ὑπάρχειν χωρὶς ὑπάρξεως, οὕτως οὐδὲ ἐνεργεῖν χωρὶς ἐνεργείας ἐστίν>. Οὗτοι τοίνυν ἀνελόντες τὴν θείαν ἐνέργειαν, καὶ διὰ τοῦ λέγειν ἀδιάφορον εἶναι τῇ οὐσίᾳ ταύτῃ συναλείψαντες, πεποιήκεσαν τὸν θεὸν οὐσίαν ἀνενέργητον. Καὶ οὐ τοῦτο μόνον, ἀλλὰ καὶ αὐτὸ τὸ εἶναι τοῦ θεοῦ τελέως ἀνεῖλον καὶ ἄθεοι γεγόνασιν ἐν τῷ κόσμῳ· <τῆς γὰρ θείας τε καὶ ἀνθρωπίνης ἐνεργείας ἀναιρουμένης οὔτε θεὸς ἔσται οὔτε ἄνθρωπος> ὁ αὐτὸς Μάξιμός φησιν. Ἀνάγκη γὰρ πᾶσα πρὸς ἀθεΐαν διαπίπτειν τὸν ἀδιάφορον ἐπὶ θεοῦ λέγοντα τῆς τοῦ θεοῦ οὐσίας τὴν ἐνέργειαν· ἀπὸ γὰρ τῶν οἰκείων ἐνεργειῶν ὅτι ἔστι μόνον ὁ θεὸς γινώσκεται. Τῷ τοίνυν ἀθετοῦντι τὰς θείας ἐνεργείας καὶ μὴ ὁμολογοῦντι τὴν πρὸς τὴν οὐσίαν

is. Furthermore, because the great Basil has revealed everywhere in his writings that "no activity can exist independently,"[95] those who contend that the essence of God does not differ from His activity, have surpassed even Sabellius in impiety. For he made only the Son and the Spirit without existence (*hypostasis*), but those people make the essence of God, which has three hypostases, without existence (*hypostasis*).

XXXII. B. But they also cite some words of the saints as evidence which declare that the essence and the activity of God are one. Do the saints then, on that account, fall into the same absurdities?

O. Not at all.

B. How is that?

O. Because they call them one, but not indifferent, i.e., the same and not the same in different manners. Hence, you will find them saying in one place "the same" and in another "different", because, in their view, they are both. And because we know that, we are fully aware of the difference too, when we hear them say that those things are the same. And when, at other times, we hear them make differences, we also know about the unity, from other texts. The person who does not understand and accept it in that way, will come into opposition to himself and fall into opposite evils, just like Sabellius in his fight against Arius. For Arius, hearing that the highest position was for the Father, did not see at the same time in other texts both that He was one and that He had the same honor (as the Son and the Spirit). But Sabellius, hearing that He was one, did not clearly understand the difference between the cause and its effects which is proclaimed in many other places in the divinely inspired texts.

XXXIII.B. Then why has the most brilliant patriarch Gregory of Nyssa revealed that there is no difference between uncreated (Father) and uncreated (Son)?[96]

O. Because uncreated things as such do not differ from each other. But that they do not differ from each other in the sense of being cause and its effect that is the opinion of Sabellius or the polytheists among the

αὐτῶν διαφορὰν ἀναγκαίως ἕψεται τὸ ἀγνοεῖν εἶναι τὸν θεόν. Ἀλλὰ καὶ τοῦ μεγάλου Βασιλείου πολλαχοῦ τῶν λόγων ἀποφηναμένου <μηδεμίαν ἐνέργειαν αὐθυπόστατον ὑπάρχειν> οἱ μηδὲν διενηνοχέναι λέγοντες τῆς ἐνεργείας τὴν οὐσίαν τοῦ θεοῦ καὶ τὸν Σαβέλλιον τῇ δυσσεβείᾳ ὑπερέβαλον· ὁ μὲν γὰρ ἀνυπόστατον ἐποίει τὸν υἱόν τε καὶ τὸ πνεῦμα μόνον, οἱ δὲ ἀνυπόστατον ποιοῦσι τὴν τρισυπόστατον οὐσίαν τοῦ θεοῦ.

XXXII. ΒΑΡΛ. Ἀλλ᾽ ἐκεῖνοι καί τινας προτείνονται ῥήσεις τῶν ἁγίων ἓν λεγούσας τὴν οὐσίαν καὶ τὴν τοῦ θεοῦ ἐνέργειαν. Ἄρ᾽ οὖν καὶ οἱ ἅγιοι τοῖς αὐτοῖς παρὰ τοῦτο περιπίπτουσιν ἀτόποις;

ΟΡΘΟΔ. Οὔμενουν.

ΒΑΡΛ. Τίνα τρόπον;

ΟΡΘΟΔ. Ὅτι ἓν ἐκεῖνοι λέγουσιν, ἀλλ᾽ οὐκ ἀδιάφορον, τουτέστι ταὐτὸ καὶ οὐ ταὐτὸ κατὰ διαφόρους τρόπους. Διὸ ποτὲ μὲν εὑρήσεις ταὐτό, ποτὲ δ᾽ ἄλλο λέγοντας ὡς ἀμφοτέρων ὄντων. Καὶ τοῦθ᾽ ἡμεῖς εἰδότες, ὅταν ἀκούσωμεν αὐτῶν ταῦτα ταυτιζόντων καὶ τὴν διαφορὰν οὐκ ἀγνοοῦμεν. Ὅταν δ᾽ αὖθις ἐκείνων διαφορούντων, ἡμεῖς ἴσμεν ἀλλαχόθεν καὶ τὴν ἕνωσιν. Ὁ δὲ μὴ ταῦθ᾽ οὕτω κατανοῶν καὶ προσιέμενος ἀντιπεριστήσεται κατ᾽ αὐτὸς αὑτοῦ τοῖς ἐκ διαμέτρου περιπίπτων κακοῖς, ὡς Σαβέλλιος εἶχε πρὸς τὸν Ἄρειον. Ὁ μὲν γὰρ ἀκούων τὸ μεῖζον ἐπὶ τοῦ πατρὸς οὐκ ἀλλαχόθεν συνεώρα καὶ τὸ ἓν καὶ τὸ ὁμότιμον. Σαβέλλιος δὲ τὸ ἓν ἀκούων τὴν τοῦ αἰτίου πρὸς τὰ ἐξ αὐτοῦ διαφορὰν οὐκ ἐνενόει τρανῶς ἀλλαχοῦ πολλαχοῦ τῶν θεοπνεύστων γραφῶν κηρυττομένην.

XXXIII. ΒΑΡΛ. Καὶ πῶς ὁ Νύσσης φανότατος φωστὴρ Γρηγόριος <ἀκτίστου πρὸς ἄκτιστον μηδεμίαν εἶναι διαφορὰν> ἀπεφήνατο;

ΟΡΘΟΔ. Ἧι ἄκτιστα τὰ ἄκτιστα πρὸς ἄλληλα διαφορὰν οὐκ ἔχει. Κατὰ δὲ τὸ αἴτιον καὶ αἰτιατὸν μὴ πρὸς ἄλληλα ταῦτα διαφέρειν, Σαβελλίου λέγειν ἢ τῆς καθ᾽ Ἕλληνας ἔστιν ὡς πολυαρχίας· ἢ γὰρ ἀρχαὶ πολλαὶ

Greeks. For either there are many principles, when there are many uncreated things without a cause; or there is absolutely one principle, when even the uncreated Son does absolutely not differ from the uncreated Father in essence or in the sense of being cause and effect respectively. Moreover, we must also consider what the discussion is about and what that uncreated is which does not differ from the uncreated according to someone. For if the discussion is about divine activities or divine hypostases then he cannot be counted among the pious believers who says that they do not differ from each other and from the essence, except in the way we have stated. But if the discussion is about the divine superessentiality, as is the case with Gregory, the luminary patriarch of Nyssa, then "there is no difference" must not only be accepted for the fact that it is uncreated but for all other aspects. For one divine essence does not tolerate one difference in itself. For one, as such, is altogether indivisible.

XXXIV. B. It seems to me that in this point as well you have reached the truth precisely. And I think that no one who wants to be pious disbelieves you although the supporting words (of the fathers) have provided them with enough useful things to attack you. For they still have those words which support their belief that the uncreated activity does not differ from the divine essence.

O. They say, therefore, that the divine nature does not have divine activity. For besides that (divine nature), there is nothing, if nothing in any way is different from it. But nevertheless, bring forward for examination whatever statement of theirs you think has any strength.

B. How about Damascene's saying, "The divine is simple and uncomposed. And what is built up from many and different things is composed. If, then, we say that the uncreated, that which has no beginning or body, that which is good and is creative and so forth, are essential differences in God, that which is built up from that kind of thing is not simple but composed."[97] Because father Damascene said that, they claim that he probably believed that the divine essence did not differ from the divine activity lest they make God composed from many and different things.

πολλῶν ὄντων ἀγενήτων τε καὶ ἀναιτίων ἢ μία παντάπασίν ἐστι, μηδὲ τοῦ ἀκτίστου υἱοῦ πρὸς τὸν ἄκτιστον πατέρα καθ᾽ ὑπόστασιν ἢ κατὰ τὸ αἴτιον καὶ αἰτιατὸν ὅλως διαφέροντος. Πρὸς δὲ τούτῳ δεῖ σκοπεῖν καὶ περὶ τίνος ὁ λόγος καὶ τί ποτ᾽ ἄρ᾽ ἐκεῖνο τὸ ἄκτιστόν ἐστιν, οὗ μηδεμίαν ἔφη τις εἶναι πρὸς τὸ ἄκτιστον διαφοράν. Εἰ μὲν γὰρ περὶ θείων ἐνεργειῶν ἢ θείων ὑποστάσεών ἐστιν ὁ λόγος, οὐκ ἔσθ᾽ ὅπως ἂν εἴη τοῖς εὐσεβέσιν ἐναρίθμιος ὁ μὴ πρὸς ἀλλήλας τε καὶ τὴν οὐσίαν διαφέρειν ταύτας λέγων, ὅτι μὴ τὸν τρόπον ὃν εἰρήκαμεν. Εἰ δὲ περὶ τῆς θείας ὑπερουσιότητός ἐστιν ὁ λόγος, καθάπερ ἄρα καὶ τῷ Νυσσαέων φωστῆρι Γρηγορίῳ, τὸ <μηδεμίαν εἶναι διαφορὰν> μὴ κατὰ τὸ ἄκτιστον μόνον ἐκληπτέον, ἀλλὰ κατὰ πάντα· μία γὰρ οὐσία θεία μηδεμίαν διαφορὰν ἐπιδεχομένη καθ᾽ αὑτήν. Τὸ γὰρ ἕν, ᾗ ἕν, ἀδιαίρετόν ἐστι παντάπασι.

XXXIV. ΒΑΡΛ. Σφόδρα μοι δοκεῖς κἀν τούτῳ τῆς ἀληθείας ἐς τὸ ἀκριβὲς καταστοχάσασθαι. Καὶ οὐκ οἶμαί τινα τῶν εὐσεβεῖν ἐθελόντων ἀπειθεῖν, οἷς γε μὴν προὔργου τὸ ἀντιλέγειν πρὸς ὑμᾶς οὐκ ἐπιλελοίπασιν αἱ συνηγοροῦσαι ῥήσεις· ἔτι γὰρ ἔχουσιν αἷς ἐρειδόμενοι μηδὲν διαφέρειν τῆς θείας οὐσίας τὴν ἄκτιστον ἐνέργειάν φασιν.

ΟΡΘΟΔ. Φασὶν οὖν ὡς οὐκ ἔχει θείαν ἐνέργειαν ἡ θεία φύσις· πλὴν γὰρ αὐτῆς οὐδέν, εἰ μηδὲν μηδαμῆ διενήνοχεν αὐτῆς. Πρόφερε δ᾽ ὅμως εἰς ἐξέτασιν ὅτιπερ ἔτι τῶν ἐκείνοις λεγομένων ἰσχύν τινα νομίζεις ἔχειν.

ΒΑΡΛ. Τοῦ Δαμασκηνοῦ πατρός, <τὸ θεῖον ἁπλοῦν ἐστι> γράφοντος <καὶ ἀσύνθετον· τὸ δὲ ἐκ πολλῶν καὶ διαφόρων συγκείμενον σύνθετόν ἐστιν. Εἰ οὖν τὸ ἄκτιστον καὶ ἄναρχον καὶ ἀσώματον καὶ ἀγαθὸν καὶ δημιουργικὸν καὶ τὰ τοιαῦτα οὐσιώδεις διαφορὰς εἴποιμεν ἐπὶ θεοῦ, τὸ ἐκ τοσούτων συγκείμενον οὐχ ἁπλοῦν ἔσται, ἀλλὰ σύνθετον>. Τοῦτο τοῦ Δαμασκηνοῦ γράφοντος πατρὸς ἀδιάφορον ἐκεῖνοί φασι λέγειν εἰκότως τὴν θείαν οὐσίαν καὶ τὴν θείαν ἐνέργειαν, ἵνα μὴ ἐκ πολλῶν καὶ διαφόρων σύνθετον τὸν θεὸν

That, then, is their contention and they think that everything which differs from the divine essence is created in whatever way and therefore they speak against you because you introduce the difference between essence and activity in God.

XXXV. O. It seems to be a good idea now to repeat about them what the Lord said to the Sadducees: "You are wrong because you know neither the scriptures nor the power of God."[98] For by completely rejecting that, they have done and suffered approximately the same things as Sabellius and Arius and those who before and after them advocated such wicked heresies. For each one of them did not believe the God-inspired Scripture in every respect. They clung to some part of it and had their ears stuffed as it were against other texts; they madly advanced against the one and only pious religion which is acknowledged by everyone, opposing to each other the voices of the saints and the spirit; they misused those pieces which they had cut off, and misinterpreted them and held them against the true believers. For Sabellius, after having heard from the saints that the Son is not another God beside the Father, should have tried to hear and learn whether He can be different in another way. He would have learned: "by essence." But, as if he were deafened against the words of the saints which proclaimed that, he was the first who wrongly conceived a contraction of the divinity by showing that Father and Son are in all respects the same. In the same way those who recently heard from the father of Damascus [John Damascene] "that we do not call the uncreated and good and eternal and that kind of thing essential differences in God,"[99] should have taken the trouble to search out how they *do* have to speak and think about those things. But they should not have perverted his other statements about these things and those of the other saints, nor should they coin in their turn new terms: fusion and cutting off and contraction which do not fall short of the divinity of Sabellius,[100] (but they do) by saying those things and that all divine activity does not differ from God's essence. In the same way even Arius would not be despicable if, along with the difference in Father and Son he had the reputation of also accepting the unity.

ποιήσωσι. Ταῦτ᾽ ἄρα καὶ πᾶν τὸ διαφέρον τῆς θείας οὐσίας ὁπωσδήποτε κτιστὸν ἡγοῦνται, καὶ ὑμῖν ὡς διαφορὰν ἐισάγουσιν ἐπὶ θεοῦ τῆς οὐσίας καὶ τῆς ἐνεργείας ἀντιλέγουσιν.

XXXV. ΟΡΘΟΔ. Καλῶς ἔχειν οἶμαι καὶ ἐπ᾽ αὐτῶν εἰρῆσθαι νῦν, ὃ και πρὸς τοὺς Σαδδουκαίους ὁ κύριος εἶπεν, ὅτι <πλανῶνται μὴ εἰδότες τὰς γραφὰς μηδὲ τὴν δύναμιν τοῦ θεοῦ>· ταύτην γὰρ ἠθετήκασι τελέως παραπλήσια πράξαντές τε καὶ παθόντες Σαβελλίῳ καὶ Ἀρείῳ καὶ τοῖς πρὸ αὐτῶν καὶ μετ᾽ αὐτοὺς τῶν πονηρῶν αἱρέσεων προστάταις. Τούτων γὰρ ἕκαστος οὐκ ἐν πᾶσι τῇ θεοπνεύστῳ πεπιστεύκασι γραφῇ· μορίων δὲ τινων ταύτης ἀντεχόμενοι καὶ πρὸς τἄλλα τὰς ἀκοὰς ὥσπερ βεβυσμένας κεκτημένοι, κατὰ τῆς ἀνωμολογημένης ἐκ πάντων μιᾶς εὐσεβείας φρενοβλαβῶς ἐχώρησαν ἀντιπαρατάξαντες ἀλλήλαις τὰς τῶν ἁγίων καὶ τοῦ πνεύματος φωνάς, καὶ τοῖς ὑπ᾽ αὐτῶν ἀποσπασθεῖσιν ἐκείνοις παραχρώμενοι καὶ παρερμηνεύοντες αὐτὰ καὶ κατὰ τῶν εὐσεβῶν προφέροντες. Ἔδει γὰρ τὸν Σαβέλλιον ἀκούσαντα παρὰ τῶν ἁγίων, ὡς οὐκ ἔστιν ἕτερος θεὸς ὁ υἱὸς παρὰ τὸν πατέρα, ζητεῖν προσακοῦσαι καὶ μαθεῖν, εἴπερ ἄλλον τρόπον ἕτερός ἐστιν· ἤκουσε γὰρ ἂν ὅτι καθ᾽ ὑπόστασιν. Ὁ δὲ πρὸς τὰς τοῦτο κηρυττούσας ῥήσεις τῶν ἁγίων καθάπερ ἐκκεκωφημένος συστολὴν πρῶτος κακῶς ἐπενόησε θεότητος ἀδιάφορον παντάπασιν ἀποφηνάμενος πατέρα καὶ υἱόν. Οὕτω τοίνυν καὶ τούτους ἀκούσαντας ἀρτίως τοῦ Δαμασκηνοῦ πατρός, ὅτι <τὸ ἄκτιστον καὶ ἀγαθὸν καὶ αἰώνιον καὶ τὰ τοιαῦτα οὐ λέγομεν διαφορὰς οὐσιώδεις ἐπὶ τοῦ θεοῦ>, ζητεῖν ἐχρῆν καὶ πῶς δεῖ λέγειν καὶ φρονεῖν περὶ αὐτῶν. Ἀλλὰ μὴ τὰς ἄλλας περὶ τούτων αὐτοῦ τε καὶ τῶν ἄλλων ἁγίων παραγραψαμένους ῥήσεις καινοτομεῖν αὖθις συναλοιφὴν καὶ περιτομὴν καὶ συστολὴν θεότητος τῆς Σαβελλίου μὴ ἀποδέουσαν, λέγοντας ταῦτά τε καὶ πᾶσαν ἐνέργειαν θείαν ἀδιάφορον τῆς οὐσίας τοῦ θεοῦ. Τὸν αὐτὸν δὲ τρόπον οὐδ᾽ Ἄρειος ἀπόπτυστος ἂν ἦν, εἰ

For he would not have counted Him who *was* with the Father from the beginning with the beings which *have received* a beginning, just as now those people drag down into the sphere of creatures the activities which are around God from the beginning when they learned that they are sometimes different from the divine nature. Nevertheless, one would perhaps see that the composition which they speak about--and because of that they fall into those sorts of impieties--is accomplished rather from saying that the things which are seen around the divine essence in a physical way do not differ from it. For the divine Cyril said to the Eunomians who also declare that God is composed because of that, "If you suppose that God becomes composed because He has nature and judgment or will, consider also this: the Father possesses the ability of generating in a physical way and of creating through the Son by way of making and in spite of that He is not composed; for those things are the fruit of His one nature. The same argument will prevail concerning good and indestructible and invisible and all other characteristics which belong to God's nature."[101] And again, "If what belongs only to God is absolutely also His essence He will be composed for us out of many essences; for there are many things which belong only to Him by nature and to no other being. For He is king and lord and indestructible and invisible and, in addition, innumerable other things which the divine Scriptures say about Him. If, therefore, all the things which are with Him lie in the order of essence, why, then, will the simple not be composed? This is a most absurd thing to think."[102] Neither have we ever talked about conditions or aptitudes in relation to God nor did we learn them from the fathers, and neither about essential differences, because neither had we heard about many divine essences. But we were taught by the fathers that there were a great many activities, and every one of them uncreated, of the one and simple essence, the holy and venerable trinity. And so you, if you want to be pious, do not call, "the uncreated, that which is without beginning, the good, the eternal and those kinds of characteristics" essential differences in God. Nor refer to them as qualities nor even essences, but place them around the essence; so too did Damascene[103] himself and before him the great Athanasius;[104] when they had enumerated all those things, they say that they are not nature, but around nature. And the great Basil[105] called them not-enhypostatic activities even of the spirit although they are with the spirit from eternity. And else-

μετὰ τῆς ἐπὶ πατρὸς καὶ υἱοῦ διαφορᾶς ἐνηχεῖτο στέργων καὶ τὴν ἕνωσιν. Οὐ γὰρ ἂν τὸν ἀπ᾿ ἀρχῆς συνόντα τῷ πατρὶ τοῖς ἀρχὴν εἰλοφόσι συνηρίθμει, καθάπερ εἰς κτίσμα κατασπῶσιν οὗτοι νῦν τὰς περὶ θεὸν ἀπαρχῆς οὔσας ἐνεργείας, ἡνίκ᾿ ἂν ἔστιν ὡς διενηνοχέναι πύθωνται τῆς θείας φύσεως. Καίτοι τὴν σύνθεσιν ἣν οὗτοι προφασιζόμενοι τοιαύταις δυσσεβείαις περιπίπτουσιν ἴδοι τις ἂν ἐκτελουμένην μᾶλλον ἐκ τοῦ μὴ διαφέρειν λέγειν τῆς θείας οὐσίας τὰ περὶ αὐτὴν φυσικῶς θεωρούμενα. Πρὸς γὰρ τοὺς Εὐνομιανούς, σύνθετον κἀκείνους τὸν θεὸν παρὰ τοῦτο λέγοντας, φησὶν ὁ θεῖος Κύριλλος <εἰ σύνθετον οἴεσθε γίνεσθαι θεὸν διὰ τὸ φύσιν ἔχειν καὶ κρίσιν, ἤτοι θέλησιν, ὁρᾶτε καὶ τοῦτο· ἔχει τὸ γεννᾶν ὁ πατὴρ φυσικῶς, ἔχει καὶ τὸ κτίζειν δι᾿ υἱοῦ δημιουργικῶς καὶ οὐ παρὰ τοῦτο σύνθετός ἐστι· μιᾶς γὰρ φύσεως τὰ τοιαῦτα καρπός. Ὁ δὲ αὐτὸς κρατήσει λόγος ἐπί τε τοῦ ἀγαθοῦ καὶ ἀφθάρτου καὶ ἀοράτου καὶ ὅσα πρόσεστι τῇ θείᾳ φύσει>. Καὶ πάλιν· <εἰ ὅπερ ἂν ὑπάρχῃ μόνῳ τῷ θεῷ, τοῦτο πάντως αὐτοῦ ἔσται καὶ οὐσία, ἐκ πολλῶν ἡμῖν οὐσιῶν συγκείσεται· πολλὰ γάρ ἐστιν, ἃ μόνῳ μὲν αὐτῷ κατὰ φύσιν ὑπάρχει, ἑτέρῳ δὲ τῶν ὄντων οὐδενί. Καὶ γὰρ βασιλεὺς καὶ κύριος καὶ ἄφθαρτος καὶ ἀόρατος καὶ πρὸς τούτοις ἕτερα μυρία περὶ αὐτοῦ λέγουσιν αἱ θεῖαι γραφαί. Εἰ τοίνυν ἕκαστον τῶν αὐτῷ προσόντων ἐν οὐσίας τάξει κείσεται, πῶς οὐκ ἔσται σύνθετος ὁ ἁπλοῦς; Ὅπερ ἐστὶν ἐννοεῖν ἀτοπώτατον>. Ἕξεις μὲν οὖν καὶ ἐπιτηδειότητας οὔθ᾿ ἡμεῖς ἔφημεν οὔτε παρὰ τῶν πατέρων ἐδιδάχθημεν ἐπὶ θεοῦ, ἀλλ᾿ οὐδ᾿ οὐσιώδεις διαφοράς, ἐπεὶ μηδὲ πολλὰς οὐσίας θείας. Τῆς δὲ μιᾶς καὶ ἁπλῆς οὐσίας, τῆς ἁγίας καὶ προσκυνητῆς τριάδος ἐνεργείας εἶναι πλείστας καὶ ἀκτίστους πάσας ὑπὸ τῶν πατέρων μεμυήμεθα. Καὶ σὺ τοίνυν, εἰ θέλεις εὐσεβεῖν, <τὸ ἄκτιστον καὶ ἄναρχον καὶ ἀγαθὸν καὶ αἰώνιον καὶ τὰ τοιαῦτα> μήτε διαφορὰς οὐσιώδεις ἐπὶ θεοῦ λέγε, μήτε ποιότητας, ἀλλὰ μηδὲ οὐσίας, ἀλλὰ περὶ τὴν οὐσίαν, ὡς ὁ αὐτὸς Δαμασκηνὸς

where again he says: "When we learned about benefactor and judge, good and just and those sorts of words we were instructed that they indicate differences of the activities; but we cannot learn anything more through the concept of the activities concerning the nature of the active one"[106]

XXXVI. It is clear, however, also precisely from what you have now brought forward that those things are both uncreated and are not indifferent from the essence, as those people contend; for that which has no beginning and is uncreated is not created, but neither is it essence. How can that which is not essence, then, be not different from the essence? And will they perhaps not be reluctant to call the uncreated itself and what has no beginning, either divine essence, just as Eunomius did with ungenerated, or created, because it is no essence? But we say that the eternal and the good which have the same position as the uncreated, and that which is without beginning are both uncreated and not essence. And why do I speak about the eternal and the good? For concerning the simple itself--on account of which they say that all those characteristics which are with God by nature do not differ from the divine nature--we know that it is uncreated and we know that it is not the nature of God; for the theologian Gregory says: "The simplicity is not His nature." Because, however, God is the creator of the natural simplicities in minds and bodies, He has the simplicity which belongs to Him by nature as an activity. The same theologian contends that the Son, too, is a beginning, but says: "That, the beginning, is not His nature, just as that which has no beginning is not the nature of the not beginning."[107] Nevertheless, because God is the creator of the natural beginnings in every being, He has the beginning as an inborn activity.

XXXVII. It is clear, then, from many points, that the uncreated activity is not the essence of God. One could call it God's essence because it makes essence and God's nature because it is with Him by nature, in complete accordance with the theologians. For he says: "It is the nature

καὶ πρὸ αὐτοῦ ὁ μέγας Ἀθανάσιος πάντα τὰ τοιαῦτα ἀπαριθμησάμενοι οὐ φύσις ταῦτά ἐστί φασιν, ἀλλὰ περὶ τὴν φύσιν. Ὁ δὲ μέγας Βασίλειος καὶ ἐνεργείας οὐκ ἐνυποστάτους ταῦτα προσηγόρευσε τοῦ πνεύματος ἀϊδίως αὐτῷ προσούσας. Καὶ ἀλλαχοῦ πάλιν, <εὐεργέτην>, φησί, <καὶ κριτὴν, ἀγαθόν τε καὶ δίκαιον καὶ ὅσα ἄλλα τοιαῦτα μαθόντες ἐνεργειῶν διαφορὰς ἐδιδάχθημεν· τοῦ δὲ ἐνεργοῦντος τὴν φύσιν οὐδὲν μᾶλλον διὰ τῆς τῶν ἐνεργειῶν κατανοήσεως ἐπιγνῶναι δυνάμεθα>.

XXXVI. Ὅτι μέντοι καὶ ἄκτιστα ταῦθ᾽ ἐστι καὶ ἀδιάφορα τῆς οὐσίας οὐκ ἔστι, καθάπερ οὗτοι διατείνονται, καὶ ἀφ᾽ ὧν νῦν προήνεγκας αὐτῶν κατάδηλον· αὐτὸ γὰρ τὸ ἄναρχον καὶ ἄκτιστον κτιστὸν οὐκ ἔστιν, ἀλλ᾽ οὐδὲ οὐσία. Τὸ μὴ ὂν τοίνυν οὐσία πῶς ἀδιάφορον ἔσται τῆς οὐσίας; Τάχα δ᾽ οὗτοι καὶ αὐτὸ τὸ ἄκτιστον καὶ ἄναρχον οὐκ ὀκνήσουσιν ἢ οὐσίαν εἶναι λέγειν θείαν, καθάπερ ὁ Εὐνόμιος τὸ ἀγέννητον, ἢ κτιστὸν ὅτι μὴ οὐσία; Ἡμεῖς δὲ καὶ τὸ αἰώνιον καὶ τὸ ἀγαθὸν τῷ ἀκτίστῳ καὶ ἀνάρχῳ συντεταγμένα καὶ ἄκτιστα καὶ οὐκ οὐσίαν εἶναι λέγομεν. Καὶ τί λέγω τὸ αἰώνιον καὶ τὸ ἀγαθόν; Αὐτὸ γὰρ τὸ ἁπλοῦν, δι᾽ ὃ πάνθ᾽ οὗτοι τὰ φυσικῶς προσόντα τῷ θεῷ μηδὲν διαφέρειν τῆς θείας φύσεώς φασι, καὶ ἄκτιστον ἴσμεν καὶ φύσιν τοῦ θεοῦ οὐκ ἴσμεν ὄν· <οὐ γὰρ δὴ φύσις αὐτῷ ἡ ἁπλότης>, φησὶν ὁ θεολόγος Γρηγόριος. Καίτοι ποιητὴς ὑπάρχων ὁ θεὸς τῶν ἐν νοῖς τε καὶ σώμασιν ἁπλοτήτων φυσικῶν, ὡς ἐνέργειαν ἔχει τὴν ἁπλότητα προσοῦσαν φυσικῶς. Ὁ αὐτὸς δὲ θεολόγος καὶ τὸν υἱὸν ἀρχὴν εἰπών, <ἀλλ᾽ οὐ τοῦτο φύσις αὐτῷ ἡ ἀρχή>, φησίν, <ὥσπερ οὐδὲ τῷ ἀνάρχῳ τὸ ἄναρχον>. Καίτοι τῶν ἐν ἑκάστῳ φυσικῶν ἀρχῶν δημιουργὸς ὑπάρχων ὁ θεὸς ὡς ἐνέργειαν ἔμφυτον ἔχει τὴν ἀρχήν.

XXXVII. Πολλαχόθεν ἄρα δῆλον ὡς οὐκ ἔστιν οὐσία τοῦ θεοῦ ἡ ἄκτιστος ἐνέργεια. Λεχθείη δ᾽ ἂν οὐσία ὡς οὐσιοποιὸς καὶ φύσις ὡς φυσικῶς προσοῦσα τῷ θεῷ, καὶ τοῦτο κατὰ τοὺς θεολόγους· <φύσις γάρ>, φησίν, <τῷ θεῷ

of God to create and to save."[108] But it is necessary for the person who wants to reach the truth to distinguish the meanings of each of those words. For our discussion deals with the superessentiality which lies beyond in hidden places. For we ascertain that the divine illuminations and activities differ from it. For while that remains altogether imparticipable and unseen and without a name, God makes Himself known by them in many ways and He is participated in through them, because they are not at all separated from it. For He is one God in essence and activity: the Father, the Son and the Holy Spirit.

XXXVIII. B. Enough also about these things. Now you must also remove every other obstacle by solving all the contrarities; for in that way you would gain the highest glory in defense of the pious truth.

O. What do you mean? Shall we jeopardize our soul in defense of the truth with the help of God and should we not be willing to toil on behalf of the argument?

B. What, then, does the great Basil mean when he says that all the things which are said and thought about God signify one thing, writing in his *Letter to Eustathius*, "all conceptions and terms proper to God are of equal honor one with another, through the fact that there is no discrepancy in them in the indication of the subject. For the designation "good" does not lead the mind to one object and that of "wise" and "powerful" and "just" to another (one), but whatever terms you use, the thing that is signified by them all is one. And even if you call Him God, you have indicated the same one whom you also had in mind, when you used the other terms."[109] And in his *Refutations Against Eunomius*, he says: "And so, examining each of those terms, one would find various concepts for only one substrate underlying all things according to the essence."[110]

XXXIX. O. These are not even obstacles, unless also the light of day produces invisibility because it has that characteristic for owls on account of the feeble perception of their eyes! But alas, the wiles of the Evil one! For the fact that one does not reach the meaning of the writer

τὸ παράγειν καὶ σώζειν>. Διαστέλλειν δὲ τὰς σημασίας ἑκάστου τῶν ὀνομάτων ἀναγκαῖον τὸν ἐφικνεῖσθαι τῆς ἀληθείας ἐφιέμενον. Ἡμῖν γὰρ ὁ λόγος περὶ τῆς ἐν ἀποκρύφοις ὑπεριδρυμένης ὑπερουσιότητος· ταύτης γὰρ διαφέρειν τὰς θείας ἐλλάμψεις καὶ ἐνεργείας ἰσχυριζόμεθα. Μενούσης γὰρ αὐτῆς ἀμεθέκτου καὶ ἀνεκφάντου καὶ ἀνωνύμου παντάπασι διὰ τούτων ὁ θεὸς πολυτρόπως γνωρίζεταί τε καὶ μετέχεται, μηδαμῶς χωριστῶν ὑπαρχουσῶν ἐκείνης. Ἐν οὐσίᾳ γὰρ καὶ ἐνεργείᾳ εἷς ἐστι θεός· ὁ πατὴρ καὶ ὁ υἱὸς καὶ τὸ πνεῦμα τὸ ἅγιον.

XXXVIII. ΒΑΡΛ. Ἀπόχρη καὶ περὶ τούτων. Δεῖ δέ σε καὶ πᾶν ἄλλο σκῶλον ἐκποδὼν ποιεῖσθαι λύοντα τὰς ἀντιθέσεις πάσας· οὕτω γὰρ ἂν εἴης τὸ κράτος κατὰ κράτος ὑπὲρ τῆς κατ' εὐσέβειαν ἀληθείας ἀνελόμενος.

ΟΡΘΟΔ. Τί λέγεις; Τὴν ψυχὴν θήσομεν ὑπὲρ τῆς ἀληθείας τοῦ θεοῦ συναιρομένου, καὶ καμεῖν περὶ τὸν λόγον οὐ θελήσομεν;

ΒΑΡΛ. Πῶς οὖν ὁ μέγας Βασίλειος ἕν φησι πάντα σημαίνειν τὰ ἐπὶ θεοῦ λεγόμενά τε καὶ νοούμενα, γράφων ἐν τῇ *Πρὸς Εὐστάθιον ἐπιστολῇ,* ὅτι <πάντα τὰ θεοπρεπῆ νοήματά τε καὶ ὀνόματα ὁμοτίμως ἔχει πρὸς ἄλληλα τῷ μηδὲν παρὰ τὴν τοῦ ὑποκειμένου διαφωνεῖν σημασίαν; Οὐ γὰρ ἐπ' ἄλλο τι ὑποκείμενον χειραγωγεῖ τοῦ ἀγαθοῦ ἡ προσηγορία, ἐφ' ἕτερον δὲ ἡ τοῦ σοφοῦ καὶ τοῦ δυνατοῦ καὶ τοῦ δικαίου· ἀλλ' ὅσαπερ ἂν εἴποις ὀνόματα, ἕν διὰ πάντων τὸ σημαινόμενόν ἐστι. Κἂν θεὸν εἴπῃς, τὸν αὐτὸν ἐνεδείξω, ὃν καὶ διὰ τῶν λοιπῶν ὀνομάτων ἐνόησας>. Ἐν δὲ τοῖς *Πρὸς Εὐνόμιον ἀντιρρητικοῖς,* <καὶ οὕτως ἄν τις>, φησί, <τῶν ὀνομάτων ἕκαστον ἐφοδεύων ποικίλας εὕροι τὰς ἐπινοίας ἑνὸς τοῦ κατὰ τὴν οὐσίαν τοῖς πᾶσιν ὑποκειμένου>.

XXXIX. ΟΡΘΟΔ. Ταῦτ' οὐδὲ σκῶλά ἐστιν, εἰ μὴ καὶ τὸ τῆς ἡμέρας φῶς ἀβλεψίας πρόξενον, ὅτι ταῖς γλαυξὶ γίνεται τοιοῦτον διὰ τὴν ἐκ τῶν ὀμμάτων αὐτῶν ἐξίτηλον ἀντίληψιν. Ἀλλ' ὢ τῆς ἐπηρείας τοῦ πονηροῦ! Τὸ μὲν

in those kinds of words can (only) be the result of a lack of natural faculty or of a mind which doesn't pay the right attention. But the fact that one even strays into the contrary opinion is clearly connected with the activity of the evil spirit; it is a clear opposition to the endeavor of the saints and a trick to try and direct upon the saints themselves the arrows which *they* shoot at the opponent. Perhaps also now they are standing around them as some public executioners breaking and twisting the tongue and hand in their writings and even the mind itself; but they remain stronger than that sort of cavillings, not only as to the meaning which the people who were caught in that quibbling have been able to save unaltered even then, but in all other things as well; for they are steadfast. It is therefore possible for him who so desires to direct the mind's eye towards them and to discern the infallible concepts in them. For according to Solomon, "Those things are all obvious to those who understand and right to those who find knowledge."[111] For the great Basil says: "Some of the divine names bear upon relation (or participation), some on value, some on activity, but none of them signifies essence."[112] Still they falsely affirm that he says the complete opposite, namely, that all of the names which are predicated of God, signify the same and bear upon the divine essence. And Basil shows that that is the voice of the false doctrine of Eunomius. Sometimes he brings forward in his *Refutations* to him that man's expression which makes that clear. Sometimes he concludes that, based on the opinions of that man, the expression is most absurd. For he says: "If, then, Eunomius considers absolutely nothing conceptually, to the extent that he does not seem to honor God by human names, he will acknowledge that everything which is said about God is, equally, essence. And if all these expressions tend to have one signification, it is absolutely necessary that the meaning of the words is interchangeable just as is the case with things which have many names. And what would be more absurd than this confusion, to take away the proper signification of each word and make new laws which run counter to the common usage and the teachings of the Spirit?"[113] And again: "If we would employ all the divine

γὰρ ἐν τοῖς τοιούτοις μὴ καταστοχάζεσθαι τῆς διανοίας τοῦ γράφοντος γένοιτ' ἄν τινος ἀφυΐας ἢ διανοίας οὐκ ἐφιστάσης καλῶς. Τὸ δὲ καὶ εἰς τὴν ἐναντίαν ἀποβουκολεῖσθαι δόξαν τῆς τοῦ πονηροῦ πνεύματος ἐνεργείας σαφῶς ἐξῆπται, σαφὴς ἀντιπαράταξις ὂν πρὸς τὴν τῶν ἁγίων σπουδὴν καὶ μηχανή τις ἐπ' αὐτοὺς στρέφειν ἐπιχειροῦσα τὰ παρ' αὐτῶν ἀφειμένα πρὸς τὸν ἀντικείμενον βέλη. Τάχα καὶ νῦν οἷά τινες οὗτοι δήμιοι περιεστᾶσιν αὐτοὺς ἀκρωτηριάζοντες καὶ στρεβλοῦντες τὴν ἐν συγγράμμασι γλῶττάν τε καὶ χεῖρα καὶ τὸν νοῦν αὐτόν, κἂν ἐκεῖνοι τῶν τοιούτων ἐπηρειῶν διατελοῦσι κρείττους, οὐ τὴν γνώμην μόνον, ἣν καὶ τότε διετήρησαν ἄτρεπτον οἱ ταῖς ἐπηρείαις ἐκείναις ἐνσχεθέντες, ἀλλὰ καὶ τἄλλα πάντα· καὶ γὰρ ἀσφαλεῖς. Ἔξεστι δὴ τῷ βουλομένῳ πρὸς αὐτοὺς ἀνατείνειν τὸ τῆς διανοίας ὄμμα καὶ ἀθρεῖν ἐν τούτοις τὰς ἀδιαστρόφους ἐννοίας· κατὰ γὰρ τὸ σολομώντειον ἔπος <πάντα εὐθέα ἐστὶ τοῖς νοοῦσι, καὶ ὀρθὰ τοῖς εὑρίσκουσι γνῶσιν>. Ὁ μὲν γὰρ μέγας Βασίλειος τῶν θείων ὀνομάτων <τὰ μὲν σχέσεως εἶναι>, φησί, <τὰ δὲ ἀξίας, τὰ δὲ ἐνεργείας, σημαντικὸν δ' οὐσίας οὐδέν. Οὗτοι δὲ πᾶν τοὐναντίον λέγειν αὐτὸν συκοφαντοῦσιν, ὡς οὐδὲν τῶν ἐπὶ θεοῦ λεγομένων ὀνομάτων, ὃ μὴ τὸ αὐτὸ σημαίνει καὶ τῆς θείας οὐσίας ἐστι σημαντικόν. Καὶ ὁ μὲν τῆς Εὐνομίου κακοδοξίας δείκνυσι ταύτην εἶναι τὴν φωνήν. Ἔστι μὲν οὗ τῶν πρὸς ἐκεῖνον *Ἀντιρρητικῶν* καὶ τὴν τοῦτο σαφῶς δηλοῦσαν ἐκείνου ῥῆσιν προτιθείς, ἔστι δ' οὗ συνάγων ὡς ἀτοπωτάτην ἐκ τῶν ἐκείνῳ δεδογμένων· φησὶ γάρ· <εἰ μὲν οὐδὲν ὅλως κατ' ἐπίνοιαν ὁ Εὐνόμιος θεωρεῖ, ἵνα μὴ δόξῃ ἀνθρωπίναις τὸν θεὸν σεμνύνειν προσηγορίαις, πάντα ὁμοίως οὐσίαν ὁμολογήσει τὰ ἐπιλεγόμενα τῷ θεῷ. Καὶ εἰ ταῦτα πάντα πρὸς ἓν σημαινόμενον τείνει, ἀνάγκη πᾶσα ταὐτὸν ἀλλήλοις δύνασθαι τὰ ὀνόματα, ὡς ἐπὶ τῶν πολυωνύμων. Καὶ ταύτης τί ἂν γένοιτο τῆς συγχύσεως ἀτοπώτερον, ἀφελόμενον τὴν ἰδίαν ἑκάστου τῶν ὀνομάτων σημασίαν ἀντινομοθετεῖν τῇ τε κοινῇ χρήσει καὶ τῇ διδασκαλίᾳ

names by referring them to the essence, we would not only show that God is composed, but also that He is a composition of unequal things, because every one of these words always signifies another thing."[114] These and comparable words are spoken by the great Basil. And those who ascribe the opposite to him and oppose themselves to us in these respects, do approximately the same thing as if someone would attribute the characteristics of darkness to light, being himself in the dark concerning light.

XL. That great Basil, however, has often said that "it is clear lunacy to claim that there is not a specific signification underlying each divine name."[115] And because he has been accused of introducing polytheism, on account of these words, by Eunomius with his false doctrines--just as we have been accused, and for the same reason, by those Eunomians who have only newly appeared on the scene--he says, for his defense as well as for ours: "Even if all the proper names of God on account of their own signification are many and various, and sometimes also admit of different reasonings, nevertheless for Him to whom they refer and to whom they belong, i.e., God, they are of equal honor one with another. For each of them does not lead the mind to different gods but the person who uses those terms indicates one God by all of them."[116] And in the text after this, teaching how God is one around Whom are all the things which are signified by those terms, he says: "He is one according to the essence, because He who underlies all those terms is one according to the essence."[117] "For," he says, "just as grain is one thing according to its substance, it changes its names in relation to the various properties which are seen in it and it becomes seed and fruit and food and it gets as many names as the forms it takes, so it is approximately with the Lord; for He is in Himself whatever He is according to His nature, but when He is called after His various activities, He has not one name in all those cases, but He receives His name in accordance with each concept which arises in us from the activity."[118] That, then, is what he said and with the

τοῦ πνεύματος>; Καὶ πάλιν· <εἴπερ εἰς τὴν οὐσίαν φέροντες ἅπαντα τὰ θεῖα ὀνόματα καταθήσομεν, οὐ μόνον σύνθετον, ἀλλὰ καὶ ἐξ ἀνομοιομερῶν συγκείμενον τὸν θεὸν ἀποδείξομεν, διὰ τὸ ἄλλο καὶ ἄλλο ὑφ᾽ ἑκάστου τῶν ὀνομάτων σημαίνεσθαι>. Ταῦτα καὶ τὰ τοιαῦθ᾽ οὕτω φησὶν ὁ μέγας Βασίλειος. Οἱ δὲ τἀναντία προσμαρτυροῦντες αὐτῷ καὶ ἡμῖν ἐν τοῖς τοιούτοις ἀντικείμενοι παραπλήσιόν τι ποιοῦσιν, ὥσπερ ἂν εἴ τις τὰ τοῦ σκότους ἴδια προσεμαρτύρει τῷ φωτί, σκοτεινὸς ὢν περὶ τὸ φῶς αὐτός.

XL. Ὁ μέντοι μέγας ἐκεῖνος πολλάκις εἰρηκὼς ὅτι <μανία σαφὴς μὴ ἴδιον σημαινόμενον ἑκάστῳ τῶν θείων ὀνομάτων ὑποβεβλῆσθαι λέγειν>, καὶ διὰ τοὺς τοιούτους λόγους ὡς πολυθεΐαν εἰσάγων ὑπὸ τῆς Εὐνομίου κακοφροσύνης ἐγκληθεὶς - καθάπερ καὶ ἡμεῖς καὶ διὰ τὴν αὐτὴν αἰτίαν ὑπὸ τῶν ἀρτιφανῶν τούτων Εὐνομιανῶν - ὑπὲρ ἑαυτοῦ καὶ ἡμῶν ἀπολογούμενος, <εἰ καὶ πάντα>, φησί, <τὰ θεοπρεπῆ ὀνόματα παρὰ τὴν ἑαυτῶν σημασίαν πολλὰ καὶ διάφορα, καὶ διαφόρους ἔστιν ὡς ἐπιδέχεται λόγους, ἀλλὰ παρὰ τὸν ἐφ᾽ οὗ λέγεται καὶ οὗ ἐστιν ὀνόματα, ὅς ἐστιν ὁ θεός, ὁμοτίμως ἔχει πρὸς ἄλληλα. Οὐ γὰρ ἐπ᾽ ἄλλον καὶ ἄλλον θεὸν χειραγωγεῖ τούτων ἕκαστον, ἀλλ᾽ ἕνα διὰ πάντων θεὸν ὁ ταῦτα λέγων ἐνδείκνυται>. Κἀν τῇ μετ᾽ αὐτὴν ῥήσει διδάσκων, πῶς εἷς περὶ ὃν ἐκεῖνα πάντα τὰ ὑπὸ τῶν ὀνομάτων σημαινόμενα, <κατὰ τὴν οὐσίαν>, φησίν, <ὡς ἑνὸς ὄντος κατ᾽ αὐτὴν τοῦ πᾶσιν ἐκείνοις ὑποκειμένου>. <Καθάπερ γάρ>, φησίν, <ὁ σῖτος ἕν τι πρᾶγμα κατὰ τὴν ὑπόστασιν ὤν, πρὸς τὰς ἐπιθεωρουμένας αὐτῷ ποικίλας ἰδιότητας ἐξαλλάσσει τὰς κλήσεις καὶ σπόρος γινόμενος καὶ καρπὸς καὶ τροφή, καὶ ὅσα γίνεται τοσαῦτα ὀνομαζόμενος, παραπλησίως καὶ ὁ κύριος· ἔστι μὲν καθ᾽ ἑαυτὸν ὅ, τι ποτὲ κατὰ τὴν φύσιν ἐστι, ταῖς δὲ τῶν ἐνεργειῶν διαφοραῖς συνονομαζόμενος οὐ μίαν ἐπὶ πάντων ἴσχει προσηγορίαν, ἀλλὰ καθ᾽ ἑκάστην ἔννοιαν τὴν ἐξ ἐνεργείας ἐγγινομένην ἡμῖν μεταλαμβάνει τὸ ὄνομα>.

following words the divine theologian Gregory of Nyssa took Eunomius to task who tried to attack the great man, by writing: "Why, then, by those words, is our argument refuted which says that it is possible that, according to the different activities and the relation to the results many names are applicable to the Son of God Who is one according to the underlying subject, just as the grain, which is one, is, on account of the various concepts about it, distributed over different names."[119] And the great Dionysius says that there are many different manifestations of God and that the many different divine names which are celebrated by us belong to them; he then adds: "And each of them does not signify different things, but they all belong to one God."[120] For mind is also each of the sciences[121] and the human mind is judge and takes care of the weaker people. But according to its essence it underlies all those activities since it is one according to that essence. Our mind, however, possesses thinking as an acquired characteristic by learning from experience or by instruction; that is the same as suffering, when the mind becomes thinking.[122] But God does not get His characteristics from suffering for He does not acquire anything. However, since He is always so, He manifests Himself as such to us through His activities. Not only the Father, but the Son and the Holy Spirit as well. For all the things which the father has also belong to the Son because He has the same things and He exists apart from the characteristics which belong to Him according to His substance; the same (is true) for the Spirit. And just as our mind, invisible for our perception and incorporeal because it does not undergo any addition or dimunition by those things, is not therefore composed, so God, being good and wise and foreseeing everything from eternity and not undergoing any change by those things, cannot be called composed on account of them. That is the way to understand the words of the great Basil and so he makes his defense for himself and for us, even if those who cannot discern the right meaning in the words think they bring it forth against us, although in fact they bring it forward against themselves.

Ταῦτ᾽ ἄρα καὶ ὁ Νύσσης θεῖος Γρηγόριος ταυτῇ τὸν Εὐνόμιον ᾔσχυνεν, ἐπιλαμβάνεσθαι τοῦ μεγάλου πειρώμενον γράφων· <τί οὖν ὁ λόγος ἡμῶν διὰ τῶν εἰρημένων ἐλέγχεται ὁ εἰπὼν δυνατὸν εἶναι πολλὰς ἐφαρμόζεσθαι προσηγορίας κατὰ τὰς τῶν ἐνεργειῶν διαφορὰς καὶ τὴν πρὸς τὰ ἐνεργούμενα σχέσιν ἑνὶ κατὰ τὸ ὑποκείμενον ὄντι τῷ υἱῷ τοῦ θεοῦ, ὡς καὶ ὁ σῖτος εἷς ὢν ἐκ τῶν ποικίλων περὶ αὐτοῦ νοημάτων, διαφόροις ἐπωνυμίαις ἐπιμερίζεται>; Ὁ δὲ μέγας Διονύσιος πολλὰς καὶ διαφόρους εἰπὼν προόδους τοῦ θεοῦ καὶ τούτων εἶναι τὰς παρ᾽ ἡμῶν ἐξυμνουμένας πολλὰς καὶ διαφόρους θεωνυμίας, εἶτά φησι· <καὶ μὴ ἄλλο καὶ ἄλλο τούτων ἑκάστην εἶναι, ἀλλ᾽ ὡς ἑνὸς θεοῦ τούτων ἁπασῶν οὐσῶν>· νοῦς γὰρ ἐστι καὶ τῶν ἐπιστημῶν ἑκάστη· καὶ κριτής ἐστι καὶ προνοητὴς τῶν ὑποδεεστέρων ὁ ἀνθρώπινος νοῦς· ἀλλὰ καὶ κατ᾽ οὐσίαν ὑπόκειται ταῖς τοιαύταις ἐνεργείαις πάσαις εἷς ὑπάρχων κατ᾽ αὐτήν. Ὁ μὲν οὖν ἡμέτερος νοῦς ἐπακτὸν ἔχει τὸ φρονεῖν, τῷ πείρᾳ τινὶ μαθεῖν ἢ διδασκαλίᾳ, ταὐτὸ δ᾽ εἰπεῖν παθεῖν, γινόμενος τοιοῦτος. Ὁ δὲ θεὸς οὐκ ἐκ τῶν παθημάτων· προσλαμβάνει γὰρ οὐδέν. Ἀλλ᾽ ἀεὶ τοιοῦτος ὢν ἐκ τῶν ἐνεργειῶν ἡμῖν δείκνυται τοιοῦτος· οὐχ ὁ πατὴρ μόνος, ἀλλὰ καὶ ὁ υἱὸς καὶ τὸ πνεῦμα τὸ ἅγιον· πάντα γὰρ ὅσα ἔχει ὁ πατήρ, ταῦτά ἐστιν ὁ υἱός, ὡς τὰ αὐτὰ ἔχων καὶ αὐτὸς χωρὶς τῶν καθ᾽ ὑπόστασιν ἰδίων, ὡσδαύτως καὶ τὸ πνεῦμα. Καὶ τοίνυν καθάπερ ὁ ἡμέτερος νοῦς ἀόρατος αἰσθήσει καὶ ἀσώματος ὑπάρχων, ὅτι μηδεμίαν ἐπιδέχεται κατ᾽ αὐτὰ πρόσληψιν ἢ μείωσιν, οὐκ ἔστι διὰ ταῦτα σύνθετος, οὕτως ὁ θεὸς ἀγαθός, σοφός, προνοητὴς ὢν ἐξ ἀϊδίου καὶ μηδεμίαν κατ᾽ αὐτὰ προσιέμενος μεταβολήν, παρὰ ταῦτα σύνθετος οὐκ ἂν λεχθείη. Τοῦτον ἔχει τὸν τρόπον καὶ τὰ τοῦ μεγάλου Βασιλείου, καὶ οὕτως ὑπὲρ ἑαυτοῦ καὶ ἡμῶν ἀπολογεῖται, κἂν οἱ μὴ συνορᾶν δυνάμενοι τὸν ἐν τοῖς εἰρημένοις νοῦν καθ᾽ ἑαυτῶν προφέροντες καθ᾽ ἡμῶν οἴωνται προάγειν.

XLI. B. But those who do not accept the difference in these things cite not only Eunomius as the one who proclaims not to believe those who unite the activity with the essence, but they also condemn you for agreeing with him.

O. Eunomius called the Son the activity of the Father, and he heaped calumny on those who made Him one with the Father by essence while he himself truly acted in a most reprehensible manner. Hence, the argument had no effect upon us; for our argument dealt with the common divine powers and activities of the Father, Son and Spirit. But Eunomius called whatever activity he talked about created and only the essence uncreated; and all the uncreated (he called) essence. How then would he not be the opponent of the truth and of us who make a great effort to show that the divine illumination is an uncreated activity, but not an essence? And how would he not be truly in agreement with those who tear away from there above and drag down to the creation the illumination and activity which differs from the divine essence in whatever way, and who teach that all the uncreated is essence, just as he does? What do you think? Shall we say that Sabellius too makes them one in a beautiful manner, since Eunomius condemns those who make them one? Not at all. For it is possible to make the activity one with the essence in an evil way just like the followers of Barlaam, and to make a distinction between them in a pious fashion-- but not the way Eunomius does! Nevertheless, even if one says that the Son is in another manner the activity of the Father, He is one and not one with the Father: in the first case by essence, in the second, by the hypostases. But we talk about the common activity of the Father, Son and Spirit on account of which we come to know whatever God is.

XLII. B. Those activities from which we learn about God they call manifestly created. And they confirm simply that air and earth and sea and that sort of thing are the activities. For they say that God is only to be known from his creatures; and that the uncreated activity is similar to the essence and unknowable, being in every respect the same as that one.

XLI. ΒΑΡΛ. Ἀλλ' οἱ τὴν ἐπὶ τῶν τοιούτων διαφορὰν μὴ προσιέμενοι καὶ τὸν Εὐνόμιον προβάλλονται παραγγέλλοντα μὴ πείθεσθαι τοῖς ἑνοῦσι τῇ οὐσίᾳ τὴν ἐνέργειαν καὶ ὡς συμφθεγγομένους ὑμᾶς ἐκείνῳ κατακρίνουσιν.

ΟΡΘΟΔ. Εὐνόμιος ἐνέργειαν ἔλεγε τοῦ πατρὸς τὸν υἱόν, καὶ τοὺς ἑνοῦντας αὐτὸν ἐκείνῳ κατ' οὐσίαν ἐβδελύττετο, βδελυρίας ὢν ὡς ἀληθῶς ἀνάμεστος αὐτός. Ὥστ' οὐδὲν πρὸς ἡμᾶς ὁ λόγος· ἡμῖν γὰρ περὶ τῶν κοινῶν πατρός, υἱοῦ καὶ πνεύματος θείων δυνάμεών τε καὶ ἐνεργειῶν ὁ λόγος. Ἀλλὰ καὶ κτιστὴν ἔλεγεν ὁ Εὐνόμιος, ἣν δήποτ' ἔλεγεν ἐνέργειαν, τὴν δ' οὐσίαν μόνην ἄκτιστον καὶ πᾶν ἄκτιστον οὐσίαν. Πῶς οὖν οὐχ ὑπεναντίος ἐκεῖνος τῇ τ' ἀληθείᾳ καὶ ἡμῖν εἰς τὸ δεῖξαι ἄκτιστον ἐνέργειαν τὴν θείαν ἔλλαμψιν, ἀλλ' οὐκ οὐσίαν εἶναι ποιουμένοις τὸν ἀγῶνα; Πῶς δ' οὐχὶ τούτοις ὡς ἀληθῶς συμφθέγγεται τοῖς διασπῶσιν ἐκεῖθεν καὶ εἰς κτίσμα κατασπῶσι τὴν διαφέρουσαν ὁπωσδήποτε τῆς θείας οὐσίας ἔλλαμψίν τε καὶ ἐνέργειαν καὶ πᾶν ἄκτιστον οὐσίαν ὡς ἐκεῖνος δογματίζουσι; Τί δέ, καὶ τὸν Σαβέλλιον ἐροῦμεν καλῶς ἑνοῦν, ἐπειδήπερ Εὐνόμιος κατακρίνει τοὺς ἑνοῦντας; Οὐμενουν· ἔστι γὰρ καὶ ἑνοῦν κακῶς τῇ οὐσίᾳ τὴν ἐνέργειαν, καθάπερ οἱ τῷ Βαρλαὰμ ἑπόμενοι, καὶ διακρίνειν εὐσεβῶς, ἀλλ' οὐχ ὡς ὁ Εὐνόμιος. Καίτοι κἂν τὸν υἱὸν ἐνέργειάν τις τρόπον ἕτερον εἴπῃ τοῦ πατρός, ἓν καὶ οὐχ ἕν ἐστι μετὰ πατρὸς, τὸ μὲν τῇ οὐσίᾳ, τὸ δὲ ταῖς ὑποστάσεσιν. Ἡμῖν δὲ περὶ κοινῆς ἐνεργείας πατρός, υἱοῦ καὶ πνεύματος ὁ λόγος, ἀφ' ἧς γινώσκομεν ὅ, τι ἐστὶν ὁ θεός.

XLII. ΒΑΡΛ. Ταύτας τὰς ἐνεργείας ἐξ ὧν ὁ θεὸς γινώσκεται, φανερῶς ἐκεῖνοι τίθενται κτιστάς· καὶ ἁπλῶς τὸν ἀέρα, τὴν γῆν, τὴν θάλασσαν καὶ τὰ τοιαῦτα, ταύτας ἰσχυρίζονται τὰς ἐνεργείας εἶναι. Φασὶ γὰρ ἐκ τῶν κτισμάτων μόνων τὸν θεὸν γινώσκεσθαι· τὴν δ' ἄκτιστον ἐνέργειαν ἐπίσης εἶναι τῇ οὐσίᾳ καὶ ἄγνωστον, οὖσαν ἐκείνῃ κατὰ πάντα τὴν αὐτήν.

O. Since they reveal that all activity which is not the same as, and not completely similar to, the essence of God, is created--well, let us now (in order not to prolong the discussion) with the help of one of the saints put them to shame and refute them because their manner of thinking is evil. Let the great and colorful Basil then put them to shame by the words in his *Refutations*: "Is it not patently ridiculous to say that the creative power is the essence; and again that the foreseeing and foretelling powers, and simply to confirm that all activity is the essence?"[123] And would he not be much more ridiculous who would suggest that those creative and foreseeing and foretelling powers are created since they are divine activity, but different from his essence? Horror! With how much impiety have they filled countless souls since they draw (water) from their own cistern, (they) who drag the uncreated activities of God down to creatures and who disparage those who know the difference between uncreated essence and activity as being impious polytheists. For they make God a creature through each activity and they act downright outrageously against the saints of God themselves. And let us again listen to the revealer of God: "We say that we know the greatness of God and the power and the wisdom and the goodness and foresight with which He takes care of us, and the justice of His judgement, not His essence itself."[124] Let the new theologians speak! What do they mean by air, earth and sea? For these things are known to us but they differ from the essence of God, which is not only uncreated but completely unintelligible as well. But let us attend to what he says thereafter. Continuing his argument, he says: "For his activities are manifold but his essence is simple."[125] Have you heard yet another difference between the uncreated essence and the uncreated activities of God? And further on: "We say that we know our God from His activities but we do not pretend to get close to His essence."[126] He means, of course, the things which he mentioned before: wisdom, justice, greatness, goodness, the activity and power to foretell, to foresee,

ΟΡΘΟΔ. Ἐπεὶ τοίνυν οὗτοι πᾶσαν ἐνέργειαν, ἥτις οὐχ ἡ αὐτὴ καὶ ἀδιάφορός ἐστι τῇ οὐσίᾳ τοῦ θεοῦ, κτιστὴν εἶναι ἀποφαίνονται, φερ᾽ ἡμεῖς ἀρτίως, ἵνα μὴ μηκύνωμεν, δι᾽ ἑνὸς τῶν ἁγίων ἐντρέψωμεν αὐτοὺς καὶ ἀπελέγξωμεν κακῶς φρονοῦντας. Ἐντρεπέτω τοίνυν αὐτοὺς ὁ πολὺς καὶ μέγας Βασίλειος γράφων ἐν τοῖς *Ἀντιρρητικοῖς*· <πῶς οὐ καταγέλαστον τὸ δημιουργικὸν οὐσίαν εἶναι λέγειν, τὸ προνοητικὸν πάλιν οὐσίαν, τὸ προγνωστικὸν πάλιν ὡσαύτως, καὶ ἁπαξαπλῶς πᾶσαν ἐνέργειαν οὐσίαν τίθεσθαι>; Ἆρ᾽ οὖν οὐ μακρῷ καταγελαστότερος ἂν εἴη ὁ τὸ δημιουργικὸν τοῦτο, τὸ προνοητικόν τε καὶ προγνωστικόν, ὡς ἐνεργείας μὲν ὄντα θείας, τῆς δ᾽ αὐτοῦ οὐσίας ἕτερα, τιθέμενος κτιστά; Φεῦ! Ὅσης ἀσεβείας ὅσας ἐνέπλησαν ψυχάς, ὡς ἐκ δεξαμενῆς τῆς ἑαυτῶν ἀντλοῦντες οἱ πρὸς κτίσμα κατασπῶντες τὰς ἀκτίστους ἐνεργείας τοῦ θεοῦ καὶ τῶν διαφορὰν εἰδότων ἀκτίστου οὐσίας τε καὶ ἐνεργείας ὡς δυσσεβῶν κατεπαιρόμενοι καὶ πολυθέων· δι᾽ ἑκάστης γὰρ ἐνεργείας κτίσμα τὸν θεὸν ποιοῦσι καὶ εἰς αὐτοὺς ἄντικρυς ὑβρίζουσι τοὺς τοῦ θεοῦ ἁγίους. Ἡμεῖς δ᾽ ἔτ᾽ ἀκούσωμεν τοῦ θεοφάντορος· <τὴν μεγαλειότητα τοῦ θεοῦ εἰδέναι λέγομεν καὶ τὴν δύναμιν και τὴν σοφίαν καὶ τὴν ἀγαθότητα καὶ τὴν πρόνοιαν, ᾗ ἐπιμελεῖται ἡμῶν, καὶ τὸ δίκαιον αὐτοῦ τῆς κρίσεως· οὐκ αὐτὴν τὴν οὐσίαν>. Εἰπάτωσαν τοίνυν οἱ καινοὶ θεολόγοι· τί τούτων ἀήρ, τί δε γῆ, τί δὲ θάλασσα; Γινωσκόμενα γὰρ παρ᾽ ἡμῶν διενηνόχασι τῆς οὐκ ἀκτίστου μόνον, ἀλλὰ καὶ ἀπερινοήτου παντάπασιν οὐσίας τοῦ θεοῦ. Ἀλλ᾽ ἐχώμεθα τῶν ἐφεξῆς· μικρὸν γὰρ προϊών, <αἱ μὲν γὰρ ἐνέργειαι αὐτοῦ>, φησί, <ποικίλαι, ἡ δὲ οὐσία ἁπλῆ>. Ἤκουσας καὶ ἄλλην διαφορὰν πρὸς τὴν ἄκτιστον οὐσίαν τῶν ἀκτίστων τοῦ θεοῦ ἐνεργειῶν; Καὶ πάλιν· <ἡμεῖς δὲ ἐκ τῶν ἐνεργειῶν γνωρίζειν λέγομεν τὸν θεὸν ἡμῶν, τῇ δὲ οὐσίᾳ αὐτοῦ προσεγγίζειν οὐχ ὑπισχνούμεθα>, δηλονότι τῶν αὐτῷ προειρημένων· τῆς σοφίας, τῆς δικαιοσύνης, τῆς μεγαλειότητος, τῆς ἀγαθότητος, τῆς προγνωστικῆς, τῆς δημιουργικῆς, τῆς

to create, and similar things. Is one of them created? What, then, does the word mean which they cite: "For His activities descend to us but his essence remains there, inaccessible"?[127]

Which of the elements or which of those things which are composed out of them or are bound together in a physical manner come down from above? But listen again to the same man how we know again about the uncreated activities but not the uncreated essence of God: "For the created things show His power and wisdom and craft, but not the essence itself; and neither do they manifest necessarily all the power itself of the Creator."[128] The people, then, who say that the uncreated essence of God is, in all respects, the same as the uncreated activities, also believe, it seems, that that essence is intelligible and participable by way of those activities.

XLIII.B. They say that God, who is undivided and simple, is completely participated in by those who participate in Him. The things which partake in Him partake, therefore, in both His essence and His activity. Otherwise God would be divisible if He is participated in according to His activity but not according to His essence.

O. How could a person then avoid aligning with the Messalians[129] if he does not turn from them who now cherish the same doctrine? For they thoroughly hold to this nonsense that those who have reached the summit of what they call virtue partake of the essence of God. But now there have appeared those men who strive to surpass even that evil notion; they despise the fathers who explicitly state that according to His essence God is imparticipable for everyone, but that He becomes participable in another way: these people state that He is participable for everyone according to His essence. And their pretext is so decent! He says: "Lest God suffer division, when He is participated in according to one aspect and not according to another." Has he shown that God is divisible who a little while ago said that he knows His power and goodness and wisdom but not His essence?

B. Come on! For the man who firmly proclaimed that God is simple, is (precisely) the great Basil.

προνοητικῆς ἐνεργείας καὶ δυνάμεως καὶ τῶν παραπλησίων. Ἆρ᾽ ἔστι τούτων τι κτιστόν; Τί δὴ τὸ ἐπαγόμενον, <αἱ μὲν γὰρ ἐνέργειαι αὐτοῦ πρὸς ἡμᾶς καταβαίνουσιν, ἡ δὲ οὐσία αὐτοῦ μένει ἀπρόσιτος>; Τίνα τῶν στοιχείων ἢ τῶν ἐκ τούτων συγκειμένων ἢ καὶ συνδουμένων φυσικῶς καταβαίνει ἄνωθεν; Ἀλλὰ πόθεν τὰς ἀκτίστους ἐνεργείας αὖθις, ἀλλ᾽ οὐχὶ τὴν ἄκτιστον οὐσίαν τοῦ θεοῦ γινώσκομεν, ἄκουσον πάλιν τοῦ αὐτοῦ· <δυνάμεως> γάρ, φησί, <καὶ σοφίας καὶ τέχνης, ἀλλ᾽ οὐχὶ τῆς οὐσίας αὐτῆς ἐνδεικτικά ἐστι τὰ ποιήματα· καὶ οὐδὲ αὐτὴν πᾶσαν τοῦ δημιουργοῦ τὴν δύναμιν ἀναγκαίως παρίστησιν>. Οἱ γοῦν ταὐτὸ παντάπασι λέγοντες ταῖς ἀκτίστοις ἐνεργείαις τὴν ἄκτιστον οὐσίαν τοῦ θεοῦ, καὶ ταύτην κατ᾽ αὐτὰς καταληπτὴν καὶ μεθεκτήν, ὡς ἔοικεν, ἡγοῦνται.

XLIII. ΒΑΡΛ. Τὸν θεὸν ἀμερῆ ὄντα καὶ ἁπλοῦν ὅλον φασὶ μετέχεσθαι παρὰ τῶν μετεχόντων. Ὥστε καὶ τῆς οὐσίας καὶ τῆς ἐνεγείας αὐτοῦ μετέχει τὰ μετέχοντα. Εἰ δὲ μή, μεριστὸς ἔσται ὁ θεὸς κατ᾽ ἐνέργειαν, ἀλλ᾽ οὐ κατ᾽ οὐσίαν μετεχόμενος.

ΟΡΘΟΔ. Τί οὖν ἔτι μεσσαλιανοὺς ἐκτρέποιτ᾽ ἄν τις, εἰ μὴ καὶ τοὺς νῦν ἐκείνοις ὁμοδόξους; Ἐκείνων γὰρ ἄντικρύς ἐστι τὸ παραλήρημα τουτί, τοὺς εἰς ἄκρον τῆς κατ᾽ αὐτοὺς ἀρετῆς ἐληλακότας τῆς οὐσίας μετεσχηκέναι τοῦ θεοῦ. Νῦν δ᾽ ἀναπεφήνασιν οἱ καὶ τὴν κακόνοιαν ταύτην ὑπερβαλέσθαι φιλοτιμούμενοι, καὶ τῶν πατέρων ἀλογήσαντες διαρρήδην λεγόντων κατ᾽ οὐσίαν εἶναι τὸν θεὸν πᾶσι παντάπασιν ἀμέθεκτον, ἑτέρῳ δὲ τρόπῳ μεθεκτὸν γίνεσθαι, τοῖς πᾶσι μεθεκτὸν τοῦτον οὗτοι κατ᾽ οὐσίαν τίθενται. Καὶ ἡ πρόφασις ὡς εὐπρεπής· <ἵνα μὴ μερισμόν>, φησί <πάθῃ θεὸς κατά τι μὲν μετεχόμενος κατά τι δ᾽ οὔ>. Ἆρ᾽ οὖν μεριστὸν ἔδειξεν αὐτὸν ὁ μικρὸν ἀνωτέρω φήσας εἰδέναι τὴν δύναμιν αὐτοῦ καὶ τὴν ἀγαθότητα καὶ τὴν σοφίαν, ἀλλ᾽ οὐ τὴν οὐσίαν;

ΒΑΡΛ. Ἄπαγε· καὶ γὰρ ὁ τὸν θεὸν ἀφαλῶς ἁπλοῦν κηρύξας ὁ μέγας ἐστὶ Βασίλειος.

XLIV. O. Hence, when we know His activity but not His essence, we do not commit an outrage to the supernatural character of His simplicity. And when we participate in His activity but not in His essence, do we make the undivided divisible? You heard him also say: "The activities of God are manifold, but His essence is simple."[130] Just as He who is manifold according to His activities is not manifold and divided according to His essence, so in the same way, He will not be participable according to His essence although He is participated according to His activities. And since we participate in God in various ways--for each of the beings participate in Him differently--we will therefore participate in Him according to His activities, according to which He is also mainfold. But we shall not participate in Him according to His essence; for according to His essence He is the least manifold in whatever way you look at it. No, but we know His goodness and power and wisdom. How much can we know of each of them? For how can a limited knowledge grasp that infinity, or rather the infinities of that wisdom, that power, that goodness? But he says: "God also reveals Himself to people on the mountain itself, on the one hand by coming down from His proper watchtower, (and) on the other hand, by leading us up from our humble state here on earth in order that the Incomprehensible ("uncontainable") is contained by a created nature in at least a moderate and most safe way."[131]

XLV. How then is He participated in and contained wholly when He is contained in a moderate way? And how is He not divided, when He is contained in a moderate way and remains altogether Incomprehensible ("uncontainable")? And how is it possible that Paul is recorded to have met with a short beam of the great light?[132] How can the short be the whole? And how can it appear on the one hand and not on the other, when it is not divided? And what are the divisions of the Spirit in the same Paul?[133] And why do we get not the fullness, but "from the fullness of Christ"[134] according to the most theological apostle, although He is altogher undivided? And how is the Spirit not poured out "upon all the flesh," but does it "flow out from the spirit of God"?[135] And how did those who went up the mount of Thabor with Jesus see a dim light

XLIV. ΟΡΘΟΔ. Τὴν οὖν ἐνέργειαν, ἀλλ᾽ οὐχὶ τὴν οὐσίαν γινώσκοντες αὐτοῦ, τὸ τῆς ἁπλότητος αὐτοῦ ὑπερφυὲς οὐ λυμαινόμεθα. Τῆς δὲ ἐνεργείας, ἀλλ᾽ οὐχὶ τῆς οὐσίας μετέχοντες, μεριστὸν τὸν ἀμερῆ ποιοῦμεν; Ἀκήκοας δὲ αὐτοῦ καὶ τοῦτο λέγοντος, ὡς <αἱ μὲν τοῦ θεοῦ ἐνέργειαι ποικίλαι, ἡ δὲ οὐσία ἁπλῆ>. Καθάπερ οὖν ποικιλλόμενος κατὰ τὰς ἐνεργείας κατ᾽ οὐσίαν οὐ ποικίλλεται οὐδὲ μερίζεται, οὕτω καὶ μετεχόμενος κατὰ τὰς ἐνεργείας μεθεκτὸς οὐκ ἔσται κατὰ τὴν οὐσίαν. Ἐπειδὴ δὲ καὶ ποικίλως ὁ θεὸς μετέχεται - διαφόρως γὰρ τῶν ὄντων ἕκαστον αὐτοῦ μετέχει -, κατὰ τὰς ἐνεργείας ἄρα καὶ μεθέξομεν αὐτοῦ, καθ᾽ ἃς δήπου καὶ ποικίλλεται. Κατ᾽ οὐσίαν δὲ οὐ μεθέξομεν αὐτοῦ· καὶ γὰρ κατ᾽ αὐτὴν καθ᾽ οἱονδήτινα τρόπον ἥκιστα ποικίλλεται. Οὐ μὴν, ἀλλὰ καὶ γινώσκομεν αὐτοῦ τὴν ἀγαθότητα καὶ τὴν δύναμιν καὶ τὴν σοφίαν. Πόσον δ᾽ ἂν γνοίημεν ἑκάστης τούτων; Πῶς γὰρ πεπερασμένη γνῶσις τὴν ἀπειρίαν ἐκείνην περιλήψεται, μᾶλλον δὲ τὰς ἀπειρίας τῆς σοφίας ἐκείνης, τῆς δυνάμεως, τῆς ἀγαθότητος; Ἀλλὰ <καὶ ἐν αὐτῷ>, φησί, <τῷ ὄρει θεὸς ἀνθρώποις φαντάζεται, τὸ μέν τι καταβαίνων αὐτὸς τῆς οἰκείας περιωπῆς, τὸ δὲ ἡμᾶς ἀνάγων ἐκ τῆς κάτωθεν ταπεινώσεως, ἵνα χωρηθῇ μετρίως γοῦν γενητῇ φύσει καὶ ὅσον ἀσφαλὲς ὁ ἀχώρητος>.

XLV. Πῶς οὖν μετρίως χωρούμενος ὅλος μετέχεταί τε καὶ χωρεῖται; Πῶς δὲ μετρίως μὲν χωρούμενος εἰσάπαν δὲ μένων ἀχώρητος οὐ μερίζεται; Πῶς δὲ βραχείᾳ τοῦ μεγάλου φωτὸς ἀκτῖνι ὡμιληκὼς ὁ Παῦλος ἀναγέγραπται; Τὸ βραχὺ πῶς ὅλον; Πῶς δὲ κατά τι μὲν φαινόμενον, κατά τι δ᾽ οὔ, μὴ μεριστόν; Τί δ᾽ οἱ παρ᾽ αὐτῷ τῷ Παύλῳ μερισμοὶ τοῦ πνεύματος; Πῶς δ᾽ οὐχὶ τὸ πλήρωμα, ἀλλ᾽ <ἐκ τοῦ Χριστοῦ πληρώματος> κατὰ τὸν θεολογικώτατον λαμβάνομεν τῶν ἀποστόλων, ἀμερίστου παντάπασιν ὑπάρχοντος; Πῶς δ᾽ <ἐπὶ πᾶσαν σάρκα> μὴ τὸ πνεῦμα, ἀλλ᾽ <ἀπὸ τοῦ πνεύματος ἐκχεῖται> τοῦ θεοῦ; Πῶς δ᾽ ἐπὶ τὸ θαβώριον οἱ τῷ Ἰησοῦ συναναβάντες ἀμυδράν, ἀλλ᾽ οὐχ ὁλόκληρον εἶδον

but not the full splendor of His divinity? The great Basil stated well that "the activities of God are manifold but His essence is simple."[136] And again: "The holy Spirit is simple according to His essence but manifold according to His activities."[137] For all those things belong to the activities of God. And according to them we participate in God in a moderate way and, according to them, we see and think of Him dimly, one person more, the other less, one by his intelligence, the other by a godlike power; each of us participates in them in agreement with his own purity and reflects on them and on the basis of them draws his conclusions about Him who is altogether imparticipable and unthinkable according to His essence. Nevertheless, one could well state that God as a whole is participated in and thought of on the basis of those activities according to a pious insight; for the divine is divided in an undivided way and not as bodies. But His goodness and His wisdom are not a part of Him and the greatness or the foresight are not other parts. But He is wholly goodness and wholly wisdom and wholly foresight and wholly greatness. For because He is one, He is not cut up in agreement with each of those activities, but in relation to each of them He is properly whole; through each of them He is known as one and simple and undivided, as being everywhere present and active as a whole.

XLVI. In that way those who participate in the activity of God participate in God as a whole, but not because we also participate in His essence in itself which is imparticipable and simple and undivided, and (we do) that all at the same time, but everyone differently. Further, those who in that way believe that God as a whole is participated in, (since with each of the participants nothing of what is with God remains imparticipable) mix and dissolve all things to one. Or rather, by referring each being to nothing, they simply do away with all things, because they have annihilated the one in each thing and caused an indiscernible confusion in the beings; or (rather) they sowed that confusion in them through erroneous thinking. For since everything participates in God--for God who created the all is absent in nothing--and since everything which participates participates in God as a whole (for the undivided is not in the least divided); and since that which participates in God as a whole is, according to them, not bereft of any part of God, it will not be that some of the beings are not living, others without reason, others immaterial spirits or something else of all things,

ἐκείνου τῆς θεότητος αὐγήν; Καλῶς ἄρ' εἶπεν ὁ μέγας Βασίλειος ὅτι, <αἱ μὲν ἐνέργειαι τοῦ θεοῦ ποικίλαι, ἡ δὲ οὐσία ἁπλῆ<. Καὶ πάλιν· τὸ πνεῦμα τὸ ἅγιον ἁπλοῦν τῇ οὐσίᾳ, ποικίλον ταῖς δυνάμεσι>. Ταῦτα γὰρ πάντα τῶν τοῦ θεοῦ ἐνεργειῶν ἐστι· κατὰ ταύτας γὰρ τοῦ θεοῦ μετέχομεν μετρίως καὶ κατὰ ταύτας ὁρῶμεν καὶ νοοῦμεν τοῦτον ἀμυδρῶς, κἂν ὁ μὲν μᾶλλον ὁ δ' ἧττον, καὶ ὁ μὲν διανοίᾳ ὁ δὲ θεοειδεῖ δυνάμει, κατὰ λόγον τῆς ἑαυτοῦ καθάρσεως ἕκαστος μεταλαγχάνων τε τούτων καὶ περὶ τούτων διανοούμενος κἀκ τούτων ἀναλογιζόμενος τὸν κατ' οὐσίαν ἀμέθεκτον παντάπασι καὶ ἀπερινόητον. Ὅλος δ' ὅμως ἐκ τῶν ἐνεργειῶν τούτων ὁ θεὸς μετέχεσθαί τε καὶ νοεῖσθαι λέγοιτ' ἂν καλῶς κατ' εὐσεβῆ διάνοιαν· ἀμερίστως γὰρ μερίζεται, καὶ οὐχ ὡς τὰ σώματα τὸ θεῖον. Ἀλλ' οὐδὲ μέρος μέν τι αὐτοῦ ἐστιν ἡ ἀγαθότης, μέρος δ' ἡ σοφία, μέρος δ' ἕτερον ἡ μεγαλειότης ἢ ἡ πρόνοια. Ἀλλ' ὅλος ἐστὶν ἀγαθότης καὶ ὅλος σοφία καὶ ὅλος πρόνοια καὶ ὅλος μεγαλειότης· εἷς γὰρ ὢν οὐ πρὸς ἑκάστην τούτων συνδιατέμνεται, ἀλλὰ πρὸς ἑκάστην ὅλος οἰκείως ἔχει, καὶ δι' ἑκάστης ἑνιαίως καὶ ἁπλῶς καὶ ἀμερῶς, ὅλος παρὼν καὶ ἐνεργῶν πανταχοῦ γνωρίζεται.

XLVI. Οὕτως ὅλου τοῦ θεοῦ μετέχουσιν οἱ τῆς ἐνεργείας τοῦ θεοῦ μετέχοντες, ἀλλ' οὐχ ὅτι καὶ τῆς οὐσίας καθ' αὐτὴν αὐτοῦ τῆς ἀμεθέκτου καὶ ἁπλῆς καὶ ἀμεροῦς μετέχομεν, καὶ ταῦθ' ὁμοῦ πάντες καὶ διαφόρως ἕκαστος. Ἔτι οἱ οὕτω νομίζοντες μετέχεσθαι ὅλον τὸν θεόν, ὡς ἐφ' ἑκάστου τῶν μετεχόντων μηδενὸς τῶν τῷ θεῷ προσόντων ἀμεθέκτου λειπομένου, συμφύρουσι καὶ ἀναλύουσι τὰ πάντ' εἰς ἕν· μᾶλλον δ' εἰς οὐδὲν ἕκαστον τῶν ὄντων φέροντες, ἐκ μέσου πάνθ' ἁπαξαπλῶς ποιοῦνται, τὸ ἐν ἑκάστῳ ἓν ἀνῃρηκότες, καὶ σύγχυσιν ἀδιάκριτον ἐμποιήσαντες, μᾶλλον δὲ ἐννοήσαντες κακῶς τοῖς οὖσιν. Ἐπεὶ γὰρ πάντα μετέχει τοῦ θεοῦ - καὶ γὰρ οὐδενὸς ἀφέστηκεν ὁ συνιστὰς τὸ πᾶν -, τῶν δὲ μετεχόντων ἕκαστον ὅλου μετέχει τοῦ θεοῦ - μερίζεται γὰρ ἥκιστα τὸ ἀμερές -, τὸ δ' ὅλου τοῦ θεοῦ μετέχον

but all things will be beings, living and rational, both intelligent and spiritual, and their contraries at the same time; for if something does not partake in one of these things, it does not participate in God as a whole. Thus, according to them, all things would be ruined because they are annihilated by each other.

XLVII. Lest that happen, the things which are only sensible do participate and they participate in God as a whole because He is undivided, but only according to their being. But they do not partake of the vivifying power of God in whatever way, lest, when their own proper being is taken away, heaven itself is done away with together with the foundation of everything under the sky, i.e., the four elements and the beings without soul and perception which come forth from them. And things which have the property to live only according to perception participate through that perception in God as a whole, God who is participated in in every respect in an undivided way, but not also on the level of reason or intellect lest the irrational beings become rational. But because they do not participate also on the level of reason, it is not true, therefore, that they do not participate in God as a whole. And the beings which participate in God on the level of reason or intellect do not all participate on the level of spirit as well, lest the wicked continue to be divine and spiritual people although they still abide in their wickedness. In that way, too, divine and spiritual people, participating in the grace of God but not in His essence, also participate in God as a whole. As a whole, because God, being present and active in them as a whole through the proper grace in a unified and simple and undivided way, is also known by them as a whole. But they do not in the least participate in His essence because they do not continue to be gods by their nature.

XLVIII. Furthermore, according to those who think that each of the participants participates in all things of God since He is undivided, no one who participates in the Holy Spirit will acquire one or two graces of the Spirit, but he will abstain from nothing because he has all since he participates in the Spirit as a whole. What does Paul mean when he says: "To one is given the utterance of wisdom, and to another the utterance of knowledge according to the same Spirit, to another the gifts of healing, to another the working of miracles"?[138] And again: "Are we all apostles? Are we all prophets? Do we all speak in tongues? Do we all interpret?"[139]

κατ᾽ αὐτοὺς οὐδενὸς στέρεται τῶν τοῦ θεοῦ, οὐ τὰ μὲν ἄζωα τῶν ὄντων ἔσται, τὰ δὲ ἄλογα, τὰ δὲ ἄϋλα πνεύματα ἤ τι τῶν ἁπάντων ἕτερον, ἀλλὰ πάντα καὶ ὄντα καὶ ζῶντα καὶ λογικά, νοερά τε καὶ πνευματικὰ καὶ τὰ ἀντιδιῃρημένα ἅμα· εἰ γάρ τί τινος τούτων ἀμοιρεῖ, οὐχ ὅλου μετέχει τοῦ θεοῦ. Φροῦδα τοίνυν τὰ πάντ᾽ ἔσται κατ᾽ αὐτοὺς δι᾽ ἀλλήλων ἀναιρούμενα.

XLVII. Ἵν᾽ οὖν μὴ τοῦτο γένηται, τὰ μὲν αἰσθητὰ μόνον, μετέχει μέν, καὶ ὅλου μετέχει τοῦ θεοῦ ὡς ἀμεροῦς, ἀλλὰ κατὰ τὸ εἶναι μόνον. Τῆς δὲ ζωοποιοῦ τοῦ θεοῦ δυνάμεως οὐ μετείληχεν οὐδ᾽ ὁπωσοῦν, ἵνα μὴ τῆς αὐτῶν ἰδιότητος ἀνῃρημένης, οὐρανὸς αὐτὸς ἐκ μέσου γένοιτο, καὶ τῶν ὑπ᾽ οὐρανὸν ἁπάντων ἡ κρηπίς, ἡ τῶν στοιχείων δηλονότι τετρακτὺς καὶ τὰ ἐξ αὐτῶν ἄψυχά τε καὶ ἀναίσθητα. Τὰ δὲ κατ᾽ αἴσθησιν μόνην πεφυκότα ζῆν μετέχει μὲν δι᾽ αὐτὴν ὅλου τοῦ ἀμερῶς μετεχομένου παντάπασι θεοῦ, ἀλλ᾽ οὐχὶ καὶ λογικῶς ἢ νοερῶς, ὡς ἂν μὴ λογικὰ γένοιντο τὰ ἄλογα. Οὐ μὴν ὅτι μὴ καὶ λογικῶς μετέχει οὐχ ὅλου μετέχει τοῦ θεοῦ. Τὰ δὲ λογικῶς ἢ νοερῶς τοῦ θεοῦ μετέχοντα οὐ πάντα καὶ πνευματικῶς, ἵνα μὴ καὶ οἱ πονηροὶ θεῖοι καὶ πνευματικοὶ διατελῶσιν ὄντες, ἔτ᾽ ἐπὶ τῆς πονηρίας μένοντες. Οὕτω τοίνυν καὶ οἱ θεῖοι καὶ πνευματικοὶ τῆς τοῦ θεοῦ χάριτος, ἀλλ᾽ οὐχὶ τῆς οὐσίας μετέχοντες τοῦ θεοῦ μετέχουσι καὶ ὅλου τοῦ θεοῦ. Ὅλου μὲν, ἐπειδήπερ διὰ τῆς οἰκείας χάριτος ἑνιαίως καὶ ἁπλῶς καὶ ἀμερῶς ὅλος ὁ θεὸς παρὼν καὶ ἐνεργῶν ἐν αὐτοῖς καὶ δι᾽ αὐτῶν γνωρίζεται· τῆς οὐσίας δ᾽ ἥκιστα μετέχουσιν, ἐπεὶ μηδὲ φύσει θεοὶ διατελοῦσιν ὄντες.

XLVIII. Ἔτι κατὰ τοὺς νομίζοντας τῶν τοῦ θεοῦ πάντων μετέχειν ἕκαστον τῶν μετεχόντων, ἐπειδήπερ ἀμερής, οὐδεὶς τῶν πνεύματος ἁγίου μετόχων γεγονότων ἑνὸς ἢ δύο χαρισμάτων τεύξεται τοῦ πνεύματος, ἀλλ᾽ οὐδενὸς ἀφέξεται πάντ᾽ ἔχων, ὡς ὅλου τοῦ πνεύματος μετέχων. Πῶς οὖν φησιν ὁ Παῦλος, <ᾧ μὲν δίδοται λόγος σοφίας, ᾧ δὲ λόγος γνώσεως κατὰ τὸ αὐτὸ πνεῦμα, ἄλλῳ δὲ χαρίσματα ἰαμάτων, ἄλλῳ δὲ ἐνεργήματα δυνάμεων>; Καὶ

Hence, not the person who has all, but the one who participates in only one thing participates in the spirit as a whole, because it is undivided. A person who participates in the power of making miracles or in the gift of healing participates therefore in the spirit as a whole, even if he has no part in the wisdom of the spirit and the other graces; and the holy Spirit is not divided for that reason. And if he does not participate in the essence of the spirit, too, will the divine then undergo a division? And why the person who participates in the grace of the spirit does not possess all things of the spirit, will be explained by father Chrystostom, for he says: "A person does not receive everything lest he think that grace is nature."[140] People who think that they participate in all things of God and in His very essence seem to adhere to that false doctrine (that grace is nature), or, rather, they say so openly, opposing themselves to those who theologize in the spirit. But we know that the participant does not even participate in the prophetic power itself, or in all the healing power or in any other activity of the spirit whatsoever. And nevertheless, he participates in the essentially imparticipable and altogether undivided God as a whole through the moderate participation in the grace which is divided in an undivided way when it is participated in. For the same man says again: "If we, when we partake of the fire which is by all means a body, divide it and do not divide it, how would not the same happen in the case of activity, especially of activity derived from the incorporeal essence?"[141]

XLIX. But do you understand that we participate in the divine activity but not in His essence and that the activity in which we participate is divided in an undivided way? Hence, the same theologian says: "Holy Writ calls the grace of the Spirit sometimes fire and then again water, showing that these are not names of the essence, but of the activity."[142] Distinguishing clearly what is said about Jesus by the Baptist, his forerunner, namely that (God) "gives the Spirit without measure,"[143] he says: "He calls the activity there spirit, for it is the activity that is divided. And if the activity

πάλιν· <μὴ πάντες ἀπόστολοι; Μὴ πάντες προφῆται; Μὴ πάντες γλώσσαις λαλοῦσι; Μὴ πάντες διερμηνεύουσιν>; Οὐκοῦν οὐχ ὁ πάντ᾽ ἔχων, ἀλλ᾽ ὁ καὶ ἑνὸς μετέχων ὅλου τοῦ πνεύματος ὡς ἀμεροῦς μετέχει. Τῆς τοῦ θαυματοποιεῖν τοιγαροῦν δυνάμεως ἢ τοῦ τῶν ἰαμάτων χαρίσματος μετεσχηκώς τις ὅλου μετέχει τοῦ πνεύματος, κἂν μὴ τῆς σοφίας τοῦ πνεύματος καὶ τῶν ἄλλων χαρισμάτων εὐμοιρῇ, καὶ οὐ παρὰ τοῦτο μεμέρισται τὸ πνεῦμα τὸ ἅγιον· ἂν δὲ μὴ καὶ τῆς οὐσίας τοῦ πνεύματος μετάσχῃ, μερισμόν τινα πείσεται τὸ θεῖον; Ὅτου δὲ χάριν οὐ πάντ᾽ ἔχει τὰ τοῦ πνεύματος ὁ μετεσχηκὼς τῆς τοῦ πνεύματος χάριτος, ὁ Χρυσόστομος ἐρεῖ πατήρ· <οὐ πάντα γάρ>, φησί, <λαμβάνει τις, ἵνα μὴ φύσιν εἶναι τὴν χάριν νομίσῃ>, ὃ κακῶς φρονεῖν ἐοίκασι, μᾶλλον δὲ καὶ φανερῶς φασιν ὑπεναντίως τοῖς ἐν πνεύματι θεολογοῦσιν οἱ τῶν τοῦ θεοῦ πάντων καὶ αὐτῆς τῆς οὐσίας μετέχειν ἀξιοῦντες. Ἡμεῖς δ᾽ ἴσμεν ὡς οὐδ᾽ αὐτῆς τῆς προφητικῆς δυνάμεως ἢ τῆς ἰαματικῆς ἢ ἄλλης ἡστινοσοῦν ἐνεργείας τοῦ πνεύματος ἁπάσης μετείληχεν ὁ μετασχών, καὶ ὅμως ὅλου μετέχει τοῦ κατ᾽ οὐσίαν ἀμεθέκτου καὶ ἀμεροῦς παντάπασι θεοῦ διὰ τὴν μετρίαν μετοχὴν τῆς χάριτος, ἀμερίστως αὐτῆς ἐν τῷ μετέχεσθαι μεριζομένης. <Εἰ γὰρ τοῦ πυρὸς μετέχοντες>, κατὰ τὸν αὐτὸν αὖθις φάναι, <καὶ ταῦτα σώματος ὄντος, καὶ μερίζομεν καὶ οὐ μερίζομεν αὐτό, πῶς οὐκ ἂν γένοιτο τοῦτο ἐπὶ τῆς ἐνεργείας, καὶ ἐνεργείας τῆς ἐξ ἀσωμάτου οὐσίας>;

XLIX. Ἀλλ᾽ ὁρᾷς ὅτι τῆς θείας ἐνέργειας, ἀλλ᾽ οὐ τῆς οὐσίας μετέχομεν, καὶ ὡς ἀμερίστως μερίζεται ἡ ἐνέργεια ἧς μετέχομεν; Διὸ πάλιν ὁ αὐτός φησι θεολόγος, ὅτι καὶ <τοῦ πνεύματος τὴν χάριν ἡ γραφὴ ποτὲ μὲν πῦρ, ποτὲ δὲ ὕδωρ καλεῖ, δεικνῦσα ὅτι οὐκ οὐσίας ταῦτα ὀνόματα, ἀλλ᾽ ἐνεργείας>. Διευκρινῶν δὲ τὸ περὶ τοῦ κυρίου Ἰησοῦ τῷ βαπτιστῇ καὶ προδρόμῳ εἰρημένον, ὅτι <οὐκ ἐκ μέτρου δίδωσιν ὁ θεὸς τὸ πνεῦμα>, <πνεῦμα>, φησίν, <ἐνταῦθα τὴν ἐνέργειαν λέγει· αὕτη γάρ ἐστιν ἡ μεριζομένη. Εἰ δὲ ἡ ἐνέργεια ἀμέτρητος πολλῷ μᾶλλον ἡ

is without measure, the more so the essence."[144] And the divine Maximus says: "The saints get the same activity as God;"[145] this is proved by the fact that they accomplish miracles by themselves or by others. But it is impious even to think that something attains the same essence as God, even if those who, in accordance with the Messalians[146] believe that the essence of God is participated in, seem to hold to that opinion.

L. B. Solve yet one more problem for me in a clearer fashion and I will believe you in every respect.

O. Which one?

B. Why is God not composed when He has both an eternal essence and an eternal activity?[147]

O. I have almost solved even that problem by what I just said. For the divine is one and simple in its essence; and that "one" is, in an appropriate way, a whole in relation to all the things which we properly think about it, and not divided in relation to each individual part of them. For it is, as a whole, goodness, and, as a whole, wisdom and, as a whole, justice and, as a whole, power in our thoughts. Not because it *becomes* such, not even when it is thought, but because it is such from eternity and because it manifests itself through His works to us who are born later. For we have come to understand that He has been moved to produce the universe by His goodness, and also that He accomplished it completely since He has the power, and that He composed it in wisdom, and holds it together and rules it with foresight. But what that "one" is according to His essence and what genuine name can get, in accordance with that essence, that which produces and arranges the universe in an unspeakable wisdom and power and goodness--no one has understood that yet to this very day.

LI. It is possible to give you the solution to this problem also on the basis of these words. Nevertheless, on your behalf, we will add a few more words, showing that simplicity is more akin than duplicity to the supernatural powers of all sorts; for by the power of God we evidently happen to mean here His activity.[148]

οὐσία>. Ὁ δὲ θεῖος Μάξιμος <καὶ ἐνεργείας τῆς αὐτῆς γίνεσθαι τῷ θεῷ τοὺς ἁγίους> φησί, δεῖγμα δὲ καὶ τὰ παρ᾽ αὐτῶν ἢ δι᾽ αὐτῶν ἐπιτελούμενα θαύματα. Τῆς αὐτῆς δὲ οὐσίας γενέσθαί τι τῷ θεῷ καὶ ἐννοῆσαι ἀσεβές, εἰ καὶ τοῦθ᾽ οὕτω φαίνονται δοξάζοντες οἱ κατὰ μεσσαλιανοὺς μετέχεσθαι τὴν οὐσίαν τοῦ θεοῦ νομίζοντες.

L. ΒΑΡΛ. Ἕν ἔτι μοι λῦσον ἐμφανέστερον καὶ πάντα σοι πείθομαι.

ΟΡΘΟΔ. Τὸ ποῖον ἕν;

ΒΑΡΛ. Πῶς οὐκ ἔστι σύνθετος ὁ θεὸς καὶ οὐσίαν καὶ ἐνέργειαν ἀΐδιον ἔχων;

ΟΡΘΟΔ. Σχεδὸν καὶ τοῦτο διὰ τῶν εἰρημένων λέλυται· κατ᾽ οὐσίαν γὰρ ἓν καὶ ἁπλοῦν ἐστι τὸ θεῖον· τὸ δ᾽ ἓν τοῦτο πρὸς πάντα τὰ πρεπόντως παρ᾽ ἡμῶν περὶ αὐτὸ νοούμενα ὅλον οἰκείως ἔχει, μὴ πρὸς ἕκαστον τούτων μεριζόμενον· ὅλον γὰρ ἀγαθότης καὶ ὅλον σοφία καὶ ὅλον δικαιοσύνη καὶ ὅλον δύναμις νοεῖται παρ᾽ ἡμῶν. Οὐχ ὅτι οὐδ᾽ ὅτε νοεῖται τοιοῦτο γινόμενον, ἀλλ᾽ ὅτι τοιοῦτον ἐξ ἀϊδίου, καὶ ἡμῖν ὑστερογενέσιν οὖσι διὰ τῶν αὐτοῦ ποιημάτων ἐκφαινόμενον. Ὅτι μὲν γὰρ ἀγαθότητι προαγαγεῖν κεκίνηται τὸ πᾶν, γεγόναμεν ἐν περινοίᾳ· καὶ ὅτι δυνατῶς ἔχων πάντως ἐξετέλεσε, καὶ ὡς ἐν σοφίᾳ συνεστήσατο καὶ προνοίᾳ συνέχει καὶ διοικεῖ. Τί δέ ποτε τὸ ἓν ἐκεῖνο κατ᾽ οὐσίαν, καὶ τί ποτ᾽ ἂν ὀνομασθείη κυρίως κατ᾽ αὐτὴν τὸ προάγον καὶ διεξάγον ἐν ἀπορρήτῳ σοφίᾳ καὶ δυνάμει καὶ ἀγαθότητι τὸ πᾶν, οὐδέπω καὶ τήμερον ἐπέβαλεν οὐδείς.

LI. Ἔστι μὲν οὖν καὶ ἀπὸ τῶν εἰρημένων τοῦ νῦν ζητουμένου σοι πορίσασθαι τὴν λύσιν. Σὴν δ᾽ ὅμως χάριν καὶ ἕτερ᾽ ἄττα προσεροῦμεν, δεικνύντες ὡς ταῖς τῶν δυνάμεων ὑπερφυέσι καὶ παντοδαπαῖς ἁπλότης μᾶλλον ἢ διπλόη σύντροφος· ἐνέργειαν γὰρ ἐνταυθοῖ τῶν λόγων πάντως τὴν τοῦ θεοῦ δύναμιν ἐτυγχάνομεν καλοῦντες.

ΒΑΡΛ. Τοῦτο καὶ αὐτὸς συνῆκα τοῖς προειρημένοις ἐμπεριειλημμένον. Ὁ γὰρ μέγας Βασίλειος ποῦ μὲν

B. I understood that myself, enclosed as it was by what has been said before. For the great Basil said somewhere that "the being of God is simple but His activities are manifold"[149] and somewhere else: "The holy Spirit is simple by its essence but manifold by its powers;"[150] in that way he showed that by the powers he means the activities. And against the doctor Eustathius you cited him as writing and showing earlier that the term divinity is not an indication of His essence but "of an overseeing or active power;"[151] further, as alleging that the three hypostases have one divinity whether one calls the nature or the activity divinity, for also here he called power and activity the same.[152] But also the God-revealer from the Areopagus called the deifying grace "power,"[153] which father Chrysostom called activity.

LII. O. Listen again to the great Basil when he very clearly states: "That power is activity which signifies all essence, of which only the non-being is deprived."[154] Since, then, that is power which we call the eternal activity of God, the divine would, more than anything else, be composed if that which has power would be composed because of that power. For each of the other things takes part in some powers but does not take part in most of them. But God, being almighty (power), is not deprived of any power. If, then, composition is in a thing through the powers, then nothing can be more composed than God. But even each of the beings is so far from being composed through the powers in it that in the case of bodies too the more simple ones have more powers than the more composite ones. For nothing is more simple than the four elements in bodies. Who is called "mother of all"? Is it not the earth, which, apart from the things of the same rank, is able to create from itself almost all the other things according to the divine order? How, then, can what has more powers be more simple if being composed is the consequence of having the powers? But from agriculture, too, one can learn that bodies which have many powers are rather the more simple. For one does not put dung which is not perfectly mature upon the meadows; but when it is mature and after some time returns to the state of being absolutely simple, then the knowledgeable farmer puts it under vegetables and all kinds of plants, because it

εἰπὼν ὅτι<ἡ μὲν οὐσία τοῦ θεοῦ ἁπλῆ, αἱ δὲ ἐνέργειαι ποικίλαι>, ποῦ δ' ὅτι <τὸ πνεῦμα τὸ ἅγιον ἁπλοῦν τῇ οὐσίᾳ ποικίλον ταῖς δυνάμεσιν>, ἔδειξεν ὡς ἐνεργείας τὰς δυνάμεις λέγει. Καὶ πρὸς τὸν ἰατρὸν δὲ Εὐστάθιον γράφοντα προήνεγκας αὐτὸν δεδειχότα πρότερον ὡς οὐκ οὐσίας, ἀλλ' <ἐποπτικῆς ἢ ἐνεργητικῆς δυνάμεως ἔνδειξιν ἡ προσηγορία φέρει τῆς θεότητος>· εἶτ' ἐπενεγκόντα μίαν εἶναι τῶν τριῶν προσώπων, εἴτε τὴν φύσιν εἴτε τὴν ἐνέργειαν ὀνομάζει τις θεότητα· κἀνταῦθα γὰρ ἐνέργειάν τε καὶ δύναμιν τὸ αὐτὸ προσεῖπεν. Ἀλλὰ καὶ ὁ ἐξ Ἀρείου Πάγου θεοφάντωρ <δύναμιν> προσηγόρευσε τὴν θεουργὸν χάριν, ἣν ὁ Χρυσόστομος πατὴρ ἐκάλεσεν ἐνέργειαν.

LII. ΟΡΘΟΔ. Ἄκουσον αὖθις καὶ τοῦ μεγάλου Βασιλείου λέγοντος ὁριστικῶς, <ἐνέργειά ἐστιν ἡ δηλωτικὴ πάσης οὐσίας δύναμις, ἧς μόνον ἐστέρηται τὸ μὴ ὄν>. Ἐπεὶ τοίνυν δύναμίς ἐστιν, ἣν ἀΐδιον ἐνέργειαν καλοῦμεν τοῦ θεοῦ, εἰ τὸ ἔχον δύναμιν σύνθετον ἔσται δι' αὐτήν, παντὸς μᾶλλον σύνθετον τὸ θεῖον εἴη ἄν. Τῶν μὲν γὰρ ἄλλων ἕκαστον τινῶν μὲν εὐμοιρεῖ δυνάμεων, πλειόνων δ' ἀμοιρεῖ· ὁ δὲ θεὸς παντοδύναμος ὑπάρχων οὐδεμιᾶς ἀμοιρεῖ δυνάμεως. Εἰ τοίνυν διὰ τὰς δυνάμεις πρόσεστιν ἡ σύνθεσις, οὐδὲν ἄρα συνθετώτερον θεοῦ. Ἀλλὰ τοσοῦτον ἀπέχει τοῦ εἶναι σύνθετον διὰ τὰς ἐν αὐτῷ δυνάμεις καὶ τῶν ὄντων ἕκαστον, ὥστε κἀπὶ τῶν σωμάτων πλείους ἔχει δυνάμεις τῶν μᾶλλον συνθέτων τὰ ἁπλούστερα· τῶν γὰρ τεσσάρων στοιχείων ἐν σώμασιν ἁπλούστερον οὐδέν. Τίς οὖν καλεῖται παμμήτωρ; Οὐχ ἡ γῆ, χωρὶς τῶν ὁμοστοίχων, τἄλλα μικροῦ πάντα παρ' ἑαυτῆς προάγειν κατὰ τὸ θεῖον δυναμένη πρόσταγμα; Πῶς οὖν ἡ πλείους ἔχουσα δυνάμεις ἁπλουστέρα, εἴγε ταῖς δυνάμεσιν ἕπεται ἡ σύνθεσις; Ἀλλὰ καὶ ἀπὸ τῆς γεωργίας ἔνι διδαχθῆναι, ὡς πολυδύναμα τῶν σωμάτων μᾶλλον τὰ ἁπλούστερα. Τὴν γὰρ κόπρον οὐκ ἐπιτιθέασιν ἀκατέργαστον ταῖς πρασιαῖς· ὅταν δὲ πεφθεῖσα διὰ χρόνου πρὸς τὸ ἀκριβῶς ἁπλοῦν ἐπαναλύσῃ, τότε λαχάνοις καὶ φυτοῖς παντοίοις

has good qualities for everything and can feed everything. Do you also see in the case of the bodies that the most simple things are the most powerful?

LIII. After (some) investigation you could discover the same thing in incorporeal beings as well. Truly, all the intelligible things take part in more and greater powers than the bodies. By their capacity to act also through bodies, they make their powers even twice their own. But they are so much more simple than bodies that they do not even tolerate a comparison made between them on that account. If, then, the more powerful are also the more simple, the most powerful is also the most simple. And that would be the genuinely simple which is far from any composition. For the composition is derived from impotence, so to speak. For, because none of the created things can be and exist by themselves in a completely simple and unmixed fashion, it necessarily needs the combination with something else; therefore, it is immediately made as a composite being right at the moment of birth.

LIV. B. It seems to be a good argument; for even being before the created things annihilates matter. But even if one says that bodies are not composed through the powers in them they nevertheless possess corporeal qualities and are almost evidently composed of different essences; for the fact that all things are mixed through all things seems to me to be true only in sensible beings and in that way it is reasonable that these beings are composed and called so. But what other composition could one imagine for the angels and the rational souls, except through the powers which are in them by nature?

O. Angels and souls do have powers, whatever they may have, but they are not composed on account of them by nature, except that they suffer more than act according to them. In view of the powers according to which they suffer, it is clear that they do not lack composition; for they put away ignorance--and because that was in them previously they belonged to composite things on that account; and they acquire knowledge--and through that addition they can be counted among composite things.

ὑποβάλλουσιν οἱ τοῦ γεωργεῖν ἐπιστημόνως ἔχοντες, ὡς πρὸς πάντα πεφυκυῖαν καὶ πάντα δυναμένην τρέφειν. Ὁρᾷς κἀκ τῶν σωμάτων ὡς πολυδυναμώτερα τὰ ἁπλούστερα;

LIII. Τοῦτο δ' ἴδοις ἂν κἀπὶ τῶν ἀσωμάτων ἐξετάζων. Καὶ πάντα γε μὴν τὰ νοερὰ πλειόνων εὐμοιρεῖ δυνάμεων καὶ μειζόνων ἢ τὰ σώματα· τῷ τε πεφυκέναι καὶ διὰ σωμάτων ἐνεργεῖν διαπλασίους ἑαυτῶν ποεῖται τὰς δυνάμεις. Ἀλλὰ τοσοῦτόν ἐστιν ἁπλᾶ μᾶλλον τῶν σωμάτων, ὡς μηδὲ σύγκρισιν ἐπιδέχεσθαι κατὰ τοῦτο πρὸς αὐτά. Εἰ τοίνυν τὰ πολυδυναμώτερα καὶ ἁπλούστερα, τὸ παντοδύναμον καὶ ἁπλούστατον· καὶ τοῦτ' ἂν εἴη τὸ κυρίως ἁπλοῦν καὶ πάσης συνθέσεως ἀπηλλαγμένον. Ἡ γὰρ σύνθεσις ἐξ ἀδυναμίας, ὡς εἰπεῖν, ἐστίν· ἐκ γὰρ τοῦ μὴ δύνασθαι καθ' ἑαυτό τι τῶν γενητῶν μονοειδῶς καὶ ἀμιγῶς παντάπασιν εἶναί τε καὶ ὑφεστάναι, τῆς πρὸς ἕτερον ἐξ ἀνάγκης δεῖται συμπλοκῆς, διὸ κἀν τῇ γενέσει σύνθετον εὐθὺς ἀπετελέσθη.

LIV. ΒΑΡΛ. Καλῶς ἔχειν ὁ λόγος μοι δοκεῖ· καὶ γὰρ καὶ τὸ εἶναι πρὸ τῶν γενητῶν τὴν ὕλην ἀναιρεῖ. Ἀλλὰ τὰ μὲν σώματα, κἂν μὴ διὰ τὰς ἐν ἑαυτοῖς δυνάμεις σύνθετά τις εἴπῃ, σωματοειδεῖς τε φέρουσι ποιότητας καὶ σχεδὸν φανερῶς ἐξ οὐσιῶν διαφόρων σύγκειται· τὸ γὰρ πάντα ἐν πᾶσι μεμίχθαι καλῶς ἔχειν ἐν μόνοις τοῖς αἰσθητοῖς ἐμοὶ δοκεῖ, καὶ τοῦτον τὸν τρόπον σύνθετα ταῦτα εἰκότως ἐστί τε καὶ λέγεται. Τῶν δ' ἀγγέλων καὶ τῶν λογικῶν ψυχῶν τίνα τις ἂν ἐπινοήσειεν ἑτέραν σύνθεσιν, εἰ μὴ διὰ τὰς προσούσας αὐτοῖς ἐκ φύσεως δυνάμεις;

ΟΡΘΟΔ. Ἔχουσι δυνάμεις, ἃς δήποτ' ἔχουσιν, ἄγγελοί τε καὶ ψυχαί, ἀλλ' οὐχὶ διὰ ταύτας σύνθετοι πεφύκασιν, ἀλλ' ὅτι κατὰ ταύτας μᾶλλον πάσχουσιν ἢ ἐνεργοῦσι. Καθ' ἃς τοίνυν πάσχουσι, φανεροὶ γίνονται συνθέσεως οὐκ ἀμοιροῦντες· ἀποτίθενται γὰρ ἄγνοιαν, ἀφ' ἧς πρότερον προσούσης τῶν συνθέτων ὑπῆρχον δι' αὐτήν, προσλαμβάνονταί τε γνῶσιν, δι' ἣν προσθήκην

In the case of the wicked angels or souls the composition is visible contrariwise. And because God only acts according to His divine powers and does not suffer too, He alone is really simple in a supernatural way. He absolutely does not undergo dimunition or increase, He does not put away things and He does not acquire things. Because He is almighty in that fashion, He is the most simple of everything. Moreover, none of those incorporeal beings changes according to their essence unless one would say that beginning itself and being born are a change according to their essence. But according to their choice, for better or for worse they seem to be changing and that which changes--but not according to the essence!-- shows that it was composed before, since the virtue or vice, smaller or greater, from which it withdrew, was present in the essence before that; and it (also) shows that it is composed now because it has acquired from outside (the virture or vice) with which it has obviously come together. But that which only acts without changing or acquiring anything from the things outside itself--how can that be composed through the activities? Hence, the divine is simple and almighty.

LV. Moreover, every angel is simple and so is all rational soul in the same or approximate manner. But none of these things is simplicity; for they are simple by participation both in comparison with the bodies and the beings which are composed of the incorporeal and body. In some sense they are simple, in another not, through the attitudes in them and through what they suffer and the changes which result from them. But God is not simple by comparison or participation; for He is Himself the One who appropriately gives by Himself part of His simplicity to every being. Hence, He alone is not only genuinely simple, but also simplicity itself. You can also see that when you enquire into all the divine names. For He is not only living and wise and good, but goodness and wisdom and life as well; He is the cause for all beings of all things, He possesses everything from eternity and is able to give everything from Himself.[155] By His saving justice He offers His gift in due proportion to everyone and at the right moment, as the ruler of all beings. Hence, the divine and almighty alone is, in our view, genuinely simple.

τοῖς συνθέτοις ἂν εἶεν ἐναρίθμιοι. Κἀπὶ τῶν φαύλων ἀγγέλων ἢ ψυχῶν ἐκ ἐναντίου ἡ σύνθεσις ὁρᾶται. Ὁ δὲ θεὸς ἐνεργῶν μόνον κατὰ τὰς θείας ἑαυτοῦ δυνάμεις, ἀλλ᾿ οὐχὶ καὶ πάσχων, μόνος ὄντως ἁπλοῦς ἐστιν ὑπερφυῶς, οὐ μείωσιν, οὐκ αὔξησιν, οὐκ ἀπόθεσιν, οὐ πρόσληψιν ὅλως ὑπομένων. Οὕτω παντοδύναμος ὑπάρχων ἁπλούστατός ἐστιν ἁπάντων. Ἔτι κατ᾿ οὐσίαν μὲν οὐδὲν τρέπεται τῶν τοιούτων ἀσωμάτων, εἰ μή τις αὐτὸ τὸ ἦρχθαι καὶ γενέσθαι τροπὴν φαίη κατ᾿ οὐσίαν. Κατὰ δὲ προαίρεσιν ἐπὶ τὸ χεῖρον ἢ τὸ βέλτιον φαίνεται τρεπόμενα. Τὸ δὲ τρεπόμενον, μὴ κατ᾿ οὐσίαν δέ, δείκνυσι πρότερον μὲν σύνθετον ὑπάρχον, ἐξ ἧς ἀρετῆς ἢ κακίας ἐλάττονος ἢ μείζονος ἀπεγένετο, πρότερον προσούσης τῇ οὐσίᾳ, νῦν δὲ σύνθετον ὑπάρχον, μεθ᾿ ἧς δήπου συνεγένετο προσειλημμένης ἔξωθεν. Τὸ δὲ ἐνεργοῦν μόνον, ἀλλ᾿ οὐκ ἀλλοιούμενον οὐδὲ προσλαμβάνον ἀπὸ τῶν ἐκτὸς ἑαυτοῦ οὐδ᾿ ὁτιοῦν, πῶς ἂν εἴη διὰ τὰς ἐνεργείας σύνθετον; Οὕτως ἁπλοῦν τὸ θεῖον καὶ παντοδύναμον.

LV. Ἔτι πᾶς μὲν ἄγγελος ἁπλοῦς, καὶ πᾶσα λογικὴ ψυχὴ τὸν ἴσον τρόπον ἢ ἐγγύς· ἁπλότης δὲ οὐδὲν αὐτῶν· μεθέξει γὰρ εἰσιν ἁπλᾶ καὶ πρὸς τὰ σώματα ἢ τὰ ἐξ ἀσωμάτου τε καὶ σώματος συγκείμενα παραβαλλόμενα. Καὶ πῇ μὲν ἁπλᾶ, πῇ δ᾿ οὔ, διὰ τὰς ἐν αὐτοῖς ἕξεις καὶ τὰ πάθη καὶ τὰς ἐκ τούτων ἀλλοιώσεις. Ὁ δὲ θεὸς οὐκ ἀπὸ συγκρίσεώς ἐστιν ἁπλοῦς, οὐδ᾿ ἀπὸ μεθέξεως· αὐτὸς γάρ ἐστιν ὁ καταλλήλως παρ᾿ ἑαυτοῦ μεταδιδοὺς ἑκάστῳ τῆς ἁπλότητος. Ὥστ᾿ οὐ μόνον ἁπλοῦς κυρίως μόνος, ἀλλὰ καὶ ἁπλότης. Τοῦτο δ᾿ ἴδοις ἂν κἀπὶ πάσης θεωνυμίας ἐξετάζων· οὐ γὰρ μόνον ζῶν καὶ σοφὸς καὶ ἀγαθός, ἀλλὰ καὶ ἀγαθότης καὶ σοφία καὶ ζωή, πᾶσι πάντων αἴτιος ὑπάρχων καὶ πάντα προέχων ἀϊδίως καὶ πάντα δυνάμενος παρ᾿ ἑαυτοῦ δωρεῖσθαι. Δικαιοσύνῃ μέντοι σωστικῇ σύμμετρον ἑκάστῳ καὶ κατὰ καιρὸν προϊσχόμενος τὴν χορηγίαν ὡς ἁπάντων πρύτανις. Οὕτως ἁπλοῦν ἡμῖν κυρίως μόνον τὸ θεῖον καὶ παντοδύναμον.

LVI. And since the divine is almighty not (only) after the creation but before the creation as well, not only is His essence uncreated but likewise all His powers. Be sure that those who rage against us for that opinion are numbered among the wicked creatures! And since the deifying grace, which also has the name of divinity from the saints, is one such power, it is also necessarily uncreated itself; those who call it created "have gone astray from the womb: they have swerved from their own belly: they have spoken lies."[156] And since grace is also a gift, the person who gives it transcends it by being its cause; non-believers are unaware that whoever transcends participation is the cause of everything. Do you see that all (second) sowings of the wicked tares[157] both of that Barlaam with his false doctrines and of his companions are wholly demolished by this one argument?

LVII. The former Barlaamite: What an evil (thing) jealousy is! For, now I have discovered that those who speak against you out of envy place lies before the truth--and that, dealing with such important issues!-- and they try to disparage and destroy in every way what they would not be able to admire and to praise in a worthy fashion. And since the things which are worthy of admiration can neither be easily known nor easily grasped and procured they deprive themselves as well as all others (as far as they are concerned) of that kind of help by making that the starting point for their attack upon you. For if you say these things, being a follower of those fathers, with how much grace and insight would their writings be filled?

O. God gives the word according to His promise, my brother, to those who speak for Him. To Him alone be eternal glory. Amen!

LVI. Ἐπεὶ δ᾽ οὐ μετὰ τὴν κτίσιν, ἀλλὰ καὶ πρὸ τῆς κτίσεως παντοδύναμον τὸ θεῖον, οὐχ ἡ οὐσία μόνον, ἀλλὰ καὶ πᾶσαι αἱ δυνάμεις ἄκτιστοι αὐτοῦ, καὶ τοὺς διὰ τοῦτο μεμηνότας καθ᾽ ἡμῶν ἴσθι τοῖς πονηροῖς κτίσμασι συντεταγμένους. Ἐπεὶ δὲ καὶ ἡ θεοποιὸς χάρις, ἣ καὶ αὕτη παρὰ τῶν ἁγίων θεότης ὀνομάζεται, μία τῶν τοιούτων δυνάμεών ἐστιν, ἀναγκαίως ἄκτιστος καὶ αὕτη, καὶ <ἀπηλλοτριώθησαν αὐτῆς, ἐπλανήθησαν ἀπὸ γαστρὸς οἰκείας, ἐλάλησαν ψευδῆ> οἱ κτιστὴν λέγοντες αὐτήν. Ἐπεὶ δὲ χάρις ἐστὶ καὶ χορηγία, ὁ χορηγῶν ὑπέρκειται ταύτης τῷ αἰτίῳ, καὶ οἱ ἀπειθοῦντες τὸν ὑπὲρ μετοχὴν ὄντα τοῦ παντὸς αἴτιον ἠγνόησαν. Ὁρᾷς πάσας τὰς τῶν πονηρῶν ζιζανίων ἐπισποράς, τοῦ τε κακοδόξου ἐκείνου Βαρλαὰμ καὶ τῶν ὀπαδῶν ἐκείνου διὰ μιᾶς ταύτης ἐγχειρήσεως καθαιρουμένας ἄρδην;

LVII. Ὁ ποτὲ ΒΑΡΛΑΑΜΙΤΗΣ. Οἷον ὁ φθόνος κακόν! Νῦν γὰρ ὑπὸ βασκανίας πρὸ τῆς ἀληθείας, καὶ ταῦτ᾽ ἐπὶ τῶν τοιούτων, τὸ ψεῦδος ἔγνων τιθεμένους τοὺς ἀντιλέγοντας ὑμῖν, καὶ ἃ θαυμάζειν καὶ ἐγκωμιάζειν οὐδ᾽ ἂν δύναιντο ἀξίως, ταῦτ᾽ ἐκεῖνοι παντὶ τρόπῳ διαβάλλειν καὶ ἐξουθενεῖν πειρῶνται. Κἀπειδὴ πέφυκε μὴ γνωστὰ ῥᾷον μηδ᾽ εὔληπτά τε καὶ εὐπόριστα εἶναι τὰ θαύματος ἄξια, τοῦτ᾽ ἐκεῖνοι τιθέντες ἀφορμὴν τῆς καθ᾽ ὑμῶν ἐπιβουλῆς σφᾶς τε αὐτοὺς καὶ τοὺς ἄλλους ἅπαντας, τό γε εἰς αὐτοὺς ἧκον, ἀποστεροῦσι τῆς τοιαύτης ὠφελείας. Εἰ γὰρ σὺ τοιαῦτα φθέγγῃ τῶν πατέρων ἐκείνων γεγονὼς ἀκροατής, πόσης ἂν τἀκείνων γέμοι χάριτός τε καὶ συνέσεως.

ΟΡΘΟΔ. Ὁ θεὸς δίδωσι λόγον κατ᾽ ἐπαγγελίαν, ἀδελφέ, τοῖς δι᾽ αὐτὸν λαλοῦσιν. Ὧι μόνῳ πρέπει δόξα αἰώνιος· ἀμήν.

NOTES

1. This translation follows the critical edition of P. Christou, *Gregoriou tou Palama suggrammata*, vol. 2 (Thessaloniki, 1966). The footnotes are primarily his own, supplemented with several of ours.

2. Proverbs 2:4. "...if you shall seek it as silver, and search diligently for it as for treasures..." (Citations from the Old Testament are taken from the Septuagint, which is what Palamas would have been using; citations from the New Testament are taken from *The New Oxford Annotated Bible* (RSV) (1991). Palamas usually quotes biblical and ancient authors in a rather loose fashion.

3. Sabellius lived in Rome in the first half of the third century, A.D. He taught that the Son and the Holy Spirit were not independent manifestations of the one God. His ideas played a role in the battle between the Arians and the Orthodox. There were Sabellians up to the beginning of the fifth century in Pentapolis (Libya).

4. Eunomius lived in Kyzicos at the end of the fourth century. He was a fervent Arian and tried to prove scientifically the complete understandability of God and that God alone is one.

5. It is more likely that Gregory of Nyssa is meant here who wrote the book, *About Not Saying that There are Three Gods.*

6. Ephesians 6:19.

7. The Barlaamites tried to prove the oneness of God by philosophical arguments and not on the basis of Scripture. Palamas, on the contrary, does not submit the truth of the Bible and the Fathers to philosophical argumentation.

8. Nature is *physis* in Greek. The Orthodox plays with words here: every *physis* has to possess physical things, otherwise it would not exist. God exists and therefore God's *physis* must also possess physical things.

9. The reference is to *About Divine Activities* 9, attributed to Maximus the Confessor.

10. Maximus Confessor, *To Marinus*, J.P. Migne, *Patrologia Graeca* (Paris, 1857-66); (hereafter: P.G.) 91, 96a.

11. John Damascene, *The Orthodox Faith* 3, 15; P.G. 94, 1056C.

12. Maximus Confessor, *To Marinus*, P.G. 91, 96B and 201AB.

13. A reference to the illumination on Mount Thabor (Matt. 17:1-8) where Moses and Elijah appeared to Jesus and his three disciples who had accompanied him. The synod of June 1341 had rejected Barlaam's idea that the light on the mount was created. See *Introduction*, pp. 9-10.

14. 2 Peter 1:4.

15. Gregory of Nyssa, *On Perfection*, P.G. 46, 280B, which was addressed to Olympius and not to Harmonius.

16. Op. cit., P.G., 46, 284D.

17. Op. cit., P.G. 46, 277CD.

18. John Damascene, *On the Orthodox Faith* 3, 15; P.G. 94, 1057B.

19. John 1:16.

20. Matt. 13:43.

21. Cf. Colossians 3:4.

22. Vespers of the 7th of August.

23. Vespers of the Transfiguration of August 6.

24. Matutinae of the Transfiguration.

25. The denial of the existence of uncreated activity in God has its consequences for the experience of living in the Church of a factual communion (unity) of man with God. When the opponents of Palamas affirm that the divine grace is a creature, either they exclude the possibility of such a communion with God or they degrade God who has communion with the saints to the order of creatures.

26. Maximus Confessor, *Capita Theologica* 2, 1; P.G. 90, 1124D-1125A; *Capita alia* I, 5; P.G. 90, 1180A.

27. Basil, *Sermon on the 44th Psalm* 5; P.G. 29, 400C. Cf. also, *Sermon on the 29th Psalm* 5; P.G. 29, 317B.

28. Basil, *Sermon on the 44th Psalm* 5; P.G. 29, 400C. Cf. also *Sermon on the 29th Psalm* 5, P.G. 29, 317B.

29. Gregory of Nyssa, *Sermon* 40, 6; P.G. 36, 365A. This quote is taken from a context in which Gregory discusses the many meanings of light, one of which is the divinity.

30. Reference not found.

31. Symeon Metaphrastes, *On the Gospel of John* 1, P.G. 116, 685D.

32. Reference not found.

33. See Basil, *Sermon on Psalm* 33 9; P.G. 29, 373A.

34. Matt. 13:43.

35. Trinitarian Canon, 3rd song, song 1, troparion 1.

36. Trinitarian Canon, 4th song, song 6, on Mary who gives birth to God.

37. See note 4.

38. *De Beatitudinibus* 4; P.G. 44, 1269A.

39. See Cyril of Alexandria, *De adoratione in spiritu et veritate* 9; P.G. 68, 608A.

40. Basil, *Against Eunomius* 2; P.G. 29, 648AB.

41. Romans 1:20.

42. Psalm 18:2.

43. Maximus Confessor, *Against Thalassius* 13; P.G. 90, 293D-296A.

44. Palamas reveals here the contradiction of the Barlaamites in trying to reconcile the philosophical theory of the oneness of God with the revelation of Christ.

45. Maximus Confessor, *Capita theologica* 2,1; P.G. 90, 1124D-1125A; and I, 5; P.G. 90, 1180A.

46. *Capita theologica* 2,1; P.G. 90, 1125AC.

47. *De Beatitudinibus* 4; P.G. 44, 1269A.

48. See Cyril of Alexandria, *De adoratione in spiritu et veritate* 9; P.G. 68, 608A.

49. See Maximus Confessor, *Capita on love* 3, 28; P.G. 90, 1025B.

50. Dionysius the Areopagite, *On Divine Names* 2,7; P.G. 3, 645A.

51. *On the Divinity of the Son and the Spirit;* P.G. 46, 573D-576A.

52. In Greek, God's "power to see" is *theatike dynamis* while "divinity" is *theotes*. Gregory of Nyssa and Palamas may be playing with words here.

53. Gregory of Nazianzus, *Orationes* 39: P.G. 36, 345C.

54. *On Divine Names* 5, 2; P.G. 3, 816C.

55. Gregory of Nazianzus, *Orationes* 29, 15: P.G. 36, 93B; see also *Orationes* 40, 43; P.G. 36, 420BC.

56. Basil, *Against Eunomius* 3; P.G. 29, 656A.

57. Athanasius, *Dialogue with a Macedonian* I, 14; P.G. 28, 1313A.

58. Gregory of Nyssa, *Against Eunomius* 3, 1; P.G. 45, 604B.

59. Basil, *On the Holy Spirit* 19; P.G. 32, 156D.

60. *On Divine Names* 11, 6; P.G. 3, 953D-956A.

61. *Letters* 2; P.G. 3, 1068A-1069A.

62. *Capita theologica* 2, 86; P.G. 90, 1165AB.

63. *On Problems*; P.G. 91, 1253D.

64. See Dionysius the Areopagite, *On Divine Names* 2, 5; P.G. 3,644A.

65. *On Divine Names* 11, 6; P.G. 3, 953C.

66. Job 38:28.

67. *Against Eunomius* 2, 23; P.G. 29, 624A.

68. Psalm 33:6

69. *Sermon on Psalm* 32, 4; P.G. 29, 333B. The "breath" is the same as the Spirit.

70. *Letter* 38, 4; P.G. 32, 329C.

71. Gregory of Nazianzus, *Orationes* 20, 6; 21, 35; 39, 11; P.G. 35, 1072C, 1124CD; 36, 345CD. It has to be noted that hypostasis ("coming into existence") can also be translated as "person." Palamas is playing with words again.

72. *On Divine Names* 11, 6; P.G. 3, 956A.

73. See *Capita theologica* I, 48; P.G. 90, 1100CD.

74. *Capita theologica* I, 49; P.G. 90, 1101A.

75. *Letter* 189, 8; P.G. 32, 696AB.

76. 1 Corinthians 1:24.

77. Enhypostatic means "existing in an hypostasis," in this case, the Son. It is not the same as authypostatic which means "independent" (see chapter XXVI)

78. *Against Eunomius* 2, 32; P.G. 29, 648A.

79. Palamas explains this in *Triads* III. i. 18 as follows: "Clearly, this term [enhypostatic] is not used to affirm that is possesses its own hypostasis...By contrast, one calls "anhypostatic" not only non-being or hallucination, but also everything which quickly disintegrates and runs away, which disappears and straightaway ceases to be, such as, for example, thunder and lightning, and our own words and thoughts. The Fathers have done well, then, to call this light enhypostatic, in order to show its permanence and stability, because it remains in being, and does not elude the gaze, as does lightning, or words, or thoughts..." (translation Gendle).

80. Isaiah 11:2; Zechariah 3:9; 4:10.

81 . *Against Thalassius* 63; P.G. 90, 672C.

82. John Damascene, *On the Orthodox Faith* I, 9; P.G. 94, 836B. See also Gregory of Nazianzus, *Orationes* 30; P.G. 36, 128A. Palamas uses the etymology of words here in the same way as Plato does in

his *Cratylus*, 397D.

83. Basil, *Letters* 8, 11; P.G. 32, 265A; Cyril of Alexandria, *On Trinity* 11; P.G. 77, 1145B.

84. Gregory of Nyssa, *Against Eunomius* 2; P.G. 45, 960C.

85. Philippians 2:21.

86. Eutyches was convicted of the Arian heresy in 448. Severus may be the late emperor (461-465), but it is also possible that the copyist made a mistake and that Palamas had the famous Eusebius in mind (4th century) who also had Arian sympathies. In that case the pun on *dyssebes* would be much more significant. Eusebius wrote the *Historia Ecclesiastica* and *Praeparatio Evangelica.*

87. Basiliscus was emperor from 475-476. He tried to discredit dogmas of the Council of Chalcedon but his endeavor was thwarted by the Patriarch Akalcio of Constantinople. Zeno was emperor from 474-491 except for the years of Basiliscus' emperorship. He battled the Monophysites. He was married to Ariadne, Verina's daughter. Verina, the wife of emperor Leo I (457-474), led the opposition against Zeno. When Zeno became emperor again she was forced to become a nun.

88. Leo the Great was pope from 440-461. In 451 he succeeded in persuading the fathers of the Council of Chalcedon to accept his letter or document in which he explained the two natures of Christ, against the Monophysite view. "Old Rome" is used to distinguish it from new Rome (Constantinople). The reference to the synod of Ephesus seems to be misplaced because Leo was not pope in 431.

89. The place or topic or tenet of the trinity: God the Father and Son and the Holy Spirit as One and Three. Tetras: the divinity was added as a fourth person to these three.

90. Cyril of Alexandria (d. 444) battled against all kinds of heresy, especially against the Monophysites.

91. Psalm 43:5.

92. Aëtius (middle of the fourth century) was the teacher of Eunomius (see note 4). He believed that the nature of the Son was totally different from the nature of the Father.

93. *To Marinus*, P.G. 91, 200C.

94. *To Marinus*, P.G. 91, 96B; see also 201AB.

95. *Against Eunomius* 4; P.G. 29, 689C. The Greek word for independently is *authypostatos*. Without existence (*hypostasis*) (see below) is *anhypostatos* and God's essence is called *trishypostatos* (with three *hypostases*). It seems evident that Palamas is again playing with words. See also note 77.

96. *Against Eunomius* 1; P.G. 45, 369A.

97. John Damascene, *On the Orthodox Faith* I, 9; P.G. 94, 833B-836A.

98. Matt. 22:29.

99. See note 97.

100. Sabellius also "fused" and "contracted" the divinity to one, "cutting off" the other two.

101. Cyril of Alexandria, *Thesauri* 7; P.G. 75, 100AB.

102. Cyril of Alexandria, *Thesauri* 31; P.G. 75, 444BC.

103. John Damascene, *On the Orthodox Faith* I, 9; P.G. 94, 833B-836A.

104 . Ps. Athanasius, *Dialogue on Trinity*, P.G. 28, 1144D-1145A.

105. Basil, *Against Eunomius* 4; P.G. 29, 689C.

106. Basil, *Letters* 189, 8; P.G. 32, 696A.

107. *Orationes* 42, 15; P.G. 36, 476A.

108. Reference not found.

109. *Letters* 189, 5; P.G. 32, 689BC.

110. *Against Eunomius* 1, 7; P.G. 29, 525B.

111. Proverbs 8:9.

112. *Letters* 189, 8; P.G. 32, 696B.

113. *Against Eunomius* I, 8; P.G. 29, 528BC.

114. *Against Eunomius* II, 29; P.G. 29, 640C.

115. *Against Eunomius* I, 8; P.G. 29, 529A.

116. *Letters* 189, 5; P.G. 32, 689BC.

117. *Against Eunomius* I, 7; P.G. 29, 525B.

118. *Against Eunomius* I, 6-7; P.G. 29, 524B-525A. In Greek "grain" is *sitos,* which also means "seed," "fruit" and "food." In English the comparison does not possess the force it has in Greek because "grain" does not have more meanings.

119. Gregory of Nyssa, *Against Eunomius* II, 353; P.G. 45, 1029A.

120. Dionysius the Areopagite, *On Divine Names* 5, 2; P.G. 3, 816D-817A.

121. Mind is one and many: it is mind but it possesses many sciences.

122. Since Aeschylus, *Agamemnon* 177, it has been a tradition to say

that one learns by suffering. There is a play on the similarity of sounds here: in Greek, "learning" is *mathein* and "suffering" is *pathein*.

123. *Against Eunomius* I, 8; P.G. 29, 528B.

124. Basil, *Letters* 234, 1; P.G. 32, 868C.

125. *Letters* 234, 1; P.G. 32, 869A.

126. Ibid.

127. Ibid.

128. Basil, *Against Eunomius* II, 32; P.G. 29, 648A.

129. Messalians is the Syriac name of people "who pray" (Greek: *Euchitai*), especially against devils who take possession of men. They appear for the first time in the fourth century. They believed in one God and revered him as the Pantocrator. They also believed that they could see the very essence of God with their material eyes. The first Messalian was probably Adelphius; his successor was Eustathius.

130. Basil, *Letters* 234, 1; P.G. 32, 869A.

131. Gregory of Nazianzus, *Orationes* 45, 11; P.G. 36, 637B.

132. Acts 9:3 and 22:6.

133. 1 Corinthians 12:4-6.

134. John 1:16.

135. Joel 3:1 (in the Hebrew); 2:28 (Septuagint).

136. See note 130.

137. *On the Holy Spirit* 9, 22; P.G. 32, 108C.

138. 1 Corinthians 12:8-10.

139. 1 Corinthians 12:29-30.

140. John Chrystostom, *On the Holy Spirit* 3; P.G. 52, 817.

141. John Chrystostom, *Sermon 4 on John,* P.G. 59, 91-92.

142. *Sermon 32 on John 1*; P.G. 59, 183.

143. John 3:34.

144. *Sermon* 30, 2; P.G. 59, 174.

145. *To Marinus,* P.G. 91, 33AB; see also *On Problems,* P.G. 91, 1076C.

146. See note 129.

147. For this problem see S. Guichardan, *Le problème de la simplicité divine en Orient et en Occident aux XIVe et XVe siècles* (Lyon, 1933).

148. The activity (*energeia*) of God is not different from his power (*dynamis*), though in general these two Greek terms have a widely different meaning.

149. See note 130.

150. See note 137.

151. *Letters* 189, 8; P.G. 32, 696A.

152. Ibid.

153. *On Divine Names* 8, 1; P.G. 3, 889B.

154. This text is not found in Basil, although *Letters* 189, 8 (P.G. 32, 696A) comes very close. See also F. Diekamp, *Doctrina Patrum de Incarnatione Verbi* 14, 9 (Münster, 1907), pages 88-89; and by the same scholar, *Analecta Patristica* (Rome, 1938), pages 14-15.

155. Dionysius Areopagite, *On Divine Names* I, 3; P.G. 3,589C.

156. Psalms 58:3.

157. See Matt. 13:25.

Index

Index of Names (Roman numerals refer to paragraphs in the Dialogue)

References to the Bible

Job	38:28	XXIII
Psalm	18:2	XIV
Psalm	33:6	XXIII
Psalm	43:5	XXVIII
Psalm	58:3	LVI
Proverbs	2:4	II
Proverbs	8:9	XXXIX
Isaiah	11:2	XXVII
Joel	3:1	XLV
Zechariah	3:4, 4:10	XXVII
Matthew	13:25	LVI
	13:43	VIII, IX
	17:1-8	VI, VIII, XLV
	22:29	XXXV
John	1:16	VIII, XLV
	3:34	XLIX
Acts	9:3, 22:6	XLV
Romans	1:20	XIV
1 Corinthians	1:24	XXV
	12:4-6	XLV
	12:8-10, 12:29-30	XLVIII
Philippians	2:21	XXVIII
Colossians	3:4	VIII
2 Peter	1:4	VII